DOCTOR and the ABORIGINES

DOCTOR
and the
ABORIGINES

Charles Duguid

O.B.E., M.A., MB, Ch.B., F.R.C.S. (Glas.) F.R.A.C.S.

LONDON:
ROBERT HALE & COMPANY

ADELAIDE:
RIGBY LIMITED

First published in Great Britain 1973
Copyright © 1973 C. Duguid

ISBN 0 7091 3755 9

Robert Hale & Company
63 Old Brompton Road
London SW7 3JU

Printed in Hong Kong

Dedicated to
my children,
my grandchildren, and
my great-grandchildren

CONTENTS

ILLUSTRATIONS

FOREWORD

by Sir Mark Oliphant,
Governor of South Australia

The awakening interest of government, institutions and people generally in the welfare of the Australian Aborigines is due, in great part, to the continued efforts on their behalf of Dr Charles Duguid.

Charles Duguid was born on the shores of the Firth of Clyde at Saltcoats, a fishing town in Scotland. His father was a schoolteacher and his mother the daughter of a doctor, so that he grew up in that atmosphere of respect for learning which we associate with Scotland. Schooling was mixed with holidays on an uncle's farm and wandering in the woods and country-side. The red-headed youth knew his own mind, and was determined to follow in the footsteps of his doctor grandfather. So he studied medicine in Glasgow University when Lord Kelvin was its Chancellor. In hospital and on rounds in the poorer areas of the city, he became acutely aware of the meaning of poverty and social injustice. In 1911, he signed on as ship's surgeon for a voyage to Australia and back aboard the Orient liner *Omrah*. This trip determined his future, for he fell in love with a young Australian girl returning to Melbourne, and with Australia, which he determined to make his home. His story of life before settling in Adelaide is fascinating, showing how well equipped he was for life in the antipodes.

After practising in the country in Victoria, Dr Duguid and his wife moved to Adelaide in 1914, shortly before the first World War disrupted their lives. In 1916 he enlisted, and he tells vividly of his experiences in North Africa. There his deep humanity again became manifest. After returning to Australia, he worked as a surgeon in Adelaide before making his first trip to the interior of the continent. At the end of a visit abroad to learn the latest techniques in surgery, he learned that his wife had died suddenly of a stroke. His own loss, and concern for his motherless son of thirteen years of age, made the ensuing years a time of heartache until, in 1930 he married Phyllis Lade, an English mistress at the Presbyterian Girls' College, of which he was a member of Council.

Through a woman missionary from an island off the north coast of Australia, who was his patient, he heard much of the desperate plight of the Aborigines, and both he and his wife became dedicated to the cause of these unfortunate people, forgotten in their own homeland and subjected to cruelty and neglect. A gross miscarriage of justice, and calculated cruelty to an Aboriginal named Takiar, in the Northern Territory, added to the flames of the Duguids' anger, and in 1934 he set out for the north by train and then by motor truck, over unmade roads, to see for himself. At Alice Springs he was upset and depressed to find that the padre of the Australian Inland Mission was contemptuous of the Aborigines, and ministered only to the white families of the cattle stations! This attitude was widespread, among Commonwealth officials, as well as the graziers. Despite the expressed contempt for the Aborigines and their dirty ways, Duguid found that the part-Aboriginal population was increasing rapidly. While their lands and their way of life were being taken from them by the whites, no attempt was made to provide for education or training in any trade. It was not uncommon for punitive expeditions to be made into the surrounding country.

Dr Duguid and his wife undertook a campaign designed to make Australians aware of the plight of the Aborigines. He became President of the Aborigines Protection League, which was neither political nor sectarian, and which sought principally recognition of the serious effects upon Aboriginal life of the taking over of tribal lands by white settlers. Dr Duguid then journeyed to the Musgrave Ranges, 1,000 miles from Adelaide, and was disturbed on the way by evidence of mistreatment of Aborigines. He saw the effects of the spread of "civilization" upon the natives of the hill country, the threat of further expansion, and the reality of segregation. With the active support of the Government of South Australia, Charles Duguid determined to persuade his Church to establish a mission at Ernabella, to serve as a buffer between the few remaining Aborigines in the Musgrave Ranges and the advancing "frontier." He persuaded the then Moderator of the Presbyterian Church in South Australia to accompany him on an arduous trip to the interior. They found that Aborigines who were relatively untouched by civilisation had no concept of ownership, sharing everything within the tribe. They were splendid specimens of humanity, with great dignity.

As a result of his determined advocacy, against surprising opposition, the Presbyterian Church in Australia decided to establish a Mission on the lines advocated by Dr Duguid. On a professional visit overseas, he spoke strongly in England and New Zealand about the conditions of the Australian Aborigines. Further expeditions to the inland were made by both Dr Duguid and his wife, travelling by motor truck and camel and learning much of the wildest parts of South Australia and the people, in time of drought and after a good season. The war of 1939-1945 meant reduced government assistance for the Aborigines and further inroads upon their native lands. As a member of the Aborigines Protection Board, Charles Duguid travelled widely to the various native settlements, finding much to depress him in what he saw and what was told him of cruelty and injustice. He was much encouraged by the fine work being done by the Ernabella Mission, where the Aborigines were introduced to schooling and the civilized way of life without compulsion or interference with their native customs. However, Dr Duguid felt impelled to resign from the Board over its decision to allow violation of the Aboriginal reserve for purposes of the rocket range to be established at Woomera.

Although he no longer had an official relationship with the Aborigines, Dr Duguid continued to work assiduously on their behalf, helping to combat a disastrous outbreak of measles, to lessen the effects of tuberculosis, leprosy, nutritional deficiencies and alcohol, and continuing at all times to call attention to the duty of the white population towards those whom they had displaced. The Duguids' house was always open to Aborigines visiting Adelaide, and they earned the deep gratitude of many whom they helped in this way. For the first time, a public meeting in the Adelaide Town Hall, arranged by Dr Duguid, was addressed by Aborigines and part-Aborigines. At seventy years of age, he again visited Ernabella and much of the interior, being heartened by some improvement in the conditions of his Aboriginal flock, but much upset by mal-nutrition due to lack of protein in their diets. He arranged for some relief of this deficiency to be given by gifts of skim milk.

The Duguids paid their last visit to Ernabella and other places in the north in 1969, after drastic changes in both State and Commonwealth legislation brought to the Aborigines all the rights of other Australians, except that to own their former tribal lands. There has been enormous change since first they came to know the original people of Australia, some of which, such as the right to share drunkenness with the white man, were not pleasing. However, this Scot, this compassionate medical man, must know in his heart that he has done more for the Aborigines of his adopted country than any other person, living or dead. In his own words, with which he closes this inspiring story of his life's work ". . . to me there is one thing which remains unchanged in a ceaselessly changing world — the astonishing power of selfless love. I have seen its manifestation in many ways throughout my long life. It remains for me the ultimate solution to the world's problems."

During his life, Charles Duguid has been helped and sustained by his religion. But it is not in religion that he sees the solution, for all men, of the uncertainties and difficulties of life today, for there are too many religions. It is in "selfless love:" the common humanity of all peoples.

PREFACE

Dr John Nurser, a Cambridge University historian, stressed to me in 1969 that I should finish some writing on which I had embarked in order to record some events of my life. For my days have been spent not only in two vastly different countries, Scotland and Australia, but also in two centuries which provide even greater contrast. Anyone who reached maturity in the nineteenth century and has lived beyond the middle of the twentieth century has experienced almost shattering change.

It is common knowledge that the influences which play on a man in his childhood and youth shape his future. Scotland, with its strong emphasis on moral values, strict economy, and hard training, gave the best preparation for the new life that I set out to make for myself in Australia, which has been my home for sixty years. For a third of that time I was, like most Australians, still unaware of the grievous injustice and inhumanity suffered by the Aborigines of Australia. Once I became aware of their tragic situation I was impelled to speak out and to enlist the concern of others. During the last forty years, I have tried to channel this into effective action.

Adelaide, 1972   C.D.

DOCTOR'S GRANDSON

THE YOUNG WOMAN WAS SUFFERING FROM QUINSY OF BOTH tonsils, and the doctor could not persuade her to open her mouth so that he could have a look at them. She was in real pain and distress, but even when the doctor tried to prize her teeth apart with the handle of a spoon he had no success. He thought for a moment, then went into the kitchen. A good fire was burning there, as was usual in cottage kitchens in those days, and he told the girl's mother to put the end of a poker in the fire. As soon as it was red hot he seized the other end and rushed into the bedroom. "Open your mouth!" he ordered the shrinking girl, and brought the spluttering poker close to her face. She opened it all right—on a loud yell of terror. This burst the abscesses, she was able to move her jaws again, and the doctor had cured another patient.

He was Doctor Robert Snodgrass Kinnier, my grandfather. He practised in the area where I was born: Saltcoats, Ayrshire, on Scotland's Firth of Clyde. Those were the days when a doctor's personality and powers of improvisation were more important than his pills. Antibiotics were unknown, and many of the surgical and medical techniques which we take for granted today were undreamed of.

But in any case the hardy Scots never sent for a doctor except as a last resort. They lived a simple, rugged life, which had known little change for many years, and the old ways and customs were still commonplace. On Hallowe'en the boys blackened their faces and went round the houses begging for Hallowe'en fare of toffee, nuts, and apples. We "dooked" for apples in a big tub of water, and carved queer faces on hollowed-out turnips which were lit by candles stuck inside. Older lads and lasses came together on Hogmanay, or New Year's Eve—one of the great festivals of Scotland. Superstition had it that a lad with black hair would bring good luck to the house if he was the "firstfoot" across the threshold, so as midnight struck the blackhaired boys were welcomed with cheers and laughter. Not that the others missed out. A kiss snatched under the mistletoe earned a pair of gloves for a girl if she was quick and bold enough to get in first, and if a lad seized the kiss then she had to give him a tie.

I was not blackhaired—in fact my hair was a flaming red, with accompanying freckles. But like most lads in those days I had my share of fun. It seemed that there was always something to be seen in the little Scottish town. Men from Spain drifted through, selling oranges for three a penny at one season, and bearing ropes of brown onions slung on poles over their shoulders during the autumn. Foreign fortune-tellers carried a caged lovebird and a box of fortune cards, and for a penny or so the cards would be spread out and the bird would hop around until it chose a card and offered it to the one who wanted to know his fate.

Italians with barrel organs came from time to time. Usually they had a monkey, which crouched atop the organ and put out its paw for pennies. Sometimes they had a bear, chained to the end of a pole, which jigged around on its hind legs in a clumsy dance supposed to be in time to the music. Thin and irritable, it was a pathetic sight, and I thought it was a good thing that its smell kept people at a distance.

Saltcoats was a fishing town, and I thought fishermen to be heroes. The storms of the Atlantic swept up the Firth of Clyde, and its waters were treacherous even when they seemed to be calm. We used to swim from the rocks on summer mornings, and often there were spirited races out to sea. Then, one morning, after Archie McLean had given the customary wave and call when he was well in the lead, he disappeared. His companions found only the long slimy yellow "sea-laces" which waved up from the depths, and when the police came with grappling arms they had a hard job to draw the body up from the tendrils which entwined its legs.

I still have a photograph of six men of Saltcoats who went out in a fishing boat to help a cargo ship which had gone aground on the rocky coast a few miles to the north. The skipper of the harbour lifeboat dared not pit his craft and crew against the gale, but the Saltcoats fishermen got every man ashore. They berthed their battered fishing boat next morning to the plaudits of the townsfolk and the national press, and in due course the fishermen were summoned to Buckingham Palace to receive medals from Queen Victoria herself.

In those days, late in the nineteenth century, every village in Scotland seemed to have its simple soul. One of them was Paddy Mitchell, who called at our door with an egg in his hand and asked my mother to boil it for him. She did. And there was a middle-aged man who often called on my father for something to read. One evening he said, "I think you should use your influence to have John Tyler made the Poet Laureate. He is a very great poet."

"Who told you that, Thomas?" my father asked, to which the swift and confident answer was, "He did."

An old rascal known as Red Hot was a terror to us boys. His name came either from the heat of his temper or the colour of his hair. He lived by catching hen sparrows, painting them yellow, and selling them as canaries. "That's no' a canary you have in that cage. It's just a spug," I yelled at him one day, then dodged for my life as he lunged forward with his stick.

Katie Gas, with the tousled hair that could never have known a comb, collected rags for a living. Poor Maggie Watt was another oddity. She was a thin, sprightly middle-aged

3

woman, too often drunk, but very likeable when sober. My father often helped her to straighten out after a drinking spree, and on one occasion I saw he demonstrate her gratitude. My father was taking part in an open air religious meeting, of the type which was very common in those days, and it was constantly interrupted by a bystander. Maggie, dressed only in petticoat and blouse and with bare feet, legs, and arms, flew at him. He was twice her size, but she swarmed all over him and soon had him routed. Someone called the police, and although Maggie had been in gaol so often that the police ignored her antics whenever they could they were obliged to take some action. By that time I already had a name for "having a mind of my own," and as Maggie was dragged away I asked the police sergeant, "Why don't you arrest Maggie's husband instead? Put him in gaol for idleness! He's never done a day's work in his life, while Maggie works hard at cleaning and washing to keep the family alive. It's no wonder that she tries to forget it all in drink." But my early attempt at social reform fell upon deaf ears.

Drunkenness, especially on a Saturday night, was almost a way of life in the Scotland of that time. Men and women worked long gruelling hours, whisky and beer were cheap, and there was not much else available by way of relaxation. It was a cause of great hardship and distress, and sometimes even death. If a man reached home on a Saturday night he would be recovered from his hangover by Monday, but if he had to walk some distance in winter snow he might never reach home. The snow might melt slightly in the early afternoon sun, then freeze again as night fell, creating a treacherous surface which was hard for a sober man to walk on, let alone a drunk. One Sunday morning a milkman found the body of a man huddled against a stone dyke between Saltcoats and Stevenston, frozen to death. Probably he had given up trying to walk on the icy surface and had sat down to rest, not knowing that his feeling of warmth was due to heat leaving the body.

Even in such frigid weather, some children had to go barefoot. Either there was no money for shoes, or it had been spent in the pub. For the mass of the people, the "good old days" did not exist, and they lived on a narrow line of poverty.

4

But a change was slowly setting in, and my father spent his evenings in teaching old people in the slums to read and write. He even managed to persuade some people to spend their money on food and clothing instead of in the pubs.

He was a schoolteacher, who had become headmaster of Saltcoats Academy at the age of twenty-six. The son of a farmer, he had gone straight from the village school of Bucksburn, Aberdeenshire, to the University of Edinburgh and after that to the Edinburgh Teachers' Training College. He married the second daughter of Doctor Kinnier and I was the first of seven children of that family of Duguids. My mother was a woman of education and culture, with sound Scottish commonsense and judgement that made her a wise mother. Her father always wore the frockcoat and silk hat of a doctor of those days, and practised medicine in Saltcoats for more than fifty years. As a Free Churchman, a staunch Liberal, and a burgh councillor he was well known in the district, and his funeral in 1904 was the longest I have ever seen. "Catholic and Protestant, Churchman and Dissenter, Liberal and Tory, rich and poor—all had come," as the *Ardrossan and Saltcoats Herald* put it.

So the days of my childhood passed, in a town where the town crier still walked the streets ringing his bell and calling such announcements as "Lost yesterday in the afternoon, between Springvale Street and the Post Office, a lady's bangle. Finder will be rewarded by returning same to the Polis Office." The roads were kept in repair by stonebreakers, eternally cracking rocks down into ballast at their spot by the side of the road, and often surrounded by an audience of small boys admiring their skill. My summer holidays were often spent at a farm belonging to my uncle, William Ferrier, at Donside, Aberdeenshire. Even though harvesting and haymaking were heavy work before the days of combines, I threw myself into the farm routine with zest. A swathe of cut-hay or corn had to be fashioned into a rope and used to bind a sheaf. A number of sheaves were set up together into stocks or "stooks," and when these were dry they were pitched by long handled forks onto the high hay wagons. Finally, back at the farm, they were built into neat stacks, which were thatched with straw.

5

Another task was cutting peat, which in the 1890s was the main fuel for farmhouse fires in Aberdeenshire. Peats burn with a warm glow and a pleasing aroma, but it was a laborious job to cut it from a distant peat moss—the semi-bog in which it is found. Each farm in the district had a section of the peat moss to work, and on my uncle's section the neat oblongs of peat had been cut earlier in the year and stacked to dry. In late July, we had to drive an unsprung cart over the roadless moor, lift the peats into the cart and drive each load slowly home to the farm.

But farm life was not all work. Bordering the fields behind the farm there was a glorious wood, in which I wandered or lay on the dead leaves listening dreamily to the birds and insects. Along the dyke which separated the woods from the farm there grew a mass of wild roses, foxgloves, campions, daisies, forget-me-nots, dandelions, and the delicate Scottish bluebell, which seemed almost to tinkle in the slightest breeze.

Pedlars tramped between the farms, including frail old Mrs Garvie with her heavy basket of fish. It was always lighter when she left again after a cup of tea and a scone. Another visitor was a sanctimonious, well-dressed man who always contrived to arrive at mealtimes. "It's wonderful, John, how well you time your visits," my uncle said once, to which he replied complacently, "Guided by the Lor-r-r-d."

My uncle could be caustic. When a visitor and his twelve-year-old son were having dinner at the farm, the father constantly corrected the lad's table manners. Reprimands pattered unceasingly, until my uncle said at last, "Never mind, Dick; just do as you do at home."

"Ganglers," as we called them, called at the farm as they wandered through the countryside in search of work or shelter, and always received generosity in the form of supper and a bed in the barn straw from my aunt—though my uncle always took their tobacco and matches away until they set off again. She was as gracious as my uncle was sometimes brusque, and beloved by everyone from the servants to the many nieces and nephews who holidayed at the farm. On Sundays the family filled the back pew at the local Free Church, everyone in his Sunday best and most of the adults in black. The lengthy, closely-reasoned sermons might have been tedious to youngsters if Aunt Ferrier had not softened them by a distribution of sugar-coated peppermints called pandrops. It wouldn't have been a proper service without the pandrops.

Pedlars and ganglers made no impact upon the quiet countryside, but its ancient peace was drawing near to an end. A "gentleman's gentleman," Archie Dey, who had served for many years in the aristocratic homes of England, had an eye for business in his retirement. He was a picture of the old school of man servant, well-covered, of medium height, always deferential in manner, with a light tenor voice and a smooth round face. He never presumed to shake hands but would gently incline his head in greeting.

He hit upon the idea of building a lodge for English visitors who came to Scotland for the salmon fishing, and for this purpose rented part of a field overlooking the river. He established a solid two-storey house of grey granite, with a well-kept garden back and front, and regaled his visitors with a five-course dinner every evening, served by himself in traditional style. He acted as footman, butler, and valet to his guests, and soon gained a reputation. The invasion of fishermen from below the border was the first break in the peace of the countryside, and soon after that the old wood in which I used to wander was torn apart by granite quarrying.

The old style of Scottish country life has long since disappeared, but I cherish memories of its sturdy, self-respecting folk with their individualistic quirks of speech and manner. I remember a pair of farmers meeting on the railway platform at Stirling after an annual Highland and Agriculture Show. "Ay, fine show, man," one greeted the other.

"Ay, man, ay," he replied. "Ay, Ay."

The first farmer boarded his train, and as it began to move away he called, "Ay, ay, man," to the one standing on the platform. "Ay, ay, man; ay, ay," the other replied, and so it continued until the train had steamed into the distance, leaving them well-pleased with their conversation.

By that time, I was travelling thirty-five miles each way between Saltcoats and Glasgow every day. At the end of my

7

primary schooldays I had had to choose between accepting a job in a bank or preparing myself for university. I chose the latter course without hesitation, and entered the High School in Elmbank Street, Glasgow. It is one of Britain's oldest schools, older than Eton and nearly two centuries older than Rugby and Harrow; only Westminster, of the English schools, is more venerable. I still keep in touch with the school and in 1937 and 1954 gave addresses on the Aborigines of Australia. In 1963 I had the honour of giving the valedictory address and presenting the prizes.

Schooldays in a big city were good for a lad who came from a comfortable family, and gave plenty of opportunities to see how the "other half" of the world lived. Each afternoon, as I walked up the mound to St Enoch railway station in Glasgow, I had to pass ill-nourished, thinly-clad old men and women, and young boys and girls shivering in the wind and rain as they offered shoe laces and boxes of matches for sale. Another unforgettable memory of my schooldays was the occasion when, with other boys from the High School, I went down to the River Clyde to see off soldiers called up from the Reserves for the Boer War. The red-coated soldiers marched to the docks where the transports waited. Drinks had been given and the men looked anything but fit. Wives wrapped in shawls, with babies tucked tightly in them, clung to the soldiers. Many older women, mothers I would think, were weeping as they trudged wearily along. Young boys and girls, barefooted and poorly clad, made up the crowd.

When I finished school my father determined what studies I should undertake at university. "You'd better do an Arts course. You'll probably know what you want to be before you finish it."

I knew long before that. Since childhood, I had understood that medicine was a most worthwhile profession, and I was proud of my grandfather. Within three months of entering Glasgow University, I had decided that I wanted to be a doctor.

2

DOCTOR IN TRAINING

I WAS INSTALLED IN GLASGOW UNIVERSITY BY OCTOBER 1902, a date which is not so immensely long ago in time, but marking a period so utterly different from anything that has survived until today that it was another world. For five shillings a week, I lodged in a small room four flights up from the street. I bought a good pair of shoes for seven shillings and sixpence, and by way of relaxation I could take a three-hour paddle steamer cruise on the Firth of Clyde during the summer evenings, for a fare of one shilling. Cheapest of all was electricity, the discovery which no one then realised was to revolutionise the life of the world. The fare by electric tram, which had just replaced the horse tram, was a ha'penny a mile or three miles for a penny. The streets were still full of horsedrawn traffic, from fast moving hansoms to lumbering brewers' drays, and women's skirts swept the dusty or muddy sidewalks.

But students, and their teachers, were not so very different from those of today. My father had decided that it would be in my interest to finish the Arts course, and to overlap it with

Medicine; so I had to attend the Latin class at eight in the morning. The professor, G. G. Ramsay insisted on his students wearing the red gowns of Glasgow University to their studies, and these flapped wildly during the mad rush to be on time — because a janitor stood by the door and closed it on the stroke of eight. There was no hope of a reprieve, and after one last-minute stampede the professor told us, "When I was a student we rose early, had a good breakfast, and walked to the university. You stay in bed to the last minute, bolt your breakfast, and rush headlong to a tramcar. You are carried here. That way of life, I warn you, leads to flabbiness."

I was glad when I could devote myself fulltime to Anatomy and Physiology. For most of us, the incredibly complex structure of the human body began to take shape in our minds as we proceeded from abstract studies to the dissecting room and then to the wards, where the patients lay in resignation as our teachers discussed their afflictions.

The Professor of Medicine, Samson Gemmell, was one of the ablest and best-liked of the professors but he could be caustic and austere. He had a glass eye and when a new student seemed to stare at him he would snap — "Well, which is it?" When we were walking the wards, Professor Gemmell would sit at a bedside reviewing a medical report, surrounded by twenty students. On one occasion the student responsible for the report listened apprehensively to the professor's comments, and in his nervousness jiggled Gemmell's chair with his foot. "Sir," demanded Gemmell, "will you stop titillating my arse!" Then followed a brief dissertation on old English.

Members of the Faculty were determined that we should measure up to their own high standards of medicine and did not hesitate to put us in our places. "That may satisfy you, Mr Leslie, but it does not satisfy me. Think again," a somewhat conceited student was told when he gave an offhand answer to a question by Dr William Jack, a distinguished physician.

The Chancellor of Glasgow University at that time was one of the world's foremost scientists, Lord Kelvin. As William Thompson he had matriculated at the age of ten and had been appointed Professor of Natural Philosophy at twenty-two. He held the Chair for fifty-three years. I had an accidental meeting with him towards the end of my course, when he was an old man. From the driveway in front of the university a grass slope ran down to the River Kelvin, and in summer it was often crowded with first-year medical students basking in the sunshine. One day the old Chancellor appeared in the doorway and was greeted with loud cheers and a rush of students towards him, but I saw that he watched them apprehensively. I offered him my arm and held up my hand to the crowd, which fell back a pace or two, and the Chancellor leaned heavily on me. With halting steps he reached his carriage, which was surrounded by cheering students as his coachman drove him away.

In these days of student unrest, it is perhaps difficult to imagine students paying such honour to a university chancellor who had earned it by his academic achievements.

Immediately before the final year, which in our course was 1909, all students had to gain midwifery experience by practising in the poorer parts of the city. We lived in a students' hostel attached to a maternity hospital and were on call every night; nurses did the day work. We worked in pairs except for the afternoons, when each of us would visit a mother whom we had attended in childbirth.

All that I had seen of poverty so far was as nothing compared with the fearful conditions under which most of the poor folk existed in the slums and tenements of Glasgow. It was difficult to understand how some of them managed to exist at all, except by the power of the human spirit in adversity. One night I was given an address to which I went with my partner, George Macleod, and we found it to be in one of the poorest parts of the city. The area was mainly occupied by itinerant Irish families, and we found the patient lying in a ground-floor room with a wash house at the back. It was an easy delivery, but when I returned that afternoon I was shocked to find the baby in bed alone and the mother busy at a tub in the wash house. "You know you should be resting in bed, Mrs O'Reilly," I told her, but she said, "Sure, doctor, you needn't worry. I only took the room for two days and as soon as the washing's dry I'll be back on the road."

She was as good as her word, for when I returned on the next afternoon the room was empty—ready to be let to the next unfortunate who could afford no more than two days under a roof in which to have her baby.

Some seemed resigned to poverty, and others, like Mrs O'Reilly, were tough enough to battle on. But for many others, life was a matter of endless mental stress and physical hardship. One woman I attended, in a poor but neatly-kept home, seemed to be in great distress for several days after her baby was born. "Is your husband not about?" I asked one afternoon, and she answered sadly, "He left me and the children, five of them, ten years ago. This baby is not his child. I've struggled on and the children have been happy, but I don't know what we'll do now."

I had noticed religious pictures on the walls, and asked if she would like me to contact her church. "No, no," she said quickly. "The priest hasn't been near me since he saw I was pregnant."

Haltingly she added, "There's a . . . Salvation Army Woman two streets away. She'd come, I think, if you asked her."

I did, and next time I called to see the mother I found a change so great that I have never forgotten it. There is no doubt that it was the work and influence of the Salvation Army lass, of the breed which in those days had to survive hardships almost as great as those suffered by the people whom they tried to help.

One of my most difficult cases was in a very rough quarter of the city. The patient lay in a dirty bed built into the wall of the single room which acted as kitchen, living room, and bedroom for the whole family. Blanket and sheet were both the same dirty grey, and lice crawled over them as well as over the patient.

As the patient endured her seemingly endless labour, her grandmother sat by the fire. "I think ye could do wi' a cup o' tea," she said at last, and poured more water into the teapot, already half-full of leaves, which sat stewing on the hob. I looked at the almost black brew and protested, "That's too strong for me."

"Och, no, it's verra guid," she said, and continued to hand

round cups of tea. As soon as she moved across to look at the patient we emptied them down the sink, but the sight of our empty cups made her move to refill them.

Labour continued for hours, and at intervals my colleague and I went out to stretch our legs and breathe the comparatively fresh air of the street. In the silence of the night, our measured steps on the pavement made heads poke out of upper windows. "Ye're no' the polis, are ye?" someone called but when we reassured them the heads soon disappeared. Perhaps a few of them might have been taking guilty consciences back to bed with them. The baby was born at last.

I might call the next case "Amazing ignorance of an Irish couple." It brought the "doctors" into contact with two young women, a blonde and a brunette, who fortunately for the Irish husband and his wife were not so ignorant of the facts of life. The girls reported to the hospital that a doctor was needed at once, and gave the address. They said that, "The woman has been in labour some time, but refuses to believe her pain has anything to do with a baby."

The two young women, better dressed than one would have expected from the address given, were standing in front of the hospital when my friend and I came out. "We can take you to the spot quickly" the brunette said. "We live on the same stairhead as the woman who's having the baby." We had never been escorted before, but to refuse would have been difficult. After thirty minutes walk, during which the young women did most of the talking, we were led to a third storey stairhead of a tenement building and directed to the door on the right. The girls' flat was opposite. The blonde lass said, "If you're not needed right away, there's aye a cup o' tea on the hob." They left the door ajar.

The flat on the right was a well kept, tidy home. The couple had been married twenty years, but had no children. The woman was well in labour, and after examining her I said, "You are going to have a baby."

"No," she said in a very Irish brogue. "It cannot be—it is the inflammation." To which I replied, "You'll soon have the inflammation in your arms!"

The husband, thoroughly puzzled, was asked to wait on

the stairhead; the girls took him into their flat. No preparation of any kind had been made for the arrival of a baby and as there was no woman to help we shared the duties. When the room showed some semblance of order the father was called and the two girls came with him. He immediately kissed his wife and looked at the new arrival in some amazement. Next day when I called I was welcomed by a relaxed couple full of pride; the mother, aged forty, had "the inflammation" in her arms.

At last the final examinations came, the first great milestone in a medical career. I had developed a special interest in surgery, and gained a distinction in that subject as well as winning the two John Hunter medals and the Macleod gold medal. I had already won the special award for Anatomy and Physiology—the basic subjects of surgery.

But for me life at the University was not all books. In the summer session I was very active in athletics, won the quarter and half-mile events and represented the University at the annual inter-Varsity contests. In 1909, my final year, I was in charge of the annual Scottish Universities athletic contest held that year in Glasgow. The medicos dubbed me "The Scarlet Runner!"

I soon found that medicine was to mean a busy life. When I arrived home after the graduation ceremonies I found a telegram waiting for me, asking me to act as locum tenens for a month in a Port Glasgow practice. I was on the first train next morning to this big shipbuilding town on the Clyde, and before the day was out I was launched upon the responsibilities of a busy general practice. Midwifery alone kept me well occupied, and in twenty-eight days I delivered twenty-eight babies.

Like every doctor, I learnt from my patients. I told the mother of a nine-year-old girl with the measles to keep her other four children away from her, but when I called two mornings later I heard loud merrymaking and glanced through the window to see all the youngsters in the patient's bed. They were romping together with great glee.

Didn't I tell you the child was to be isolated from the others?" I asked the mother in some vexation, but she answered,

TOP: Dr Charles Duguid as a young surgeon in the Surgical Laboratory of the University of Glasgow before the first World War. BOTTOM: This row of cottages was typical of the mining villages in which the author practised

"Doctor, d'you think I want to have measles in the house for weeks on end, one bairn after the other?"

I saw the point, and resisted the temptation to tell her that "the dregs o' the measles" could be the beginning of tuberculous disease of the lungs.

One afternoon, I was called to a farm near Port Glasgow, and found a boy of five with a fracture of the shin bone. He had been climbing up a stone dyke, and had dislodged a big stone which fell against his leg. Children of that age have fast-growing bones, so the problem was to keep the leg still and straight so that the fracture would heal without distortion. I had boards placed under his mattress, and then began to look for some kind of weights which could be used as a splint. "Have you a grandfather clock, by any chance?" I asked the farmer, and he looked at me wonderingly. "Aye, doctor," he said, and led me to a fine specimen. I opened the long door, and saw just what I needed. The farmer did not protest as I unhooked the weights, but no doubt he was wondering what a doctor needed with a clock. He soon found out as he watched me binding the weights onto the child's leg. They were long enough to reach from above his knee to below his foot, and when tightly secured with calico they made a perfect splint. The boy was a good patient, and was rewarded with a quick, clean knitting of the fracture. Nowadays, of course, he would be taken to hospital and his leg set with plaster of paris.

Near the end of my stay in Port Glasgow I received an urgent call at breakfast one morning. It was to a house in a slum area, and after climbing the rickety stairs on the outside of the house I entered the poorest and dirtiest home I have ever seen. It was furnished with upturned boxes and one chair, which was almost too knocked-about to support the box which lay upon it. In this box lay a baby of about two months old. Two children, aged four and five, stood watching me expressionlessly, as scantily and raggedly dressed as were their parents. There was not a scrap of food in the place.

With the same deep feeling of sadness which always possessed me when I entered such homes, I examined the baby. It was unkempt, its brow was cold, and its eyes sunken. The family

TOP: A scene at El Arish, near the front where British and Australian troops were fighting the Turks in 1917. Casualties are being placed in readiness for transport back to Base. BOTTOM: The author with Lieutenant Fred Coy, the Australian Light Horse officer from whose skull he removed a Turkish bullet

watched me in silence until I turned and told the father that his baby was dead, and asked him if he had any idea of when it had died. "It was alive last night," he said.

All I could say was, "You realise that I never saw your baby alive, and I can't certify the cause of death. You should have sent for me earlier."

He said nothing, and I asked the mother, "Hadn't you noticed that your baby was ailing?"

She seemed to have nothing to say, so I told them, "I'm sorry, but it's too late for me to do anything," and went on my way.

I was almost back at the surgery when I was overtaken by the father and another man, who said briskly, "Could I have a word with you, Doctor? I want to assure you that this man's baby died of natural causes during the night. It was insured two weeks ago, and it was quite well."

"Are you an insurance agent?" I asked.

"Yes, I completed the insurance. Everything was above board. There should be no difficulty about the certificate."

"You know I can't say why the child died, and I can't give you a certificate."

"Doctor," he said. "These people are very poor. This is going to be very hard on them."

"I imagine that they're poorer since you collected the insurance premium off them," I told him, and crossed the road to the surgery. He was clearly anxious that there should be no Coroner's inquest.

I had a hospital appointment waiting for me when I finished that locum, but felt like a break first. So I went to my home in Saltcoats. In that month, August 1909, there were big shoals of herring in the Firth of Clyde, and fishing boats were sailing from harbours all along the coast. They were followed by fast steam herring-collectors. I was interested to see how the herring were caught and handled, so asked Robert Reid, the owner of the *Falcon*, if I could have a night on his collector. "The shoals are easing," he said, "but we're going out at four p.m. We'll be glad to have you."

The ship plunged westward for miles before it came in sight of the herring fleet scattered over a wide stretch of sea.

I could see several collectors beside the *Falcon*. The fishing boats worked in pairs, each with its net at the stern. Within signalling or hailing distance of each other, the two boats kept watch on the surface of the sea. When one of them sighted a shoal it shot the net in an arc from the stern. The other boat picked up the end of the net from the sea and between them they enveloped the herring. Scottish fishermen used a net forty yards long, twice the length of the English net.

A flare indicating a catch sent the herring collectors at full speed to the spot. Each collector lowered a boat which was rowed to the lucky fishermen. In these boats a man stood up and bidding became fast and keen. How the bidders, with their boats bobbing up and down in the waves, knew when the bid was against them was beyond me.

Twice during the night a catch was secured by the *Falcon* and nothing impressed me so much as the skill with which the fishing boat, full of herring, approached the collector. With amazing speed it came alongside parallel to the collector and seemed to graze the side as it slowed to a halt. The herring still in the net were hoisted aboard and tumbled on to the deck of the steamer. In the moonlight it looked as if thousands of silver coins had rained from the sky. At once the men on the *Falcon* started packing the herring into flat boxes and piling them up ready for transport to market.

The ship made for port at full speed, and we entered harbour at 6 a.m. The boxes of herring were rushed ashore, loaded into a train waiting with steam up and in a few minutes it was off.

Soon after this I took up my appointment at the Western Infirmary, in Glasgow, where I began work as house surgeon to Sir William Macewen. For six months I was junior to Dr Arthur Turnbull, who achieved fame in the first World War for his determination to have British soldiers supplied with steel helmets. The men in the trenches suffered skull wounds from bullets and shell splinters, which caused many of the deaths, but Turnbull's attempts to stir the War Office into action were ignored until he jumped from the Visitors' Gallery of the House of Commons into the midst of the members. His shock tactics worked, and in 1919 I learnt that the introduction of steel helmets had saved many lives.

The Western Infirmary gave me board and lodging, but no salary. I had three wards to supervise, and was kept so busy that on some days I was hardly off duty at all. Almost every hour of the day brought some fresh emergency, but luckily there were some lighter touches. Once a man in his sixties, deeply distressed, was brought to the accident ward. He was certain that he had swallowed his false teeth.

I examined his mouth and throat and assured him that this was most unlikely, but he persisted in his belief. I was about to send him to the X-ray department when a woman of about forty rushed into the ward, panting from her run up three flights of stairs. "Here's yer teeth, Paw," she gasped. "They were on the kitchen mantelpiece."

At another time a pretty young Frenchwoman called at Outpatients, with a scratch on the ring finger of her left hand. I dressed it, and told her that she need not return. "But I am frightened of blood poisoning. I work in a sweets factory, with many dyes," she said.

I told her not to worry about the sweet colourings, but the next week she was back again. "Finger still sore," she said, and held it out daintily. I assured her that it would soon be better, and she returned a few days later with a happy smile and a big box of cigars. I hadn't the heart to tell her that I didn't smoke.

But not every patient brought light relief. A battered woman, whose appearance was so frightening that she was screened off from other patients, was brought in by ambulance. Her eyes could not be seen because of swellings caused by repeated bashing from her drunken husband's fist, and he had also kicked her so savagely between the legs that the swelling was great enough to keep her legs apart.

Her husband had been arrested, and when she was well enough to make a statement two policemen were admitted to her bedside. But she refused to make a complaint, and it was impossible to obtain a word of evidence that would condemn her husband. The police returned two days later, but with no greater success. The woman's loyalty to her husband, the drunken brute who had disabled her, was unshaken.

I felt sure that she must have felt my compassion for her,

and the day before she was to be discharged I asked quietly, "What are you going to do if your husband gets drunk again?" She shuddered slightly and looked down at her bed, but did not answer.

Life in hospital taught some lessons in public relationships. There was an unwritten law that a lawyer who requested a medical report on a client who was or had been a patient in the hospital should make a written request and enclose a fee of one guinea. In my first week of duty I had to go down three double flights of stairs to the porter's office to answer a city phone call. In those days, telephones on the various floors were for internal use only and were not connected to the outside world. On the 'phone, a pleasant voice asked, "I believe that you admitted a man named Thomas Nicholls yesterday, with a fractured skull?"

"The man's in the ward all right, but there's no question of a fractured skull," I told the caller.

"Thank you very much," he replied, and hung up. I had been tricked.

Another firm of lawyers wrote for a medical report on a man who was claiming damages from his employer. I replied that I would send the report when I received the fee of one guinea. This was sent to me with a letter from a senior partner of the firm. He said that, since my father and grandfather had done so much for the poor without thought of payment, he was astonished by my request for a fee. My reply was that perhaps it was now time the third generation received the recognised fee.

At that time, all surgeons were general surgeons. They operated on any part of the body. My chief was one of the world's greatest surgeons, but was frowned upon by the traditionalists for his sometimes startling methods—of which many have become commonplaces in modern surgical techniques. The first time that I saw Sir William plunge a pair of long narrow forceps through the surface of the brain into an abscess, in order to drain it, I was shocked. But the patient, a youth, recovered completely, and on 20 February 1969 the American neurosurgeon Donald Matson wrote to me that: "Sir William's results with abscess of the brain were never really improved on in spite of antibiotics and all the other support available to the modern surgeon." The *British Medical Journal* of 5 April 1969 printed an editorial which stressed the same point.

Sir William could take dead bone from a withered arm, insert spicules of fresh bone into the gutter which he had made, and be confident that the patient would have an efficient arm restored to him. I remember a man from whom Macewen had removed a lung riddled with tuberculous disease. The patient lived to be an old man, and it was my responsibility to examine him from time to time.

Sir William's knowledge and sureness of touch were the result of long study, careful investigation, and the application of scientific principles, but like every innovator he was not popular. Nor were those who followed his methods—as I found in my dealings with rival house surgeons. But I had no doubt that Sir William was right. He was outstanding in every branch of surgery, from removing a brain tumour to breaking legs bent by rickets and setting them straight again. Besides such work, he introduced to Scotland the technique of treating tuberculous disease of the bones and joints by immobilising them in plaster of paris.

My interest in surgery was given fresh impetus when I was appointed Junior Assistant to Professor Macewen—at the splendid salary of fifty pounds per annum, on which I had to live out. In the mornings, my work was tutoring, demonstrating, lecturing, and assisting in operations. In the afternoons I processed the tissue of tumours removed by Sir William and made a microscopic diagnosis.

Outside medicine, my main interest was politics. The Liberal convictions of my grandfather and father had influenced me strongly, and I was a keen supporter of Asquith's government in its fight against the power of the House of Lords to veto bills from the House of Commons.

In the general election of 1910 the first meeting of the Saltcoats campaign was held in the Station Square. A wagonette served as hustings for the speakers who addressed the crowd, amongst whom I stood to watch and listen. The chairman sent me two messages to join him on the wagonette, and at last I decided to plunge into the political fray. From then until election day I was busy on almost every night, and was referred to at a Tory meeting as "the schoolboy politician who seems to be so busy at this election."

"Dinna' fash yersel' aboot the young doctor — he'd flatten ye if he were here," called a stonemason in the audience. "Gi'e us yer ain story."

The Tory candidate proceeded to do so, and as it was in support of the House of Lords his "story" cost him his seat.

Our Liberal candidate already had been defeated in Ayrshire, which was a Tory stronghold, and there was talk of moving him to a safe seat. But I appealed to London to leave him with us, and we swept him through to victory on election day.

3

FIRST TASTE OF AUSTRALIA

A YEAR LATER I WAS GIVEN THE OPPORTUNITY OF SIGNING
on the R.M.S. *Omrah*, of the Orient Line, as ship's
surgeon for a voyage to Australia and back. This seemed like
an opportunity for a much needed holiday and change of
scene, so I jumped at the chance.

But I almost lost it. Sir William Macewen had given me
leave, but his senior assistant fell sick. Sir William had been
commanded to attend the coronation of King George V and
Queen Mary, and as Surgeon to the King of Scotland would
be away for a week—the very week in which I was to make
my arrangements for the voyage. He told me that I would
have to carry out his duties in his absence.

I caught the night express to London for interview by the
directors of the Orient Line, and was accepted. As I was about
to leave the office, the secretary told me to return on the
following morning to sign the ship's articles at the Board of
Trade office and be measured and fitted for uniforms. "I
can't," I told him. "I'm lecturing at Glasgow University at
nine next morning."

"Then what guarantee have we that you'll be available when you're required?"

"Only my word," I told him, and he said, "I shall have to consult the directors."

He went into the board room, leaving me on tenterhooks until he hurried back and said, "We must sign you on right away."

We ran round to the Board of Trade office, which was just about to close, and I was duly signed onto the *Omrah*. The next couple of weeks passed in a rush, but in due course I reported aboard the ship—only to find that sailing was delayed by a seamen's strike. The number of deckhands, firemen, and trimmers who had signed on was far short of requirements, so the Chief Officer had to hustle around London and collect drafts of men for the crew. I had to examine them for medical fitness, but the third draft was so drunk that the men slumped around the deck unable to stand—I refused to examine them. But the ship sailed with them!

The scratch crew had to prove its ability to handle a life-boat, so two boats were lowered to the river and rowed around under the eyes of Board of Trade officials. Luckily there were enough officers and experienced seamen to make a showing, because it was obvious that to most of the newcomers an oar was simply a strangely-shaped piece of wood. The boats went round in circles until the officers could push the crews into some kind of shape, which satisfied the officials who in any case were in a hurry to go and watch the Coronation Naval Review at Spithead.

At last we steamed out of the Thames into the English Channel, where I was to find that my experiences in fishing-boats had not immunised me against seasickness. The Channel was rough, but the Bay of Biscay was even rougher, and I was so violently sick that I could not leave my bunk. Fortunately there were no cases requiring urgent medical attention.

Lord Denman, the Governor-General-elect of Australia, was on board with his wife and staff, and Lady Denman remarked that I was not able to look after myself, to say nothing of the passengers. She dosed me with her own prescription, though whether I was cured by that or by becoming accustomed to the motion is hard to say. At least I was well enough to take care of medical clearance of the ship when we reached Gibraltar.

We sailed on to Toulon, then through the Mediterranean. It was all a thrilling experience for a young Scottish doctor who had hardly even crossed the border into England before that, and I drank in all the new sights as well as thoroughly enjoying the life on board ship, which for a doctor was a very leisurely affair after the grimness of Glasgow slums and the constant emergencies of hospital work.

But coaling at Port Said shocked me. It was an inhuman process. A plank stretched from the wharf to the deck, and up it ran a ceaseless stream of Egyptians clad in loin cloths, each with a basket of coal on his shoulder. The Egyptian in charge stood on the wharf and every now and then, with the foulest of English swearing brought down a whip on the back of one of the runners. The baskets emptied, the men ran down another plank, refilled their baskets and trotted up again.

On the first day in the Red Sea, I was called to a young fireman who had been brought on deck after collapsing in the stokehold. Most ships were fired by coal in those days, a matter which I took for granted until I climbed down the ladders into the depths of the ship and saw stokehold conditions for myself. Toiling like demons, the firemen had to lift the coal on huge shovels and sling it into the roaring fires, exposed to the searing heat which doubled the high temperatures of the Red Sea. Sodden with sweat, their teeth gleaming in blackened faces as they grimaced with the effort, they fed the fires which kept the great ship sailing elegantly onwards, with passengers sipping cool drinks under her deck awnings.

The firemen were kept supplied with coal by the trimmers, who worked in scarcely less difficult conditions in the bunkers. Not only did they have to keep coal flowing into the stokehold, but they had to shift mountains of it to keep the ship on an even keel as the bunkers were depleted with consequent shift of weight. Their sweating bodies were plastered with coal dust, which they breathed in until their lungs were suitable only for pathological studies.

No wonder the young fireman was delirious and almost maniacal, and had to be held down while I applied slabs of ice to his body. He calmed down as he began to recover from his heat-stroke, and wanted to go back to work. He knew that his mates would have to toil harder because of his absence. But I would not allow this, even though the Chief Officer was worried about the stokehold shifts being undermanned.

Another of my patients was a young woman who had been thrown off her feet when the ship pitched during the night. She was carrying her baby, and with typical maternal instinct did not throw out her arms to protect herself. Her face was badly cut and bruised, but when I was called to attend her I was seasick again. The woman was laid on a table, and a seaman stood on either side of me, holding a basin for instant use as the ship pitched and rolled. I found that the patient's nose was broken, and in the intervals between filling the basins I managed to put it temporarily to rights. Two days later, when the sea had calmed down again, I set her nose properly.

I found that a special advantage of my position as ship's surgeon was that I had the sole run of the quarantine deck, which was out of bounds to passengers and crew. This became very useful when I found myself strongly attracted to an Australian girl who was returning home with her parents on the *Omrah*, and by the time the ship reached Colombo we were engaged.

The first port of call in Australia was Fremantle. It was my job to instruct the immigrants, of whom there were a good many on board, on the Australian quarantine regulations and inspections. I held two rehearsals of the procedure which the passengers would have to go through, and explained the diseases which would prevent any of them from entering Australia. Four male immigrants reported that they were suffering from one or another of these, but after examining them I rather thought that they were afflicted by the disease of homesickness. However, they had made the declaration, so I had to leave the final decision to the Fremantle Port Doctor.

We sailed on through the Great Australian Bight, which

luckily for me did not live up to its reputation of being just as rough as the Bay of Biscay. I had seen Perth; now Adelaide lay ahead, and Melbourne, which in some ways was to remind me of Glasgow, and then Sydney and finally Brisbane. There, I saw something which I had never seen before—a family riding on horseback down the main street of the city.

I fell in love with Australia. I felt that the country was still in its infancy, and that it held challenges which were far more exciting than any which could be offered by the cramped old life at home. As we sailed back from Brisbane to Sydney, I made up my mind. I wanted to marry, which would be impossible on the fifty pounds a year which I received from the University. Good medical positions in Britain were hard to come by, and to start in general practice a man had to slave for many years as an assistant, with the hope of being taken into partnership, or have enough money to buy a practice. For me, I decided the future was in Australia. So from Sydney I wrote my letter of resignation from Glasgow University.

My fiancée was a Melbourne girl, so I met her again when the ship called at that port. There was much to talk about and the time was short, and to my horror I discovered that I had dallied too long. I rushed back to the wharf where the ship lay, just in time to see that the gangways had been heaved aboard and the mooring ropes slipped. She was just easing away from the wharf, so I tossed a parcel to the sailors on the lower deck and yelled to them to catch me when I jumped. I ran back to gather speed, took the leap, then landed safe in the arms of half-a-dozen sailors.

The voyage home went slowly; I was too anxious to wind up my affairs in Scotland and return to Australia and my wife-to-be. When I arrived in Scotland, I found a letter from Sir Donald Macallister, Principal of Glasgow University, directing me to call on him. When I did so he said that my resignation had been a surprise and asked if there had been a difference of opinion with Sir William.

"Not the slightest," I said. "I've been very happy in my work."

"It's very puzzling," he said. "We confidently expected that you would follow an academic career. You've got one foot on the ladder, but you're jumping off instead of climbing. Can you explain why?"

I told him the reason, and when he asked me to reconsider I was firm about my intention to settle in Australia — a decision I have never regretted. We parted good friends, and I was always welcomed back at the University when I returned for further study.

4

DOCTOR DOWN A MINE

T HE PROBLEM WAS HOW I WAS TO GET BACK TO AUSTRALIA.
So I looked for another post as ship's surgeon on a vessel
sailing to Australia—on which I would not return. This was
not so easy, but at last I was appointed surgeon to an immigrant
ship which would be sailing in six months' time.

To support myself in the meantime, I became assistant to
a doctor in a practice which covered four mining villages.
The experience was not to be a stimulating one. No operations
were performed, and it was made clear to me that I must not
even attempt minor surgery. I soon found that an acute
appendix was written off as a "sair belly," and that death
certificates for young children neatly described the cause of
mortality as "prematurity." Those for aged patients went to
the other extreme. According to the certificates, they had
died of "senility."

I found such things hard to swallow, but as the assistant I
was obliged to conform with my employer's instructions.
Twice, however, I rebelled. On the evening I arrived, I
examined a miner who complained of a very painful back,

and prescribed an ointment to be applied. When Dr McCluskey read my entry in the prescription book, he grunted, "That's far o'er dear for a miner's back. I'll show ye how we treat miner's backs here. See these two stock bottles? They're both water with a trace of mercuric chloride, but one's coloured with methylene blue, and the other's red with cochineal. Give the blue lotion to rub in for three to four weeks, and if the sair back's no better then change over to the red. Ye'll find that the pain soon goes after that."

"I haven't unpacked my cases, doctor," I said. "And if that ointment's not dispensed, I won't be doing so. I'll leave in the morning."

The ointment was dispensed, but the other difference of opinion between us could have been more serious. The old doctor had just sat down to lunch when I returned from the morning round. "John Currie at the high village has acute appendicitis," I reported. "There's tenderness over the appendix, his abdominal muscles are on guard, and he's in great pain with a high temperature and pulse rate. I told his mother he'll have to go to hospital."

"You should have left that to me," said the doctor. "It'll be just another case of sair belly. He can be treated at home. His mother's a wise woman, and she'll look after him."

"That boy will die if he's not operated on," I said. "The sooner it's done, the better. But in any case I've told you now, so whatever happens is your responsibility."

The doctor grunted and went on eating his lunch, but in the late afternoon he told me that he had seen the lad and arranged for him to go to hospital.

But Doctor MacCluskey was not always behind the times. Diphtheria was endemic in the mining villages, as in so many places in those days, and he insisted on a supply of anti-toxin being carried on the rounds. No doubt this saved many a child's life, to say nothing of saving the doctors' legs on calls to those who might have contracted the disease.

We relied on our legs in those days when the motor-car was still regarded as a somewhat erratic toy, but since one of the villages was a good walk over a high hill and across a moor I decided to hire a horse for one of my visits there. When I returned, Doctor MacCluskey was waiting for me. "Riding is out," he said firmly. "You must walk to the villages."

"But I paid for the ride—it was my responsibility," I protested.

The doctor laid down the law. "If anything happened to you, then as your employer I would have to pay. So no more riding while you're working here!"

So walk I did, which I daresay was good for my physical and mental health. And as I walked past a row of miners' cottages a Mrs Greig gave me an anxious call. I found her husband in bed and distressed in his breathing, but he objected when I sat him up for examination. "I dinna want ony o' they newfangled instruments you've got," he wheezed.

"But I can't find out your trouble unless I examine you."

He lay down again, and muttered, "Ah'm no' gaun to be examined."

"Och, Alec, let the doctor examine you," Mrs Greig said. "Ye've no' been out of the house for a week, and look at the time ye've lost at the pit."

I knew that something must be seriously wrong if a miner was missing work, so took out my watch and said, "Mr Greig, I'll give you two minutes to make up your mind."

The seconds ticked away, but he said nothing. I tucked the watch back in my waistcoat pocket, and said, "I'm sorry to go, but I've the top village to do as well as this one."

He still did not give in, but on my way home again Mrs Greig was waiting for me. "Alec's worse, and he's awfu' hot," she said. "If you're willing, he'd like to see you again. I was fair ashamed this mornin'."

Mr Greig sat up meekly, and when I sounded and percussed his chest I discovered a big accumulation of fluid over the right lung. His temperature was 102 degrees. I told him the situation, and said, "We can get rid of the fluid and ease your breathing if you let me use an instrument I have. It's back at the doctor's house. What d'you say?"

"I leave it to you, doctor," he said resignedly, and I told his anxious wife to scald out a tureen, fill it with boiled water and leave it to cool, and to have a big kettle boiling when I returned that afternoon.

Top: Children of the Half-Caste Home at Alice Springs in 1934. Bottom: This was the only hospital for Aborigines in the Alice Springs area in 1934

After lunch I packed my aspirator, and set off without telling Doctor MacCluskey where I was going. The operation was performed in the kitchen on the bed—recessed in the kitchen wall as so often in those days. I fitted my apparatus together and Mrs Greig gasped as I inserted the needle into her husband's back, but she was a most efficient helper and did not falter as viscous straw-coloured fluid began to run through the tube into the apparatus bottle. "You can relax now," I told Greig as I removed the aspirator, but he was speechless when he saw the fluid. "Did a' that come oot o' my back?" he asked, while Mrs Greig brought in her next door neighbour to admire the results and make all concerned a cup of tea. Greig himself could breathe freely again, and was somewhat reconciled to "newfangled instruments."

In the good old style, Doctor MacCluskey dispensed his own prescriptions, and the patients brought their own bottles to be filled. Usually these were empty whisky flasks, which they handed in at a small hatch in the wall separating the waiting room from the dispensary. One evening I glanced through the opening to see a five-year-old boy lifting a glass-stoppered lemonade bottle onto the shelf of the hatch, and said, "That's a funny bottle for medicine, son."

"There are nae drinkers in oor house," he answered solemnly.

The doctor made good use of me by sending me out to all the night-time confinements, which sometimes gave me little sleep. I decided on a measure of self-defence, and after the baby was born I would stay in the house and sleep on a couch until day dawned. Even then I would sometimes be called to another case after returning home, and on one such occasion the laird's wife sent a gig to fetch me. Half-asleep, I was being carried up the drive when I was suddenly jolted forward. "What was that for?" I asked the driver as he started off again.

"There was a pheasant on the drive. It would be as much as my job is worth to run over it."

"Next time risk the pheasant and save my back," I grumbled.

One evening the doctor was attending an unmarried girl of twenty, who was in labour with her third child. She had been

Aborigines around Alice Springs built themselves such "houses" as these out of rubbish discarded by the white man. These were photographed by the author in 1934, but similar shacks were in existence as late as 1970

in severe labour for some hours and was making little headway, so the doctor sent a note to the surgery. "Bring those new forceps of yours and don't be long," I read.

As I arrived, I heard loud screams from the patient, followed by Doctor MacCluskey's sharp, "Dae that again and I'll skelp yer arse." The yell was repeated a few minutes later, and the doctor's heavy hand came down upon the patient's buttock. I had to deliver the baby with the "new forceps," and when a safe delivery was announced the girl's father opened a bottle of whisky. A little dropped on the baby's head caused it to cry lustily, after which the grandfather poured a glass for the father (the fathers of the other two children were not present), another for the mother, and finally one for himself. The old doctor and I had to make adequate excuses to abstain.

One man owned the whole countryside, including the coal mines. He spent most of his time in London, but always returned for the quarterly Church communion. His factor (agent) employed gamekeepers to rear pheasants, and preserve them for the shooting season in the autumn. On one of my routine visits to a row of mining cottages a small dog followed me, and the woman waiting in the room where patients were seen began to exclaim at the sight of it. "Doctor, if the gamekeeper hears that ye brought a dog across the moor he'll blame ye for disturbing the pheasants, and that'll be the end of ye," one of them said.

"Hoots, woman, I didn't bring the dog. It followed me," I told her.

"It doesna' matter what ye say," another woman said. "The company'll no' stand for it."

A few days later I met the head keeper, and asked what would happen to the hundreds of young pheasants he was rearing. "They're fed here at the home farm until about two months before the visitors are due," he said. "Then they're taken a mile or so out beyond the shooting-butts, and later we move 'em about three miles further off. They fly home for their food, but when we take them further out then this feeding is cut down so that they'll look for natural food away out on the moors."

"But they'll still think that there's food at home?"

"Ay, but by the time they've been out a month or so they don't fly back until the beaters are out."

"And when the beaters disturb them they make for home — over the butts where Sir Albert's guests are waiting with their guns cocked?"

"I thought you were interested, but you've been fooling me," the keeper said angrily.

"No, not fooling you. I know this pheasant business is your livelihood, but shooting tame birds is not my idea of sport."

Another "sport," in another part of the country, riled me even more. I was spending a day at a large farm run by a father and two sons, and noticed the farmer's wife fussing over a patch of fresh-turned earth near a haystack. She was throwing pieces of straw upon it as camouflage, and when I asked "What are you up to?" she said in a subdued voice, "A fox has been raiding the fowl yard, and Bob shot it this morning. If Lord Eglinton's gamekeeper finds he's a fox short he'll enquire at the farms, and if he saw fresh earth he'd want to know what was below. Bob might lose the farm for shooting a fox. They preserve them for fox-hunting."

I had seen such a hunt when I was a schoolboy, and watched the redcoated riders go hell-for-leather through crops and over fences. The compensation for any damage was only what the factor cared to pay, since the farms were rented from the landowner who enjoyed foxhunting. The only farmer who owned his own land was James Spiers; he also shot a fox that killed his poultry — to the great consternation of the same gamekeeper who had to provide sport for his master.

The coal mines lay close to the mining villages, and one of the seams was entered through a cutting in a hillside. The foreman asked me if I'd like a trip below, and when I agreed he guided me through the cut and down the long, gloomy, steeply-sloping shaft. At the bottom I was surprised to find a swift-flowing stream, fed by seepage from within the hill, and when we had jumped over that the glistening coal seam lay before us. It was worked from two sides, connected by a hole at floor-level that was just big enough for a man to wriggle through.

The miners appreciated my coming to see them. They had not expected me to accept the invitation, and talked freely about their work. Soon they challenged me to wriggle through to the other side of the seam, and a young spark said, "None but a miner has ever gone through that hole. Ye have to lie on yer back, gae in heed first, and work yer way through."

"That's no' a job for a doctor," scolded an older man, and told me, "Once ye start, ye'll be lying on coal with the whole depth of the seam above ye. A whimper in the seam would bring it doon; ye'd be as flat as a pancake."

I knelt down and looked through the hole, and could hear voices on the other side saying, "He's no' game to come through, and I don't blame him."

That settled it. I lay on my back and worked myself through head first; through the utter blackness of the hole which was scarcely broad enough for my shoulders. The miners cheered me as I emerged, for being "game" enough to do once what they did as a matter of course.

A few days later I asked the district manager of the coal mines, "Do the owners know that the miners have to go through that rathole from one face of the seam to the other? It's inhuman, and they should put a stop to it."

His face clouded, and he said defensively, "It saves the men from coming all the way up and going down the other side again," he said.

"Maybe it's good business for the owners, but it could cost men's lives—and you can tell the company what I think about it." But I doubt whether he did.

The railway station was at the dead end of a spur railway off the main line. The old porter, born in the district, had a son and daughter who migrated to Australia, and when his wife died he decided to join them. He came to the surgery for a health certificate, and when Mrs MacCluskey saw him she said, "Jamie, I think you're making a mistake going off to Australia at your age. Everything will be very different, and I hear that clothes are very dear there."

"Och, that disna matter," he said confidently. "Australia's a hot country—ye dinna need many claes."

Two months later he sailed off to his "hot country," after

giving most of his heavy clothing to his neighbours, and I often wondered what he thought about the cold winds and rain of an Australian winter.

Soon after that I was making my own way to Australia, but at least I knew enough about the country not to give any of my warm clothes away.

5

DOCTOR DOWN UNDER

ON 21 MARCH 1912 I BOARDED THE EMIGRANT SHIP AT TILBURY, about twenty miles from London, on the evening before she was to sail, and woke up next morning to find her anchored in midstream. The emigrants were brought out in lighters, on which I had to examine them before they were allowed to board the ship. I was told to pay particular attention to their hair, and if any nits were found I was to order it to be clipped off close to the scalp. This caused a great deal of wailing, but all the affected parties, male or female, had to submit to the barber's clippers.

I escaped seasickness on that voyage, though the weather was very rough and most of the migrants suffered. The old ship ploughed slowly south, with her speed dropping to four knots in the Bay of Biscay, and then had to call in at the Canary Islands for engine repairs which the Chief Engineer claimed could not be done at sea. Such sights as the sixteenth century cathedral, and the white and rose-pink flamingoes in the public park, were a welcome relief from crowded shipboard life.

The Chief Engineer vanished soon after arrival, and for twenty-four hours there was no sign of him nor of the engine spare which he had claimed to be an essential. Late on the second day a search found him to be replenished, and he was carried on board together with his spare part.

While we were in port, the Chief Steward brought his order book to the surgery and asked me to sign for a bottle of whisky as "medical comforts." He told me that he had to have whisky on hand for emergencies.

"It's for me to decide when an emergency needs a glass of whisky to cure it," I told him, but he persisted, "It's always been routine for the ship's doctor to sign for a bottle. Just sign here."

"I'm afraid I won't follow routine," I told him, and he repaid me by having the floor rugs removed from my cabin when I was absent. The Chief Officer had them replaced.

From Las Palmas to Cape Town, the sea was calm and the voyage was peaceful, so I was able to get on with my studies. Late one night I was writing at my desk when the wireless operator knocked at my door and came in. He was so pale that for a moment I thought he was ill, and that he had come to consult me, but he held out a message form in a trembling hand. "The *Titanic's* sinking," he said.

I stared at him unbelievingly. The *Titanic* was the biggest ship ever built until that time, and before we left England the papers had been full of details about her speed, size, splendid appointments, and so on. We knew that she was on her maiden voyage across the Atlantic.

"Are you sure?" I asked him, and he nodded. "I was only able to pick up snatches, but I'm afraid she's down."

"Go back up to the wireless room and I'll join you in half an hour," I told him. "See if you can hear any more."

Thirty minutes later I climbed up to the top deck where the wireless cabin had been built, and found the operator sitting amongst the primitive instruments of those days. It seemed a long time before he turned to me and said, "Yes, she's down. D'you think I should tell the Captain?"

"He turned in two hours ago, and he can't do anything. Wait till he goes to his bath in the morning," I said.

37

Half an hour before breakfast the Captain hailed me. "Shocking news," he said in a low voice. "The *Titanic* is down—it was picked up on the wireless. But you mustn't tell a soul. We should make Cape Town this evening, and it's better for the passengers to hear it ashore."

Within two hours every one of the senior officers had told me the same thing—always in strictest confidence! By night time the story had leaked out, but the appearance of Table Mountain on the horizon took the passengers' minds off it a little. Next day, they went ashore to a subdued city, and no one seemed to talk about anything else. In these days, when the world has survived two world wars and several smaller ones, it may seem strange that people were so upset by the mere sinking of a ship. But it was a great tragedy and struck very deep—especially since the *Titanic* had been hailed as "unsinkable."

Fortunately there was much in Cape Town to distract the passengers' minds. Most of them came from English cities and they were delighted with the magnificent displays of wild flowers for sale in the streets, and excited by seeing countless squirrels running along the ground and up the trees in the fine public parks. A few joined me in the spectacular cable railway trip up Table Mountain and down again.

Those amongst us who had never visited South Africa before were astonished by the contemptuous attitude of the whites towards the blacks, but any comment was swiftly brushed aside.

I had a friend in port—Mr McNab, the Deputy Town Clerk, who had been a pupil of my father's. He showed me around the city, and my interest in politics induced me to spend an evening in Parliament. General Botha, the outstanding Boer leader in the South African War, was present but did not speak. The principal speaker was a director of a diamond mine.

When Mr McNab escorted me back again to the ship, he said in some alarm, "How are you going to get through the Roaring Forties in that old tub?"

"Well, she got us through the Bay of Biscay, so I've no doubt that she'll get us to Australia," I said but I didn't know the Roaring Forties, the stormy seas that lie south of forty degrees of latitude between the Cape of Good Hope and Australia. Three days after we left Cape Town continuous rough weather set in until we reached Melbourne and became even worse during two major storms. Thick ropes had to be run across the for'ard well deck to the women's and children's quarters, to cling onto in case a sudden lurch sent one into the scuppers or over the side, and the Captain insisted that they should be used by everyone. He reprimanded me for failing to do so.

The first great storm hit us eight days out of Cape Town. The ship was flung about for two days and nights, and many of the passengers were terriffied. But even worse was ahead, and a week later the Chief Officer came in to my cabin and woke me up. He was carrying oilskins, sou'wester, and rubber seaboots, and he yelled, "Get up at once and put these on, then go to my cabin."

He stood over me while I dressed, but I refused the seaboots. "I'm better without them," I said. "They're too clumsy for me."

But when I stepped out on deck I found that it was awash, and almost at once I was drenched by a wave which knocked me against the bulkhead. Another struck me as I struggled down the companionway to the Chief Officer's cabin. Thick teak boards had been fitted at the entrance to the alleyways to prevent water from rushing along them, and the passengers' quarters had been battened down. The Captain and all executive officers had been on watch all night.

Waves were washing well over the sides, and when the ship sank into the trough of the waves it was awesome to look up at the great wall of water on either side of her. But the sight when she rode the crest was just as fearsome. Under a lowering sky I could see nothing but white-topped mountainous waves, and the worst moment came when three waves in succession smashed onto the top deck and cascaded onto the lower decks like roaring waterfalls. The ship battled on somehow, making some progress even though she seemed to be motionless in the tumult of wind and sea. One of the great waves smashed against the wireless cabin on the top deck, almost wrecking the primitive equipment. When the operator got it working again the first message that he picked up was: "*Wakool*—are you afloat?"

But the storm passed, and for some reason I had felt no special fear of a rougher sea than I had ever dreamed possible.

An odd incident was the discovery, during morning inspection by Captain, Chief Officer, Surgeon, and Purser, that one of the lower-deck portholes had been forced open, allowing water to pour into the ship. All portholes had been secured with special wrenches, and it was soon found that one of these was missing. The passenger responsible was traced, and kept under close control for the rest of the voyage.

During the previous week the ship had been plastered with stickers advertising the I.W.W.—the initials of the International Workers of the World. The stickers were pulled off and no others appeared, but the immigrant responsible must have walked ashore at Sydney. I often wondered what role he fulfilled in Australia.

Amongst the passengers were a number of young women, some of whom were going to join their husbands in Australia. One of these had remarked several times on the very comfortable couch in the cabin where patients were examined—part of the ship's surgeon's suite. One afternoon she opened the door, walked in, and sat on the couch. It was not my time for examining patients, but she said that she felt ill. I soon found that her pulse was normal, her tongue clean, and her colour good. "Not much wrong with you," I said. "Maybe you had too much lunch. Take some exercise and see if that makes you feel better.

"No, my stomach is properly upset," she persisted with a winning smile. "I want some medicine."

I dispensed an ounce of castor oil, which cured her—and her interest in the couch—very quickly. Another lady sent me a note saying that she was in bed and very sick, so I went along to see her. I was accompanied by a stewardess, the usual thing when I was examining women in their cabins, and the passenger's face fell when she saw her. "What's the trouble?" I asked, and she said, "The food on this ship is too rough. I've never been accustomed to such food. It makes me sick and upsets my bowels."

"I inspect the food you eat, and often eat it myself," I told her. "So far as I'm concerned it's perfectly satisfactory. But if you have to use the receptacles in the cabin kindly notify the stewardess, who will report to me. Good afternoon."

In dealing with these two ladies, I was mindful of a case which had occurred about five years before. A young married woman, travelling to England in a single first-class cabin, had sent for the ship's doctor several times in the early hours of the morning. Unwisely, he had neglected to disturb a stewardess to accompany him at such times, and when the ship reached Tilbury the young woman complained to her husband that the doctor had been pestering her. The husband demanded that the shipping company should dismiss the doctor, to which they replied that if he was prepared to divorce his wife then they would dismiss their officer. This rebuff made him angry enough to complain to the British Medical Association, which found the young doctor guilty of unprofessional conduct and struck him off the roll of medical practitioners. He had qualified only two years before, and this action, which ended his professional career, was thought by many to be an over-severe punishment. But members of the medical profession enjoy a special trust, and the Association demands that their high reputation shall be maintained at all costs.

There was great excitement as the ship neared Australia, and a great washing and ironing of clothes in preparation to disembark at Melbourne and Sydney. The immigrants streamed down the gangways, some into the arms of waiting relatives and some to the bewilderment and strangeness of starting a new life in a strange land. Soon it was my turn, and I stepped ashore in Sydney to begin work as a doctor in Australia.

6

COUNTRY DOCTOR

I N SYDNEY, I WAS MET BY JOHN YOUNG OF NHILL, VICTORIA, WHO
was soon to be my father-in-law, and Professor R. D. Watt,
an old friend from Glasgow University. After a couple of days of
sightseeing we boarded the westward train, and after an
overnight trip to Cowra I began to see many things that were
strange to me. "Why don't they cut the timber for firewood
and cart it to the towns?" I asked when I saw great stacks of
dead trees burning in newly-cleared paddocks. "Because it
would cost too much to cart and cut," Mr Young told me.

"Then why are so many fine trees destroyed anyway?"

"So that more grass will grow for the sheep."

"But trees attract moisture, and give shade to the sheep in
hot weather. Isn't it a mistake to cut so many of them down?"

But I was soon made to realise that, as a "new-chum," my
role was to look and listen, and not to offer advice.

It was a slow train trip across New South Wales in those
days, and my former delight in Australia was somewhat
tempered by the sight of seemingly endless stretches of dry
brown grass—where there was any at all. I had not expected to

see the lush green of the British Isles, but this parched country-side was certainly an extreme contrast.

At Kerang, on the Victorian side of the River Murray, we were met by a car driven by Ivan Young. As we drove across the countryside, my depression and astonishment deepened. I was seeing Australia during one of its worst droughts, and in the days before very much progress had been made in water conservation and reticulation away from the cities. Everything was parched, bare, and seemingly lifeless. As we began to drive along a track through the paddocks, stopping from time to time to open and close the gates, I was staggered to see four cows and three calves in such dreadful condition that their bones seemed to be protruding through their skin. They looked like hatracks. Further on it was even worse. Some sheep were hopelessly bogged in an attempt to reach a pool of muddy water at the bottom of a dam, and several were lying on their backs feebly moving their legs. Others were still standing, but fell over as they ran away from the moving car. "Can't we put them on their feet?" I pleaded, and my future in-laws took pity on my ignorance and stopped the car. But as soon as the sheep were righted again, they fell over once more. Slowly I began to realise that nothing could be done. Until the rain fell again, the stock must perish, and I simply had to try to develop the same seeming indifference as my companions.

I gave myself away as a new chum yet again when we stopped at an hotel for lunch. As soon as I had finished a plate of boiled mutton and vegetables the waitress whisked it away, and asked, "Have a return?"

I asked, "What is a return?" I'd never heard the word applied to meals before then.

Soon after that I was reunited with my fiancée and warmly welcomed by her family. Her father had extensive country interests and had planned a trip to give me some idea of the inland, but my arrival coincided with the breaking of the drought. The skies opened and deluged the parched land, and it was two more weeks before it was possible to travel. Even then, the unpaved roads were muddy and slippery, and at one point we came to a pool stretching right across the road. "Follow the buggy tracks," Mr Young told his English chauffeur, but he didn't and the car was bogged to the axles. Mr Young jumped into the mud and tried to turn a rear wheel while the driver applied power, but it would not grip. "I don't mind tackling the other wheel, but my trousers are coming off first," I said.

By packing brush under the rear wheels we managed to edge the car out of the bog. Mr Young's sodden trousers were clinging to him, but he laughed at my mudcaked legs. "You can't pull your trousers over those," he said, so I folded the car rug round me with the tassles hanging below my knees. "You can introduce me as your friend from Scotland, still in his kilt," I said.

We pulled up at the Rainbow Hotel for lunch, and Mr Young did as I suggested. But one of the bystanders, a Scot, said, "There's nae doot the man's a Scotsman, but that's no' a kilt he's wearing."

Five months later, Irene Isabella Young and I were married at the Collins Street Congregational Church in Melbourne. The minister, the Rev. Leyton Richards, and my best man, Professor Robert Watt, were both University friends of mine.

I had decided to practise in the country for a spell, in order to learn the ways and temperament of the real Australian at close quarters, before trying my hand in the city. But my first contact was to be a fellow Scot, Hugh McLean, who called before breakfast and insisted on seeing me. He stretched out his hand with tears running down his cheeks, and said, "You're the first man from my home town that I've met since I came here twenty years ago."

He was in no need of medicine, but no doubt our long yarn together had a therapeutic effect. Our newly-made friendship continued throughout his life and was carried on by his children.

The town in which I practised was Minyip, in the Wimmera district of western Victoria. It was well under a hundred years since the Wimmera had been discovered by the explorer Major Thomas Mitchell, who is said to have named it after the Aboriginal word for a throwing stick or boomerang. The railway had been running through the district for only about thirty years, and a good many of the population were either the original pioneers of the area or their sons and daughters. After the lush countryside and cramped cities of Scotland it was strange country to me, with the seemingly endless plains undulating away to the horizon and broken only by fences, windmills, the occasional belt of trees, and the little homesteads with their barns and stables. Yet it had its own kind of beauty, which I soon came to recognise; the spaciousness of great skies overhead, the huge wheat paddocks which were emerald green in spring and a shining gold when they were ready for harvest, and the glittering clarity of the air.

The people were typical Australian country folk—as outgoing, welcoming, and democratic as the Scots, and I soon felt at home amongst them.

There were cases of typhoid fever in the district, and the doctor from whom I was taking over took me to see a very sick girl who was believed to be suffering from the disease. "This doesn't suggest typhoid to me, but a septic infection," I said when I looked at the chart. "What's the history of the case?"

The doctor said that the girl had had an attack of measles some time before. The affliction had left her somewhat hard of hearing, and lately she had complained of pain in the left ear and of increasing headaches.

By that time the girl had been in bed for three weeks. She seemed to be oblivious of her surroundings, but when I pressed gently on the bone behind her left ear she gave a piercing scream. As I had suspected she had a mastoid infection, and I told her parents that nothing would save her but an immediate operation. They agreed, and I hurried back to the surgery for my instruments.

But when I looked through the big wooden trunk which I had had made in Scotland to carry all my medical equipment, I discovered that it did not contain the necessary mallet and chisel for cutting through the mastoid bone. There was only a Macewen gouge. Unfastening and unpacking the trunk had taken some time, and when I hurried into town I found that the shops were closing. It was midday on a Saturday.

I searched the general store for anything that might be suitable, but the best I could find were two thin-bladed joiner's chisels and a croquet mallet. I returned to the surgery

45

and began to saw the handle of the croquet mallet down to size, and as I was doing so the girl's parents arrived. The father asked hesitantly, "Would you mind if we consulted another doctor?"

"By all means do so. But I have no doubt that the operation is needed, and I don't think it should be delayed too long."

They looked at each other, and after a brief talk asked me to do what I could. There was no hospital in the town, but by good fortune one of the daughters of a local farmer was a trained nurse. She helped me to prepare a room for the operation, and on the following morning we laid the patient on the table. Her hair had been cut and shaved around the mastoid area, and after exposing the bone I took up one of the joiner's chisels and the head of the croquet mallet, on which I had left just enough of the shaft to provide a handle. They had of course been sterilised by boiling.

When the required amount of bone was removed pus was found at the depth of the mastoid cavity and carefully mopped up. The cavity was then lightly packed with a narrow strip of iodoform gauze.

Within thirty-six hours the child's temperature had dropped, and she made a steady recovery. Twenty-five years later her father called on me in Adelaide, saying, "You probably don't remember me."

"Oh yes I do," I told him. "How is your daughter?"

"She's never had an illness since you operated on her, and she is now the mother of four children. My wife and I thought that you'd like to know."

I still had the chisels. I used them for many years in carpentry until the head of the larger one split, after which I kept the other in my study as a memento of my first operation in Australia.

My stay in the country achieved the desired result of teaching me more about Australia and the Australians, and was full of human interest. One day a young Scot called on me and I recognised him as the son of a brilliant family whom I had known at home, but he was poorly dressed and down on his luck. I soon found out why. I found him a job at sewing wheat bags, but he was argumentative and aggressive and quickly fell out

TOP: Part-Aboriginal children at Alice Springs in 1934. BOTTOM: This pair of newly-weds was photographed by the author on his first visit to Alice Springs

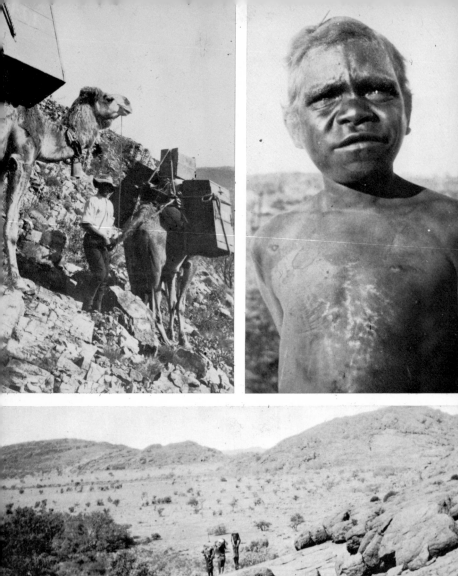

with his employer and workmates. The next I heard of him was that he was in a mental hospital, whose superintendent told me that his aggressiveness had increased. As a Celt, the young Scot was adamant on the score of Home Rule for Ireland, but another patient in the hospital took exactly the opposite tack. They argued furiously, reaching a climax when, at lunch one day, the Scot rose in his seat, lifted a large jug of milk and crashed it down on his opponent's head.

The young Scot had run away from home in his early twenties, and if he had not revealed himself to me I doubt whether his family would ever have learnt where he had gone.

My father and grandfather were so well known in parts of Scotland that I was rarely without some link with home — even if it was an unwelcome one. One day I read in a local newspaper that a set of clothes had been found near a deep irrigation channel, and that their owner, whose name was mentioned, was believed to be drowned. But I had my doubts. I knew the young man — the only son of wealthy parents but shiftless and cunning. He had left Scotland for Australia about eighteen months after his father died, and I had little doubt that for some reason he had shed the clothes and dressed in another set, in order to obscure his trail while he took off for another State. He must have been successful, because lengthy efforts failed to find the body or the man, and the clothing was never claimed.

A month after I began to practise I was called to a distant sheep property, which meant a long, cold trip by horse and buggy through the wintry landscape. When I reached the homestead a middle-aged daughter told me that her father was suffering attacks of great pain. She led me in to find a man of about seventy, clad in working shirt and trousers, lying on a couch in the kitchen. He was thin, and had the worn features of a "hard battler."

I took his temperature, listened to his heart, and was about to raise him in order to examine his back when he screamed with pain. His body arched off the couch as though in unbearable tension, and I thought immediately of two things — strychnine poisoning or a tetanus infection.

When his spasm had passed, I looked for further signs of

Top Left: This photograph of Mr G. G. Kramer with his camels shows the kind of country which camels could tackle when used as pack animals in Central Australia. Top Right: Tjaruru, described by the author as "one of the most intelligent men, of any race, whom I have ever met." Bottom: Scene in the Musgrave Ranges

one or the other of these. There was no locking of the jaw or stiffness of the neck, and the man's muscles had relaxed. His temperature was normal, and I could not find any cut in his hands or feet which might have given access to tetanus from infected earth. It seemed that I could eliminate that possibility.

As I examined the old man, I was struck by the unusual and even eerie atmosphere of the property. Usually a farmhouse would be bustling with life, and any visitor who called would be entertained by those who wanted to hear the latest news. But the house was silent, and I had seen no one but the daughter.

I probed the patient's abdomen, and felt it spring to rigidity under my fingers as the old man screamed again. His back arched in another spasm, but he slowly relaxed once more. He was clear in his mind and answered questions without hesitation, but after we had been talking quietly for about ten minutes he screamed loudly and went into yet another spasm.

I was faced with a very serious situation and went to the kitchen door to call the daughter. "Is the rest of the family around?" I asked.

She nodded.

"Ask them to come in, please."

She brought her mother and brothers into the sitting room, and I spoke to the elder son—a man between forty and fifty. My brief experience in the Australian countryside enabled me to ask, "Where do you keep the strychnine for poisoning foxes?"

"There's never been any strychnine on the station as far as I know," he said.

I asked him about the various outbuildings, but he said each time that he had never known strychnine to be kept in any of them. So I turned to the mother and said quietly, "I'm sorry, but I'm afraid that your husband is very ill and I don't think that he's likely to recover."

She grasped her daughter's arm, and they went slowly into the kitchen. The sons were silent when I told them, "In my opinion your father has somehow swallowed strychnine. It is too late to save him now. I don't know where the poison came from but I'm sure that he hasn't long to live. I'm very distressed about this, because it's my duty to put the cause of death on the certificate."

The sons still regarded me dumbly, and I thought that they must be too stunned for speech. I left the house, and was driving towards the road when I looked back and saw a horseman galloping away in the opposite direction. I was able to recognise that he was the elder son, and there was something about the wild urgency of his riding which made me know at once what he was going to do.

I was not called upon to certify the farmer's death, and though I had plenty of other things on my mind I found time to wonder what happened. But the family did not send for me again, and I had no reason for driving in their direction. I did not forget, and later in the year there was a golf tournament at which I met the doctor who served the opposite side of the district from my own. We chatted for a while, and then I asked, "By the way, were you called to see the farmer at Hilltop a couple of months ago?"

"Yes. Too late, I'm afraid. He was collapsed and dying."

"What did you give as the cause of death?"

"Why are you asking?"

"Because the family called me in too. It's my opinion that the old man was dying of strychnine poisoning. It's not too late to have the body exhumed. How do you feel about it?"

"I feel that we're doctors, not policemen. You have a right to your opinion, but there's no need to go any further."

I never met the family, nor the doctor, again.

In those days, death in the country seemed to be treated fairly casually. A day or two later the local constable called to say, "A body was found on the road a couple of miles out of town, doctor. It's in the mortuary now. Will you do a post-mortem today?"

"Are there any signs of injury?"

"Not a thing."

"How old is he?"

"Late sixties, I reckon. Probably died of natural causes."

"I hope so, anyway. I'm no pathologist, and unless it's something obvious I'm likely to be guessing."

49

"That's all right, doctor. All I want is a cause of death to put in my report."

I found an enlarged heart, which satisfied the constable, but it would not necessarily have been the sole or real cause of death.

Only a week afterwards he called me to the scene of a murder, at a little country pub about ten miles to the north. After certifying the cause of death I was glad to leave everything to the police.

One of my sorest memories of that period is of the time when a local bank manager showed me a cheque on which the signature was barely legible. "The old man's writing has got much worse lately," he said. "Would you mind taking a look at him, to see if he knows what he's doing?"

The "old man" to whom he referred was Mr McIver, eighty years old and the owner of a valuable property. He had never married, and was looked after by a young woman. A relation of hers was employed to work the land.

McIver was a Scot, and when I called on him he asked me to sing "We'd better bide a wee." I knew the song and its implications, and although I could sense the old man's emotions and nostalgia I tried to pass it off by saying, "I'm no singer, Mr McIver."

But he started to sign, then broke off and said quaveringly, "I want you to sing too." So I pulled myself together and joined in, and after that we talked for a while about the homeland which he had not seen for so long.

Then I got down to business, and asked, "Mr McIver, is it right that you want to draw money from the bank?"

"Ay, that's right. Freda needs it for the house."

"Would you mind just writing your name on this piece of paper?"

Freda, the housekeeper, drew up a little table to the old man's chair, and held the paper steady for him. With great difficulty he signed his name, which to me looked very much like the signature on the cheque.

I seized a couple more opportunities to speak about the money which he wanted to withdraw, and on both occasions he told me that Freda wanted it for the house. Eventually I gave the specimen signature to the bank manager, with McIver's explanation for the withdrawal. He seemed satisfied, and I dismissed the matter from my mind—since, strictly speaking, it was none of my business.

But a doctor in a country town becomes very closely involved in its life—far more so than in a city practice. Three months later the old man died, and after the funeral I had a visit from his nephew, Tom Donald. He looked sufficiently distressed for me to ask him what was wrong, and he said, "I've been tricked out of my uncle's farm, doctor."

"Tricked? But how?"

"They've just been reading the will. Until about three months ago, he'd willed his farm to me, but now he's turned it over to that woman who's been working for him. I let fly when the will was read——said it couldn't be right, and so forth. But the lawyer just waited until I'd finished, and said there was no doubt about the signature. He said you had satisfied the bank that the old man was able to sign his name properly, and that he knew what he was doing."

"The bank, yes. But I didn't know anything about the will."

Tom gave a hopeless shrug. "I'm not blaming you, doctor, but they've used you, I'm afraid—same as they used the old man. They must have grabbed at the chance to get his signature on a new will as soon as they could. They've got a perfect witness to say that he was in full possession of his faculties."

He meant me, of course, but I tried to persuade him that he could contest the will and said that I would do everything possible to help him. But he refused. "No, I'll not start a legal wrangle," he said. "It's a bad business, but I can take it."

He shook my hand, and drove home to his much smaller farm. He had a wife who could take it, too.

Getting around the widespread practice was a problem which made me think amusedly sometimes about the old doctor who had made me walk round the mining villages. I bought a motor-cycle, and one of the fastest trips I made on it was after a phone call from a farm many miles out. A faint, broken voice said, "My younger son has been found in the channel—please come at once."

I rode the motor-bike so fast along the rutted roads that I flew clear of the saddle on several occasions, and when I reached the farm I found a well-built lad of eight lying motionless on the ground. He had been missed for an hour, and at last was found under water in an irrigation channel, concealed under some heavy planks which had been used to bridge it. It took me only seconds to discover that his eye was insensitive to touch and that there was no heartbeat, but after a quick examination of the air passages I had sufficient hope left to make me administer artificial respiration for half-an-hour. At last I had to acknowledge defeat, and rose from the pitiful little body. The farmer said afterwards that he feared the boy to be dead even while he was calling for me.

The roads were so bad, especially in winter, that my "iron horse" would not carry me over them, and it was a tedious and difficult business to drive along the boggy tracks in a buggy. So when I received an urgent call to a farm about twelve miles away I had to take to horseback, and was plugging along when I saw another rider galloping towards me. The clods of red mud were flying from his horse's hooves, until he pulled up to say urgently, "Can you hurry along, doctor, please? The baby was born yesterday, but the mother's still losing a terrible lot of blood. They're very worried."

I dug my heels into my horse as the other rider wheeled to gallop alongside me, and we covered the remaining distance as fast as our mounts could carry us. Luckily I managed to hold on without falling into the mud.

When I reached the farm I found that the bleeding was caused by the afterbirth adhering to the womb. I gave the mother an anaesthetic and proceeded to remedy the situation, and soon the bleeding stopped. The husband, together with anxious neighbours and relations, were deeply relieved and grateful and insisted on me staying and having a meal with them. I was ready for it, and afterwards let the horse make its own pace home. The morning's gallop left me stiff and sore for a week.

For some farmers the telephone had robbed emergencies of some of their terrors. They were self-reliant folk, either the pioneers or immediate descendants of pioneers who had opened up that part of the country, and did not call the doctor unless they thought it to be absolutely essential. One of them went a little too far. He was French, and called me in halting English to say, "My wife has broken her leg. Tell me what to do and I will set it. I don't want you to come out."

"I won't give you instructions over the telephone," I said emphatically. "I'll come at once, and if you're too poor to pay me I'll look after your wife without a fee."

"No," he said. "I do not want you to come."

I ignored that and set out for his farm, wondering if he had quarrelled with his wife and hurt her in some way. But I found husband and wife to be the best of friends. She had been struggling up some stone steps with a bucket of water in each hand, slipped, and broken the outer bone of the left leg above the ankle. Her husband seemed unable to give any reason for his unwillingness to have me call on them, and wasted no time in finding boards to place beneath the bed mattress so that his wife's leg could be supported firmly. But he refused to employ help in the house while his wife was confined to bed—though he did pay his account promptly.

A very different person was the wealthy farmer who brought a twenty-six-year-old employee to my surgery, laid him on the examination couch, and dumped his belongings on the verandah. "I'm not responsible for this man's illness," he said gruffly. "He'll have to meet his own expenses."

I examined the young man, and found that his legs were flaccid and paralysed. "When did you take ill?" I asked.

"Yesterday. My legs felt weak, and this afternoon I couldn't move them."

Further examination showed that the paralysis was spreading to his abdomen. He had no pain, no loss of sensation, and his mind was perfectly clear. It was obvious that he was suffering from Acute Ascending Paralysis, which in those days meant that death was imminent. The palsy would affect his chest and arms, and when his diaphragm was affected he would find it increasingly hard to breathe.

"Would you like a cup of tea and something to eat?" I asked him, and he ate all the meal which my wife made for him. That his mind was clear, and would remain so until the

53

end, made it all the sadder, and I could not make up my mind whether to acquaint him with his fate. I did not feel that I could tell him bluntly, so said, "I'm afraid that you are very ill, George. If you'll give me your parents' address I'll send them a wire."

"Thank you," he said, but gently shook his head.

"Well, is there anyone at all I could get in touch with?"

"No, thank you,"

Two hours later, with help, I took him to the train with a note for the nearest public hospital. I explained his condition to the guard of the train, who did all that he could to make him comfortable. Three days later he died.

Not long afterwards, the farmer who had brought him to me hailed me on the street. "I believe that fellow died," he said. "You needn't send me an account. I won't pay it."

I felt my heart thumping. "You made yourself clear when you dumped his swag on my verandah," I said. "I've been told that you're of Scottish extraction. If so, then I want you to know that you're a blight on the race and the most inhuman wretch it has ever been my misfortune to meet."

Probably my words did not even sting him. I walked on, leaving him leering on the street.

The average general practitioner does not have much time or opportunity for laboratory work, but my background in this respect came in handy when a tall, strongly-built labourer came staggering into the surgery on one blazing afternoon. He had ridden over twenty miles of rough bush tracks on a heavy old-fashioned bicycle, and fainted very soon after he had complained to me of "boils that would not clear up." When he came to again I took his temperature, which was 103 degrees, then let him rest for a while and have a cup of tea before I proceeded with the examination.

The patient's left arm was swollen and firm, and the glands in his left armpit were enlarged. There was a mass of angry pustules on his forearm, and I asked, "How long have you had these?"

"About three weeks ago I was shearing lambs for a couple of weeks. Halfway through I noticed pimples on my left arm where it rubbed against the fleece. 'Yolkboils' grew on the pimples, and my arm got hard, but I didn't knock off work until the boils kept spreading."

At once I recognised the sores as the malignant pustules of anthrax and took steps to confirm my diagnosis. I made a platinum loop and transferred a thin film of fluid from a vesicle on the sores to a microscope slide, then dried and stained it in the way that I had done countless times at Glasgow University. What I saw under my microscope confirmed my suspicions—the typical rod-shaped bacilli of anthrax.

I told the patient, and added, "We'll need to get you off to hospital but you'd better have something to eat first."

With the country warmth and hospitality which were typical of her, my wife looked after him until it was time to put him on the train for the isolation hospital at Warracknabeal. Early next morning I reported the case by telegram to the Public Health Department, and then set out for the farm where the man had been shearing. Anthrax is a serious infection for man or beast, and can spread fast with fatal results. But I could not find anyone else who was suffering from "boils," and the farmer was not having any unusual problems with his sheep, so I returned home again. No reply to my telegram had arrived, so I sent an urgent wire at two p.m.

Late that afternoon the phone rang, and a voice identified itself as that of Inspector Bragg, of the Stock Department. "Headquarters have alerted me to get in touch with you," he said. "Are you quite sure that case was one of anthrax?"

"Would you be convinced if you saw anthrax bacilli from the patient under my microscope?" I asked half-jokingly.

"It's my business to know."

"Good. Then come here as quickly as you can; you'll be just in time for dinner."

Inspector Bragg arrived after a hot forty miles' drive, but the first thing he said was, "May I have a look at that microscope?"

He studied the slide carefully, then said, "It's anthrax all right. The first case I've seen for hundreds of miles around here. May I ask where you got that fine microscope?"

"I brought it out from home."

My wife called us to dinner, and we didn't talk about anthrax at the table, but later I told the Inspector about my efforts to track down the source of infection. The Stock Department moved fast, and its inspectors looked at countless animals and shearing sheds, but was no more successful than I had been. Fortunately, there was no known recurrence of anthrax at that time.

The patient was fortunate. It is very rare to see a multiplicity of anthrax lesions such as those from which he was suffering, but he made a complete though slow recovery.

A case which required less pathological knowledge was that of the two-year-old girl who complained of a "buzzing in her ear." I arrived to find that her parents were frantic with anxiety, and no wonder. The little girl was screaming wildly with pain or fear, but with the aid of a mild anaesthetic I was able to look in her ear with an auroscope. The cause for complaint appeared immediately—a large fly, buzzing vigorously. I washed it out with warm water.

Apart from medical practice, I was learning about my adopted country. Soon after I arrived in town I went to buy a newspaper, which in those days was brought in by train at about 5.30 p.m. and was always awaited by a group of men. One of them came up to me and said, "G'day, doctor. You'll be needing some hay for your horses this winter, I suppose? I've got a fine lot, and I'll drop you off a load or two. The price'll be right."

"Wait till I see the stock agent," I said. "I'll let you know."

This brought a smile to everyone's face but his, though I did not know that he and his brother had a reputation for pushing sales and driving a hard bargain. As he moved away, another man told him, "You'll have to be up early to get the better of a Scotsman, Tom!"

"I haven't been long in Australia, but long enough to know that if you want to be upsides with an Australian you never want to go to bed!" I said.

When the stock agent's clerk was consulted, he said that the "fine lot of hay" was straw blown against the rabbit fence during harvest!

Six months later I was chatting with the owner of the largest store in town when Tom's brother came up. A bit hesitatingly, he said, "Tom bought two screws from you last week, but he only needed one of them. I've brought the other back, and he'd like you to credit it to his account."

This parsimony was a family trait, though they owned one of the finest farms in the district. They attended the Presbyterian Church, which held a sale of work in autumn, and their gift was a sheaf of hay. As Tom's mother and sister walked into the church grounds just ahead of my wife and me, I heard them assuring the minister that the sheaf had been specially packed for the Church. As my wife shook hands with the minister, I looked around and asked, "What's happened to that famous sheaf of hay?"

"I threw it over the fence to the pony," he said with a broad grin.

In those days, country folk had to rely upon themselves for their entertainments even more than they do today. Amongst the great events were the matrons' and bachelors' balls, and the notices announcing them proclaimed MOONLIGHT in capital letters. "What's the great importance of moonlight?" I asked my wife, and as a country girl herself she laughed, "Most people will be coming in from the farms, and they wouldn't come to town on a winter night unless the moon was nearly full. They wouldn't be able to see the way."

The earth roads around Minyip weren't too good at the best of times, and Rene suggested that we drive out to see some friends that night so that I could test night-driving for myself. The night was dark, and the kerosene lights on the buggy were of little help. I tried to keep the horse on the smooth, worn patches which ran alongside the fences, but they would soon stray back onto the rougher sections of road. "Just hold the reins lightly," Rene said. "Let them find their own way home." I did, and found that the horses had more road sense than I had in the dark of a moonless night.

I grew to know the roads very well, and on one of them I always had trouble with a hefty bull. In Scotland, bulls had rings through their noses and were kept in special yards. If they were taken anywhere, it was under strict control.

57

Eventually I asked the stock agent if he knew about the bull, and whether he didn't think it dangerous for such a powerful creature to be roaming at large. "Oh, he's quite harmless," the agent said. "He's not hand-fed, like the bulls in your country. If you complain to the Council you'll have the whole countryside against you. He doesn't belong to anyone in particular, and just feeds at the roadside with everyone's cows. If he was shut up, the local families would soon be without milk."

As always, I was interested in politics, but found that country politics in those days was a very casual affair. A Federal election was scheduled, so I wandered down to the Institute one evening to hear the Labour candidate's side of the question. When the doors opened there was only an odd man or two to be seen. The candidate and a handful of supporters arrived, and prepared for the meeting in a leisurely way. When he rose to speak there were only thirty-one in the audience. After the zestful and argumentative political meetings in Scotland, where there was never a vacant seat in the hall and the speaker was greeted with uproarious cheers, it was difficult to believe that Australian politics was a serious business—at least in Minyip.

Scots are supposed to be canny, and at least one friend of ours might be of that opinion. About five o'clock one evening a man rang the door bell, and when I answered it he said, "I'd like to see Mrs Duguid."

"Do you know my wife?"

"I know her father well. I'm a wool buyer, and often have dinner with her family when I'm in that district."

"What is your name?"

"Robert Oliver."

"Oh yes—I've heard of you. Do come in."

Oliver stayed for dinner, and next time he saw my father-in-law he said, "You don't need to worry about your daughter's safety. I had to give my name and credentials before I was allowed to see her."

DOCTOR AT WAR

IN MAY 1914, RENE AND I MOVED TO ADELAIDE, WHERE I hoped to establish myself in practice. To begin with all went well, and I was welcomed by other members of the profession. Leaders amongst them were Sir Joseph Verco and his nephew John. Sir Joseph was the recognised consultant-physician of South Australia, the possessor of a confident and penetrating mind and a most pleasant personality. Whenever I gave a diagnosis of serious import, the patient almost invariably asked me if I would mind consulting with Sir Joseph, and such consultations helped to put me on my feet in Adelaide. I had evolved a card index system to record all my cases, and when I showed it to Sir Joseph he introduced me, with justifiable pride, to his library of manuscript volumes which contained complete records of all his cases.

John Verco became my closest friend in the profession. Those were the days of the one man practice, but John and I worked together by assisting each other at operations and we maintained a relationship of mutual help for thirty years until his death.

In 1914, the senior surgeon in Adelaide was Dr Ben Poulton. I once asked him to examine a friend of mine who was very vocal concerning her reactions to medicines prescribed for her. When he had completed the examination he began to write a prescription, and she said, "You know, Doctor, I can't take bromide and I'm susceptible to bicarbonate of soda."

"Madam, I am happy to treat you but I must refuse to consult with you," he replied.

Like so many busy, happy lives, ours was soon to be interrupted by the first World War. To begin with it meant for me, as for so many doctors, a heavier case load. The armed forces needed doctors, who had to be drawn from the civilian population. Those who were left had to take over their work. I was made responsible for the practice of Dr Arthur Powell, as well as my own, and was allotted two hospital posts. Often I was so busy that I barely had time to think about the increasingly dreadful news from the theatres of war, which seemed very far away from Adelaide. But hundreds and then thousands of Australia's young men were going to the front, and it seemed that the war would swallow up as many men as we could send to it. War meant casualties; casualties needed doctors. As a young healthy man, with ample surgical experience, I realised that I must go too, and by 1916 I was in camp as a Medical Officer. My brother Willie, who also had settled in Australia, had joined the 8th Light Horse Regiment and already was in Egypt.

In February 1917 I too sailed for Egypt, with Light Horse reinforcements aboard Transport A6. Lieutenant Kelly of the 3rd Light Horse, who was going overseas for the second time, was O.C. Troops and I was Medical Officer. Kelly, one of the finest of men, was killed in action a year later.

The ship anchored in Suez on 12 February 1917, and when I disembarked I was ordered to report to Australian Imperial Force Headquarters, Cairo. After a monotonous train journey I arrived in the city to find that the offices were closed, but the corporal on duty directed me to a nearby hotel, the National. I dumped my kit, and filled in the time before dinner by strolling through the teeming streets, thinking of Rene and of home.

When I reported next morning, the Assistant Director of Medical Services kindly offered to help me to get in touch with my brother, for which the first step was a posting to the 2nd Australian Stationary Hospital at El Arish, on the border of Egypt and Palestine. I travelled by train to Kantara, crossed the Suez Canal, and spent a night at the huge military camp at Kantara East. With its railway sidings, workshops, blacksmiths' shops, canteen, stores, and streets of hutments, it seemed more like a township than a camp. and I was delighted to hear that most of the soldiers spoke with Glasgow or Ayrshire accents. I soon found old school friends, and on the next day encountered thousands more Scotsmen when I reached Romani, the scene of the first major battle against the Turks in which the Australian Light Horse had helped to win a resounding victory.

A weary journey filled the following day, from Romani to El Arish, along the railway which rolled slowly over the desert. There was nothing to see but sand dunes, an occasional palm grove, and odds and ends of rusty metal and barbed wire which showed that war had passed that way. Indian troops predominated at the little camps where the train halted.

El Arish was the forward base, lying between the desert and the sea; it had been established after the Turks had been defeated at the battle of Romani and driven east of El Arish. The main feature was the Second Australian Stationary Hospital established in large marquees which in an emergency could take almost a thousand men.

Not far from the hospital, there was the teeming activity of stores and ammunition dumps, the digging of trenches and other defences in case of attack. Most of the work was done by men of the Egyptian Labour Corps, who toiled in companies of about 100. Dressed in long flowing garments, and each with a little red fez or a soiled cloth around his head, they were driven on by the hoarse shouts and whipcracking of their foremen. As they removed mountains of sand in little baskets it was easy to understand how the Pyramids were built by such arduous labour—huge swarms of men whose combined strength could do almost anything.

After dinner at El Arish I asked the Colonel's permission to press on in the hope of seeing my brother, one of the Light Horse "originals" whom I had not seen since he left Australia. He told me to carry on at once, and Signals said that the 8th Light Horse were at the next station—El Burg. I arrived there at four-thirty a.m., and awakened the night corporal. He said that the regiment was still there, but five minutes after I had left the train, and it had pulled out, he staggered up, saluted, and said that the regiment had moved on a week ago. He was hardly in a fit state to be sure about anything.

But I was lucky. The only tent that showed a light contained a Scottish signalman from Ross-shire, and he managed to find out that the regiment was now beyond Sheikh Zowaig. He sent them a message to say that I would be on board a water-train, and I couldn't thank him enough. Waiting contentedly for the water-train I watched the peace and beauty of a desert sunrise, then was on my way through the desert. Most of the water trucks were leaking, and at every stopping place the Egyptian work-gangs used the little jets of water as showerbaths.

The only Light Horsemen in sight when the train pulled up were a few troopers with led horses, come to meet officers who were not on board the train. They lent me one of the horses and I followed them up and down great sandhills as steep as mountainsides, until at last we came to the bivouacs near the sea. My brother's astonishment at seeing me was as great as my own pleasure. He had no idea that I was in the desert.

We spent the day and much of the night in yarning, and early next morning, while it was still dark, we rode back to a train at railhead. Willie, or "Scotty" as his mates called him, took my horse, and after a final handshake swung back into his saddle. I climbed to the top of a carriage and watched until he disappeared over the first sandhill. I never saw him again.

Next morning I reported back to the Colonel commanding the 2nd Australian Stationary Hospital at El Arish. He appointed me to work in the Isolation Department, but the senior surgeon, Dr Cavanagh Mainwaring of Adelaide, put

TOP: Filling up at Piltardi waterhole on the author's expedition into the Petermann Ranges. BOTTOM: The western end of the Petermann Ranges

in a claim for me. The first battle of Gaza was about to begin, and there would be more need for surgeons than for physicians.

The desert and its skies were swarming with activity. Masses of infantrymen and numerous batteries of heavy artillery went past us on their way to the front, and aircraft were flying to and fro all the time. Like a gathering storm, we heard the distant rumble of the guns increasing. Each medical officer was allotted a marquee in which he would treat the wounded placed under his care, and as hospital trains and ambulances began to grind past towards the front I collected a good stock of dressings, morphia, serum, syringes and other requirements, and stored them in a sterile tray which I had devised. Sterility was a constant problem in the desert. The first cases that I had to treat were men suffering from septic sores, brought down from the front before the fight began.

By 26 March 1917 the first battle for Gaza was well under way, and the first trickle of casualties began to arrive. On 28 March a train brought in 256 casualties, mostly Welshmen and East Anglians wounded with varying degrees of severity. One, shot in the neck, died soon after being admitted. Most of them, after they'd been given a hot drink and a few biscuits, drifted off into the sleep of shock and exhaustion. I was on my feet until late at night except for a snatched meal, and as I examined their wounds I got some picture of conditions up at the front. They said that they had had practically no water to wash with for the past fortnight; only a quart a day between each fourteen men. For the previous two days they had had little to drink, nothing to eat except the hard ration biscuits, and had lain out in the frigid desert nights without as much as a blanket to cover them. Such conditions were reflected in the fact that the wounds of two men, suffered only two days before, were badly septic.

One of them was suffering badly from shell shock, from a shell exploding in front of him and throwing him on to a cement gun emplacement. Another had his chest ripped open, and another had the entrance wound of a bullet beneath his chin and the the exit behind the left ear. The officers had suffered as badly as the men, and their ward was crowded out.

TOP: Tall, strong, dignified, and perfectly in harmony with their environment, these tribal Aborigines were photographed in the far north-west of South Australia in the 1930s. BOTTOM: After contact with white men's civilisation. These four tribesmen were imprisoned for spearing cattle on their own tribal territory

Whatever "romance" there might be in war was not apparent in the crowded marquees, and we surgeons had to deal with an increasing flood of wounded fed back to us by the never-ending growl of guns over the horizon. On 29 March, 320 wounded arrived at seven-thirty a.m., and after a day spent in attending to them we had to deal with a long train of open trucks which arrived at eleven that night. It was an eerie sight to see the wounded men being lifted down in the fitful moonlight. The orderlies worked like Trojans, and by midnight the casualties were all in bed and were being fed. They were all famished, but most of them relished the hot tea which was brought to them in great buckets.

By 30 March I was responsible for the wounded men in three marquees. With the help of excellent orderlies I dressed the more lightly wounded first, so that they could be cleared back down the line in open trucks, and then attended to the more serious cases. The patient courage of these men will always remain in my memory.

Soon afterwards I was put in charge of the officers' ward, and found a poor old major, shot through the lungs and very far gone. The officer in the bed next to him had been shot across the eyes, of which one at least would never see again. Next again was a young officer whom I had met in Kantara only a fortnight before, who had been with his platoon for only two days before the battle began. His face was covered with bandages, but I recognised his voice and when I spoke to him he said, "Oh, it's grand to hear a voice that you know." Though we had been together for only a few hours, he knew me better than he did the other wounded.

Many of the wounded had had their suffering increased by the arduous journey back through the desert. One of the soldiers, wounded in the arm, had taken more than three days to reach us. He had been shot on the Monday afternoon, could not find his own Medical Officer to treat him, and was given a first dressing at Brigade Field Ambulance in the evening. Then he was sent off with other wounded who had to ride two to a camel. They lost themselves, spent the night lying in the desert, started off again at dawn, found a Casualty Clearing Station, and had their wounds dressed on the

Tuesday afternoon. Next afternoon they went on again, making their way by slow stages until they were loaded into open rail trucks which brought them to our hospital. No wonder they were exhausted when we received them; they must have been tough to survive it.

On 1 April a hospital train brought us 520 casualties. Fortunately a good many of them were comparatively lightly wounded, so that we could send 400 of them back down the line, but every man had to be examined, his dressing checked or replaced, and the decision made as to whether he was fit enough to travel on or should be put to bed. The hours flew past in an endless succession of wounds to almost every part of the body, of men cheerful or silent or simply enduring, of X-ray examinations which showed chunks of metal embedded in arms, legs, chests, heads, abdomens.

Some wounds were comparatively slight, like that of the officer who had a bayonet tear in the abdominal wall. He told me that he and his men had had to march thirty miles over the desert, and were then given some bully beef and cold water and sent straight into action.

Other wounds were appalling, like that of the man with a face shattered by a bomb explosion. By the time that I saw him the wound was a week old, and the dressings had not been changed for five days. When I removed them I saw a gaping, greenish yellow wound in his cheek, with two pieces of cheekbone lying loose in the wound. The lower jaw was fractured. He could hardly speak and could not eat, and yet when I examined him after dressing the wound under an anaesthetic I found him to be contented, and very grateful for anything that could be done for him. He had been in the army since 1914.

Trainloads of casualties from the first battle of Gaza continued to arrive for as long as ten days after the action — on 2 April 500 wounded, on 3 April 286 wounded, on 4 April 500 wounded. As I went from one bed to another, I found that many of the wounds were septic. I had to dress such cases as a man with a shattered thumb, another with the flesh torn off his hip, the next with the inner part of a foot torn away by an explosive bullet, the next with what was left of his abdominal wall being ballooned out as he breathed. Another was unconscious, with part of the left side of his skull missing.

I talked to a man from the 3rd Light Horse Field Ambulance. In the battle, the Light Horse Brigade had penetrated beyond Gaza and had remained there until the morning after the British forces had been ordered to retire. No one could understand the retirement. Everyone who had been in the battle agreed that the enemy had been in full retreat, followed up by British and Australian troops until they had been ordered to withdraw.

At last the wards were almost emptied as we sent all but the most seriously wounded down to the base hospitals, and we began to clean up in readiness for the next offensive. What a prospect! The trains were rumbling past all day and night, and the hospital was passed by an endless procession of men and supplies. Another Light Horse brigade went up to the front, preceded and followed by truck loads of ammunition and artillery, Field Ambulances, battalions of infantry, hundreds of horses and thousands of camels — over a thousand camels had been killed in the first battle.

The enemy aircraft were very active, trying to hit the reservoir and ammunition dump which were part of the base at El Arish. "Funk holes" were dug everywhere, and huge Red Crosses laid out on the sand around the hospital. We saw the results of one raid on 12 April, when a hospital train brought in men who had been wounded by bombs dropped on one of our airfields. The most seriously wounded was an officer who had been asleep in his tent, and was riddled with bomb fragments.

The British Army in the desert consisted of men from many parts of the United Kingdom and what was then the British Empire. Amongst them were a number of British West Indians, and many of our fellows affected to despise them as "niggers." But when I went to a church service held one evening in their lines, I found that I had no such feelings.

Every day brought new evidence of the monster build-up for a new offensive and of the enemy's preparations to retaliate. Gunfire began to rumble again beyond the horizon, and the A.A. guns round El Arish were in action several times as the enemy attempted to raid us. Our Army Service Corps dump at railhead was being heavily shelled, and some of the shells landed on Field Ambulances. The casualties, including a medical officer, came down to us.

Tension mounted slowly, with men and materials still pouring up to the front. One day about 1,000 camels plodded slowly past—some with a stretcher fastened to each side of their saddles, others with padded seats. A grim portent of what was to come. On 14 April, an old friend was admitted to hospital, Captain William Rutherford of the Royal Army Medical Corps. We had been together at Glasgow University and Western Infirmary, and he had served in the advanced Field Ambulance during the first battle of Gaza. "No one could understand the retirement," he told me. "Our ambulance stayed out for hours after the order came, but we didn't see anything of the enemy. During the attack their shells did for our supplies, including the water, and the medical officers had two biscuits and one bottle of water in three days and no sleep from Saturday to Wednesday night, working at full pitch all the time." He was mentally and physically exhausted, and was sent down to Base.

On 17 April the artillery barrage opened at five a.m., and at seven that evening a message came from railhead that an ambulance train was on its way. It arrived in the early morning, and amongst the first casualties was Major McLauren of the 8th Light Horse. He had a broken collar bone, which I fixed when the seriously wounded were in bed. A young, well-built Light Horse lieutenant, F. H. Coy, was admitted unconscious and with no power in his limbs, but when I examined him I could find only a small scar on the front of his scalp. When I investigated the wound I found a large round bullet embedded in the skull, and when he was taken to the operating theatre for the old-fashioned missile to be removed we discovered that the skull was fractured and a portion of the brain surface damaged. This was removed, and he recovered consciousness but not, at that time, the power of his limbs.

Another hospital train arrived in the afternoon, and it was 9.30 p.m. before I finished the dressings. It was the same weary story. One ófficer, paralysed from the waist down, was shot high up in the spine. Another had a depressed fracture of the skull. Another would lose the sight of one eye, if not both. As I worked, I could hear the train loads of men, horses, and supplies moving up to the front—expendable material to be replaced when put out of action.

For the next three days, the hospital trains arrived at intervals of only a few hours. The wounded came in by hundreds at a time. One train brought in 800 at midnight on 20 April, and I had never seen men so cold. Already shocked by their wounds, they had been travelling in unlined steel trucks and vans through the chill of the desert night, and when they entered hospital their teeth were chattering and limbs quivering.

The medical officers and orderlies at El Arish kept up with the flood as best they could, but as soon as we had finished with one batch of wounded another lot came in. My long days were broken into irregular periods of dressing wounds, operating in the theatre, and snatching a meal or a couple of hours sleep whenever it was possible. There were a great many Scots among the wounded—Highland Light Infantry, Scottish Rifles, Royal Scots Fusiliers, and King's Own Scottish Borderers—infantrymen who had suffered badly in what we were beginning to realise was a disastrous action.

Whenever possible we sent men down the line to Base, in order to keep beds free for the continuing influx of more recently wounded, but by the morning of 22 April we had 928 battle casualties in hospital and the next train that arrived had to go further down the line. We hadn't a spare bed or blanket with which to deal with them.

The days became a continuous sequence of horrors in which doctors and orderlies worked in steadily growing exhaustion, unable to rest when their services were so urgently needed by so many men. For some reason, steel helmets had not yet been issued on that front, and I remember dealing with four fractured skulls in two days. As so often before, the fineness of the human spirit in adversity showed itself in many ways. Amongst our wounded was a Brigade Colonel suffering from multiple very severe wounds, not even able to speak because of massive damage to the face. Just before he lapsed into final unconsciousness he pointed to my note pad, and when I handed it to him he scrawled with his undamaged arm, "Am afraid I've given the orderlies a rotten time." I showed it to the orderlies after he had died; they were too broken up to say anything.

One poor fellow I shall never forget. His right arm and practically his whole abdominal wall had been torn away, but when I first saw him on my preliminary rounds he apologised for being in the ward. "Ah shouldna be here, sir; Ah'm no' an officer," he said.

"Never mind, Sergeant; you'll be an officer next time," I told him.

"There'll no' be a next time, sir," he replied, looking at the stump of his arm. His courage, until he passed away four days later, was something to be remembered for ever.

I knew that my brother Willie's regiment of Light Horse had been one of those engaged on 19 April, and had become increasingly anxious about him. On 22 April I heard that he had fallen, but I had to pick up the story of his death little by little. I knew that some men of the 8th and 9th Australian Light Horse Brigades were in a nearby Casualty Clearing Hospital, so in the evening I asked the Colonel in charge if I could see them. I had listened to what the Light Horsemen had to tell me for some time when the Colonel intervened and took me away. "You must get some sleep tonight," he told me. "I've poured some whisky for you."

"But I never drink whisky, Colonel," I told him.

"Never mind. You must drink it tonight. I'll see you home to your tent."

I drank it down, but lay on my bed without closing an eye. My grief, especially for my parents in Scotland, made sleep impossible. Next day the news of Willie's death was confirmed. For weeks afterwards, messages came to me from all ranks of his regiment, and some of them added a little more to the story. Bill Kane of Minyip, one of my brother's squadron, told me, "I've never seen Scotty cheerier than on the morning of the fight. 'I'm detailed despatch rider to the Colonel, Bill,' he told me. 'And I've got to pick one of the best horses.

You'd better give me yours.' While he was saddling up, he said: 'This is going to be a hot job, but we've got to see it through.' He jumped into the saddle then, said 'Cheerio,' and left the squadron to join the Colonel."

He rode as despatch rider for Colonel Maygar from two a.m. to nine a.m. on 19 April, and he could see that the 8th Light Horse were having a bad time. At nine a.m. he was told that he would not be needed as despatch rider any longer and asked permission to join his regiment, but was told "your job is finished." Later he said he felt that he must join his mates, the Colonel was unable to dissuade him and he went into the battle. He never reached the 8th Light Horse, but was shot in the thigh while still among men of another unit. They dressed his wound, but he was left behind when they were forced to retire. That night, Jack Foreman of Adelaide crept out to find him. He was in a bad way, and told Jack that a Turkish soldier had robbed him and would have left him, but a German officer ordered the Turk to bayonet him. Jack could not get him back to our lines, and he died in No Man's Land.

While the wounded were still coming in, we read the British communique on the second battle of Gaza together with the Turkish reports of the first battle—which were ridiculed by the British press. But those who had suffered in the battle, and we who were attending them, had no doubt as to the truth. The first battle was a British victory and should have been a triumph, but was thrown away by the bad generalship which ordered our troops to retire. The second battle was a massacre. The Turks, led by German officers, lost no time in reclaiming the positions which they had evacuated. They dug themselves in more strongly, brought up more artillery and other weapons, and knew all the ranges to a nicety. When the British attacked, they were mown down as they advanced across the desert. Several officers in my ward told me of seeing a line of crouching men whom they thought to be digging a trench, but when they went closer they found that every soldier was dead. The Lieutenant-Colonel of Willie's regiment wrote to me and said: "The Brigadier of this Brigade (Brigadier Royston) is over sixty years of age, and a splendid type of man. He has been soldiering since sixteen years of age and has been in every fight since South Africa. He states that the battle on the 19th was the fiercest he had ever experienced, and on such a day your brother did his duty to the end." The whole Regiment knew that Willie had "gone the second mile" after finishing his duty as a despatch rider.

Day after day went by. The guns still thundered in the distance, the troop trains and horses and camels still went up to the front, the hospital trains still came back. Not even the wounded were safe. On 5 May a Casualty Clearing Station and a Brigade Field Ambulance were attacked by four enemy aircraft, which glided down with engines shut off, machine-gunned the line of tents and dropped bombs every ten yards, and threw hand grenades at men running for shelter. They repeated the raid two nights later. Many men were horribly burned from head to foot, and a man in the dispensary tent was burnt to death. A patient who had been operated on for appendicitis three days before had a leg and an arm blown off as he lay in bed.

One of my saddest duties was that of writing letters to the mothers of boys who had died of wounds. The waste of human life had been appalling, and it still went on. It was dismaying to read the nonsense written in the newspapers when one could see the end results of warfare every day.

As the weeks passed, we had to deal with an increasing amount of sickness as well as wounds. There were a good many cases of appendicitis, boils, carbuncles, and septic sores resulting from living in desert conditions on a poor and monotonous diet. But it is the wounds that one remembers. The lad from Aberdeen with a wound in the neck reaching to the spine, who could not talk but seemed to be comforted when I told him that I knew his home town well. He died the next day. And the Glasgow boy who had been discharged from a hospital near the front, and was walking across two miles of open ground to rejoin his battalion when a shell burst hear him and took off his arm. He lay there for some hours, losing a lot of blood, until he was spotted by two R.A.M.C. officers riding that way. And the youngster with a terribly mutilated thigh . . . and another with a badly fractured skull above the left eye . . .

Not all the wounds came from enemy action. With so many horses being used, we admitted a number of men injured by horse kicks. One of them died.

The war went on, but things were happening behind the scenes. In *The Official History of Australia in the War of 1914-1918*, H. S. Gullett wrote of the first battle of Gaza that it was a: "Severe blow to the British Army, since . . . there was not a single private in the British infantry or a trooper in the mounted brigades who did not believe that failure was due to staff bungling and nothing else. The men were convinced that owing to the almost unbelievable folly of the Higher Command, they had been robbed of a victory they had actually gained." The British Commander-in-Chief was General Sir Archibald Murray, and Gullett wrote of the second battle of Gaza that: "Murray's disaster, moreover, had been entirely of his own making."

Two disasters in one month were too much for the British Government. Murray was ordered home, and relieved by General Allenby, whose first step was to close Murray's luxurious headquarters at the Savoy Hotel in Cairo. He installed his own H.Q. within twenty miles of Gaza, and the effect on morale was instantaneous.

Allenby took stock of his new command, decided on his requirements, and ordered the Medical Corps to re-examine all "B" class men. All permanently rated "B" were to be sent home at once. Nearly all those I examined came into that category.

Soon afterwards I was told that I was to be in charge of the seriously wounded on a hospital ship taking them from Suez to Australia. When I reported to the medical transport officer at Suez, he told me, "You will be busy on the voyage. Tomorrow forenoon, there'll be a row of paralysed men on stretchers on the wharf. They'll be lifted on deck by cranes, and you'll take charge of them as soon as they go aboard. Here's a list of their names."

I took the list, and saw that it included Lieutenant F. H. Coy, the man whom I admitted unconscious to El Arish with damaged skull and brain. Apparently he still had not regained the use of his limbs, but I was to share his excitement when they developed some feeling during the voyage. He was one of the lucky ones.

I had excellent nursing sisters and a good sergeant and orderlies, and needed all of them because we were kept very busy in looking after the wounded. We had a calm voyage to Colombo, where we had an unexpected break of ten days because a P & O liner ahead of us had been attacked and a number of floating mines had to be cleared. The wounded were transferred to a shore hospital, where we lived with them, and were all treated royally. But there was a great gulf between those who had been at the front and those who sympathised with them but could not possibly understand how they felt. This was emphasised at a concert given for the troops one evening, when one of the entertainers sang "If you were the only girl in the world, and I were the only boy," with great gusto. It was a very popular song in those days, but was out of character with what we'd come from. It made me feel uncomfortable, but as senior officer present I waited to see how the others reacted. An Australian fighter pilot who sat next to me, said, "This is a bit too much for me." Then a Light Horse officer, who like me had left a brother behind in Egypt, leant over and murmured, "I can't take this."

I turned to the nursing sisters and asked, "What about it?"

"We wish to leave," their senior said, so when the song was finished we left quietly.

During my time in the desert I had suffered several attacks of dysentery, and this recurred during the voyage, becoming more severe as we drew near Australia. I was able to stay on duty, but the disembarkation medical officer in Melbourne wanted me to go into hospital. I told him that I would sooner go home, as relaxation appealed to me more than medicine. My wife's old home was at Nhill, half-way to Adelaide, so I spent six weeks there, mostly in bed. Then I was allowed to go on to Adelaide, where the Senior Medical Officer examined me. I am six feet tall but weighed only nine stone seven, so he said, "You had better take two months leave on pay."

"No, thank you. I'm starting work tomorrow," I told him.

I did, and found that there was plenty to do. I did not go overseas again, but saw out the war in Adelaide. Even after the war, sick and wounded soldiers were being treated for some time in six hospitals around the city. When I was elected Vice-President of the recently-formed Returned Soldiers' League, I paid them fortnightly visits. Arthur Blackburn, V.C., was President at that time.

When the Legacy Club was formed, to help the children of fallen soldiers, I was asked to sponsor a group of teenage girls at their regular meetings. Over fifty years later, most of those girls have become mothers and even grandmothers, and I still have the opportunity to meet some of them from time to time.

8

SURGEON IN THE CITY

A S SOON AS THE WAR WAS OVER I DECIDED TO SPEND 1919 IN post-graduate study in Scotland, and to sit for the Surgical Fellowship at Glasgow at the end of it. In February, I sailed for Liverpool with my wife and young son Charlie, and we enjoyed a happy voyage except for noticing that the coloured people in Cape Town were still the underdogs, forbidden to use the amenities reserved for Europeans.

I found that many things had changed in Britain. When I used sovereigns to pay for our railway tickets from Liverpool to Glasgow, a man standing beside me remarked, "I haven't seen gold for years!" Sovereigns were common currency in my youth, but the war had obliged the country to use paper currency and gold coins were soon to become worth more than their face value.

I had changed, too. When I telephoned my brother from Glasgow, he did not recognise my voice. But when I proudly presented my wife and son to my family it was a joyful occasion, and I had the pleasure of teaching young Charlie to recognise Scottish birds as my father had taught me. We spent a fortnight in travelling Scotland, and my wife fell in love with its dark mountains, purple heather, and golden sands.

At the end of our holiday I rejoined the staff of my old hospital. Every morning, I assisted Sir Kennedy Dalziel in general surgery. Abdominal surgery was his forte. On two afternoons a week I assisted Sam Cameron in gynaecology. I was in charge of his wards, and took gynaecology out-patients. Later, I did a clinical course of gynaecology with Balfour Marshall at the Royal Infirmary, and worked with Munro Kerr in operative obstetrics at the Royal Maternity Hospital. It was a full and rewarding year, broken only by another fortnight's holiday in which I introduced Rene to more of Scotland, and at the end of it I sat the Fellowship examination. It lasted for three full days, with gynaecology and obstetrics as my special subjects.

Shortly before we were ready to return to Australia I received a letter offering me the chair of Obstetrics and Gynaecology at Cape Town. But I had not liked the atmosphere of South Africa, and even though I was pressed to accept the appointment by Dr Freeland Fergus, President of the Faculty of Physicians and Surgeons of Glasgow, I declined the honour. I told him that I did not wish to cut myself off from general surgery, and that I had come to look on Australia as my home.

A busy life was waiting for me in Adelaide, both professionally and personally. We bought a large property at Magill, about six miles from Adelaide, and for the next forty years its homestead was to be the centre of many family activities. My wife made the front garden into a thing of beauty, and my own special pride was the lawn tennis court which was the scene of regular Saturday afternoon tennis parties. The big rambling garden was used for many garden-parties and fêtes for various charities, and behind it was a vegetable garden and a big paddock in which we kept a cow, turkeys, and fowls. I have been a keen breeder of fowls for most of my life.

Most memorable of the many visitors who enjoyed the old home were my parents and my sister Janie who came from Scotland in 1925 for a stay of nearly two years. My brothers

Robert and George already had settled in Australia—George to farm and Robert to practise medicine in Adelaide. Another sister, Agnes, had come to Australia with my brother Willie before the war. She was staying with us in 1915 when an official telephoned our home to ask "Is Doctor Duguid a German?" Apparently the name was unfamiliar to him, but Agnes soon set him right—though in reporting the side of the telephone conversation which she heard, my wife said that she doubted whether the official would have understood the flow of indignant Scottish language that assailed him!

A great many Scots have settled in Australia over the years, and my father was amazed at the number of his former pupils whom he met in Melbourne and Sydney. He was even more excited by his reunion with five fellow-students of the Edinburgh Teachers' Training College. They were Mrs Brown, founder of the Wilderness School, Sir Josiah Symon, one of Adelaide's most sought after barristers, Doctor and Mrs Ramsay Smith, and William Lowrie, Professor of Agriculture.

A good deal of my professional life was spent in the Memorial Hospital, North Adelaide, which was built in memory of Methodists who had fallen in the first World War. I had a cupboard built to house my instruments and did nost of my operations at the hospital, though at that time most minor surgery such as the setting of fractures of the limbs or collarbone was still done in the home.

But there were many cases for which hospital treatment was essential. One was that of the young Scot who stepped off the pavement after posting a letter and was hit by a motorcycle going at full speed. One could have no doubt as to what had to be done; the broken end of his right shin bone was protruding through the skin, and both the leg bones were broken. I set these under anaesthetic, but after he had been six weeks in hospital an X-ray examination showed that the broken ends of the tibia were not uniting. I operated again, and plated the bone, but after another six weeks there was still no sign of healing. A colleague advised me to amputate, but I remembered the principle laid down by my old chief, Sir William Macewen of Glasgow, that a limb should never be sacrificed unless it was utterly unavoidable. The young Scot was a keen

77

football player and to rob him of a leg would be a tragedy.

Then I read an article in the *American Medical Journal* which described the good results obtained in delayed healing of fractures by giving the patient thyroid extract three times a day. I adopted this treatment, and to my great relief found that union was firm at the end of another six weeks. The young man played football again in the next season. Soon after that Sir William Macewen stayed with us when he was representing the British Medical Association at an annual meeting in Melbourne. I had the pleasure of showing him the X-ray plates of the case and the patient, and of describing how I had held firm to his teaching.

This principle of not only saving a limb, but restoring it to full function, was put to the test in a workmen's compensation case. A man in his fifties was carrying a ladder across a cement floor when he slipped and fell heavily. He was brought to my rooms in great pain and with a very swollen left knee. After examination I decided that there was no fracture and ordered complete rest, telling him that it would be many weeks before I allowed him to put weight on the injured leg. After some time I was visited by a young surgeon who asked my permission to see the patient on behalf of an insurance company. He told me that he was advising an operation which would make the knee rigid, so that the man would be restored to some kind of movement and could go back to work. "Not at all," I told him. "It's simply a matter of time. The man will be walking as well as I am if he rests the knee long enough."

I was proved correct three months after the accident, when the man returned to work with a sound knee.

Some years later, it took all my persistence to save a man's hand. He was a teacher, who had been experimenting with chemicals which exploded. The force of the blast had torn the palm of his right hand across and turned it in towards the wrist. The hand was blackened by the explosion, and the tendons of his fingers were ruptured. When I had him on the operating table it was a difficult and time-consuming task to find the correct end of each tendon so that they could be sutured together. Then the torn flesh had to be fitted back into place, and the skin brought into alignment and loosely stitched. The healing of the wound was only the beginning of another lengthy process, that of coaxing each finger back into action. But the whole process succeeded, and when I met the teacher years later he had individual action of all his fingers.

Not all surgical emergencies were the result of accidents. One day a practitioner telephoned me to say that one of his patients, a woman past middle age, was complaining of acute tenderness over the gall bladder. He asked me to consult with him, and when I arrived I found that the patient had a high temperature, a rapid pulse, and was breathing quickly. There was no doubt as to the tenderness over the gall bladder, but her rapid breathing made me examine the right lung. I found that it was solid with pneumonia, so her doctor and I agreed that there could be no surgery until the lung returned to normal. In the days before "wonder drugs" pneumonia was regarded as a considerably more serious affliction than it is today, but the woman was eventually pronounced fit for surgery. When I opened the abdomen it was easy to see why the infection had been so severe. The gall bladder was necrotic (mortified) and when gripped by the forceps it lifted in one solid piece. After its removal the patient made a rapid recovery, and went overseas two months later.

Nowadays surgeons tend to specialise, but in the 1920s a surgeon operated on a wide variety of cases. One of my most challenging tasks was the repairing of a baby's face. It had been born with a cleft palate and a complicated hare-lip, which caused it to be terribly disfigured.

I repaired the cleft palate while the baby was still an infant, but a plan to tackle the hare-lip was difficult to work out. I gave it deep thought and eventually found a clue in notes I had made when a student at Glasgow. When the boy was in his fifth year I decided to operate.

The problem with a hare-lip, so called because the child is born with the upper lip divided like that of a hare, is that the tension of the skin tends to pull apart any repair which may be made.

I realised that, to eliminate tension, I must free the skin of the cheeks over a wide area. So after incising each skin edge of the wide gap in the upper lip, I made a cut in the gums and, with an elevator, raised the cheeks off the bones on each side. This made it possible to bring the cut sides of the lip together without any sign of strain. I then placed holding stitches deep in the tissues under the skin, and finally stitched the lip together so that the edges were in accurate apposition. Two years later, the boy was shown at a Children's Hospital conference. His lip was mobile and free from strain, and he spoke with scarcely any defect.

A somewhat similar case was the girl of thirteen who was brought to me by her parents. She suffered from permanent torticallis (wry neck) due to a birth injury. The sterno mastoid muscle on the left side of the neck was contracted, so that it pulled her head to that side while her face looked to the right. There was some atrophy of the face on the affected side. Apart from interfering with the girl's normal life of school work and games this disability had affected her whole nature, and she was shy and withdrawn.

The tendon of the muscle appeared as a taut band directly under the skin, but I decided against dissection of the skin over the muscle because I knew that this would leave the girl with a large scar, thus replacing one disfigurement with another. So I made a very small cut in the skin and inserted a special knife held on the flat. When this cut through the tendon, it ruptured with a loud snap. The girl's neck was kept in plaster in an over-corrected position for three weeks, and then an adjustable plaster was fitted. After a regimen of exercise the girl returned to boarding school, no longer shy and retiring but brimful of life and happiness.

From such planned operations to an abdominal emergency was no uncommon step for a surgeon in those days. I was called to one of these by a close friend, a grandson of Dr John G. Paton, the missionary who won fame in the South Pacific. My friend asked me to see his mother, who was in great pain, and I found that she had a ruptured duodenal ulcer. I operated an hour later, and the patient, who was in her seventies, made a good recovery.

A case which presented a particular challenge was that of a boy driving his soap-box buggy down hill. He put out his right foot as a brake, and broke his leg. When I looked at the

X-rays I saw that it was a very oblique fracture, presenting me with the problem of setting the greatly over-riding ends of the bone into the correct position.

I decided upon a method which Macewen of Glasgow had taught me. When the boy was under anaesthetic I drove a stainless steel pin through his heel. This pin formed the base of a steel stirrup, from which a cord led over a pulley at the end of the bed to a small platform. Weights were placed on the platform, and we increased them gradually until the lower part of the fractured bone was drawn downwards into a satisfactory position over the upper portion of the break. The lad was back on the playing fields a few months later, and has for many years been a very active general practitioner.

As every doctor knows, not all emergencies are caused by patients. The matron had to assist me on the excision of a gall-bladder when my assistant was prevented from attending after the patient had been anaesthetised. On another occasion, the removal of a cancer from the blind end of the large bowel, my assistant fainted while I was still freeing the bowel. I was obliged to proceed, and the operation was well advanced by the time another assistant could be found. The patient lived and worked contentedly for a further quarter-century.

Fortunately that operation was on the right side, which is less involved than removing a cancer from the left side of the bowel. But even that operation could be performed success-fully, and a lady from whom I removed such a cancer was alive and well ten years later.

The commonest seat of cancer in women is the breast, and of all operations it is the one in which it is most difficult to predict the final outcome. Recurrence can occur when least expected, but the opposite is equally true. In 1929 I examined a woman in which breast cancer was so far advanced that there seemed little hope of complete recovery, but I performed a radical breast operation. I heard no more of the case after the patient had been discharged until I was visiting London in 1937, when I was stopped by her on Oxford Street and saw that she was fit and well. Such moments are the surgeon's reward.

It is similarly rewarding for the surgeon to earn the gratitude of patients who have been apprehensive about a scar in the neck following operation for goitre. To one such woman I gave the assurance that if there were any noticeable disfigurement I was sure her husband would give her a pearl necklace. When I saw her a year after the operation she said happily: "I didn't get that string of pearls!"

Caesarean section, the opening of the womb to deliver a child which cannot be born normally, was a dreaded operation at the turn of the century. It was performed only in extreme emergency, and for marked narrowness of the pelvic canal. Professor Murdoch Cameron of Glasgow improved the operative technique so greatly that it became relatively straightforward, and further progress has made the operation almost a commonplace. In fact, it is performed nowadays for reasons other than contracted pelvis, and often for conditions which would not have justified it in earlier times. I remember one of my own cases particularly well; it was the first pregnancy of a young Scotswoman with a grossly contracted pelvis. When I opened the womb I found that not one, but two babies awaited delivery, and she awoke from the anaesthetic to find a dark-haired boy and a blue-eyed girl beside her.

No subject in medicine gave me greater satisfaction than the diagnosis of an unruptured ectopic pregnancy (development of the foetus outside the womb, usually in a Fallopian tube). While I was a student in my final year, the examination of numerous cases enabled me to distinguish between an ectopic pregnancy and a threatened miscarriage. In my first year of practice in Australia I diagnosed what I believed to be such a case, but called in a consultant for confirmation. He disagreed with me, and was not convinced until the patient suffered a major intra-abdominal haemorrhage. After that I always trusted my own diagnosis, and when I operated I had the satisfaction of finding that I had saved the patient from what could have been a calamity.

9

FIRST TRIP TO THE OUTBACK

I WAS TO COME TO KNOW THE OUTBACK REGIONS OF AUSTRALIA,
and the Aborigines to whom they had once belonged, as
well as any man could who did not live there. But during my
first thirteen years in Australia I had never been north of the
Murray, and like so many Australians of those days I had only
an academic knowledge of the Aborigines. My awakening
was to come later.

My first trip north was in 1925 to Broken Hill on business
concerned with Toc H. This organisation was founded during
the war as a servicemen's centre known as Talbot House
behind the lines in France. The soldiers who enjoyed its
physical and spiritual comfort as a respite from the firing line
called it Toc H, the army signallers' method of spelling its
initials. It was run by Padre 'Tubby' Clayton, and after the
war he determined that the spirit of unselfish sacrifice which
had impelled so many men to face wounds and death should
not be submerged in the mundane things of peace. He established Toc H as an organisation which, by such methods as
youth groups and the providing of assistance to those in need,

would pay practical tribute to the memory of those who died. The organisation flourished for a long time, but of late years has been somewhat overshadowed by other "service clubs" which do similar good work.

Tubby Clayton and his offsider Pat Leonard visited Australia in 1925 to found Toc H here. Lord Forster, Governor-General of Australia, and Lady Forster, gave the first Lamp of Remembrance in memory of the two sons they lost in the war. £5,000 was given to endow the Edwin Wright Memorial Chaplaincy, in memory of Captain Wright who was aide-de-camp to Governor Bosanquet of South Australia before the war and whose death in action together with those of his two brothers put an end to that branch of the family.

Clive Carey of the Adelaide Conservatorium of Music, and I, were the first two sponsored and initiated for Toc H in Australia. Both of us had lost a brother in the war. Early in October I went with Pat Leonard to Broken Hill in the hope of starting a branch there, but even though there were many ex-soldiers among the miners the Toc H ideal of "unselfish sacrifice" did not appeal to a number of trade unionists, who doubted whether it was practical politics. On a Saturday night I attended a soldiers' smoke social where we were regaled with a speech by General Sir John Monash, commander of the Australian Army Corps in France in 1918. He spoke on how to win the next war, but did not say a word on how to win the peace.

Three days later I left by the mail-motor for Wilcannia on the Darling. The truck was crammed with passengers and baggage, which was piled high at the back, stacked under the seats and under our feet. It ground along the "road" which stretched ahead of us across the saltbush plain, with the driver negotiating the ruts and soft spots with the skill of long practice. It was in fact a main stock route, one mile wide, with a bore and tank every ten miles. Despite its overload the truck made better headway than a camel-waggon we encountered. Loaded with wool, it was bogged to the axles in sand and its team of eighteen camels could not budge it.

Hot, dry, and dusty, we rocked along until a miserable wooden structure came in sight at four in the afternoon. This was Tobar hotel, isolated on the desert with not another building for miles. After a bite of lunch we plugged on again, pausing a couple of times for billy tea and for the driver to rig a tarpaulin along the weather side of the truck to keep out the bitter wind after sunset. We reached Wilcannia at midnight, and I was given a bed in the same hotel room as a station manager who had been in hospital. "You won't get much sleep tonight," he said. "It's Race Week, and the boys are celebrating. As soon as the dance is over they'll be making for the hotel."

Sure enough, we soon heard a wild uproar in the street, and the station manager chuckled, "There's a couple of commercial travellers next door, and they've bolted themselves in. They'll be sorry for it. Best leave our door open, or they'll break it down."

He was right. The commercial travellers' door went down with a crash, and we heard sounds of chaos next door. Then half-a-dozen hefty jackeroos came bowling in to see their friend the station manager, who had had the room to himself when they left him. They didn't even notice me in the other bed, and one of them jumped onto the foot of the bed with a bottle of beer in each hand. "What am I bid?" he bellowed. "Come on, lads—make your bids!"

He swung the bottles around wildly as he swayed on the bed, and I thought that they were coming a little too close to my head. His friends hadn't even noticed me behind him, so I eased down the bed, put both feet in the small of his back, and propelled him onto the floor among his cobbers. Completely mystified, they stared at me until I asked, "Isn't it about time you opened those bottles?"

Wilcannia was a pretty spot, the River Darling there being two chains wide and spanned by a beautiful bridge. I was greatly impressed with the medical organisation of the surrounding countryside. Everyone within a radius of a hundred miles belonged to a locally-inspired medical scheme which included doctor and hospital, with no private practice in the ordinary sense of the word. It was an effective forerunner of the Government-controlled medical schemes of today.

I travelled the hundred miles or so from Wilcannia to Menindie with a commercial traveller, driving along a road which traversed sheep paddocks. He was glad of a companion, because it gave him someone to get out and open and close the gates which occurred at regular intervals.

I was fast gaining experience of outback pubs. The Boundary Hotel, midway between Wilcannia and Menindie, was merely a shed containing shelves of bottles—which did not include any soft drinks. At the Menindie hotel, a queue of men was lined up outside, trying to prove themselves to be *bona fide* travellers so that they could buy a drink after six p.m. They were surrounded by drunks who had had the forethought to buy their booze before closing time.

Next morning I drove on in Treweek's mail-truck, which was said to do a thousand miles a week. We carried bread and butter for the station homesteads as well as their mail because none of them had cows—though there were plenty of goats all the way from Broken Hill to Wentworth.

It was an uncomfortable trip. The truck jolted along through a north wind blowing a gale of fiery heat and dust. The homes and settlements looked bleak and primitive, and in those days they were a long, hard journey from each other. Pooncerie, one of the settlements, consisted only of a post office, hotel, general store, public hall, and three houses.

I was interested to see Tarcoola station, because I knew that it belonged to T. R. Hogarth of the 3rd Light Horse who was killed at Beersheba. We had just passed it when a figure ran towards us from the riverbank, yelling and waving his arms. He told the driver that his wife was sick; he hadn't been able to work for three days. "Well, there's a doctor on board," the driver said, and the man's face lit up. As we walked towards his home on the river bank he told me that he too had served in the 3rd Light Horse.

The woman was lying in the "bedroom", simply a tent inside a galvanised-iron shed open to the river on one side— and uncomfortably close to it. It was roofed with brush, and furnished with one bed, a table, and a few boxes to serve as chairs. What a reward for a man who had fought for his country—and what a plight for his wife and three children.

His wife was quite young—only twenty-six. I found that she was very low from persistent loss of blood, probably a result of her last confinement. There was not much that I could do for her under such conditions except to make her comfortable and advise her to avoid any exertion, and say that I would report the case to the Wentworth doctor. As we drove on I thought of the Bush Nurse on whom I had paid a courtesy call at Menindie, a double-certificated sister who acted as midwife, pulled teeth, and treated all accidents and sickness. The township was lucky to have her, because there was not a doctor within seventy miles. Those who lived in the outback needed to be hardy in those days.

The next stop was Burtundy Hotel, another drinking booth with half-a-dozen men sprawled around it in various stages of intoxication. Talking to those who were still sober, I found that most of them were rabbiters. They made good money from the skins, but spent the greater part in the pubs. Here, as elsewhere on the trip, I met Light Horsemen—men who had learnt horsemanship and self-reliance in these isolated outback settlements, joined up for service overseas, and then returned to an existence which did not seem to offer much future for most of them. Their eyes lit up when they found that I knew the places in Egypt where they had served, as though their desert warfare had by that time become a happy memory. One of them, who had been through the entire Egypt and Palestine campaign, got me to treat a very septic sore on his hand.

After sunset the wind rose to what seemed like hurricane force, as cold as it had been hot. One of the howling gusts blew in the windscreen, which already was cracked, and from then on we jolted along with eyes slitted against the whipping dust. The headlights showed clouds of it blowing along the road, which was so lonely that we saw only two young drovers swaying beside a cart which they were too drunk to drive, and an old rabbiter who hailed us to pass up a bag of skins and warn of fallen trees, and later a row of T-model Fords parked along the riverbank with tents slung in between—a camp of fishermen.

By the time we reached Wentworth I was smothered in red

dust. The streets were dark and empty, and I had to ring the hotel bell for a long time before a surly landlord opened the door. "Y'can't have a bath this time of night," he told me when I asked for bed and bath, so I answered, "Please yourself. A bath first, or bed as I am?"

He switched on the light to have a closer look at me, and when he saw me as a walking pillar of red dust he grunted, "You can have a bath."

Next morning I told the local doctor about the woman in the river camp near Tarcoola, and he made arrangements for her to be picked up and brought to hospital. The next stage was from Wentworth to Mildura, broken only by the driver's visit to a hotel where he waited until the winner of the Caulfield Cup had been telephoned through.

By a chance meeting with a Scot whose wife had been delivered by my grandfather, I met more Scots in Mildura than I encountered in any town in Australia; most of them were from Ayrshire towns near my own old home on the Clyde. Some of them saw me aboard the paddlesteamer on which I travelled down the Murray to Morgan to take the train for home.

I had travelled a good many miles through Australia on this trip, but hadn't seen a single Aboriginal except for one "blacks' camp" which we passed on the river bank. I still had no more than an academic interest in the subject of Australia's native people, though I had read a good deal about them when I first settled here. I felt no sense of responsibility for the disappearance of Aboriginal tribes from the banks of the Darling and the Murray. My involvement was to come later, after I had heard of the wholesale massacre of drought-stricken, defenceless tribal Aborigines by Constable Murray and his accomplices in the Northern Territory during 1928.

The years passed, busily occupied in family, professional, and public affairs. I had been convener of the committee set up to establish the Light Horse Memorial on the corner of East Terrace and North Terrace, and was proud of the splendid support given by the citizens of Adelaide—especially the relatives of those who had fallen. It was unveiled by the then Governor of South Australia, Major-General Sir Tom

Bridges, and still stands in the same place, a corner not much changed since those days though I doubt whether the memorial is often noticed by the car drivers who sweep by. Not far away is the water trough installed in memory of the "heavy horses" who served the Australian Army overseas.

Among my other associations were those with the English Speaking Union, which I helped to found in Adelaide and chaired in 1932, and with the Presbyterian Girls College. The College was founded in 1922, and is now one of South Australia's leading independent schools. Its pupils still wear the Black Watch tartan which was chosen for the kilts and bonnets of their uniform a few years after the school was founded. The Assembly of the Presbyterian Church ruled that members of the College Council, to which I belonged, should be members of or adherents to the Presbyterian Church, and as a stalwart Scot I upheld that. In the mid-1930s, after I had served as Chairman of the Council for three years, my successor induced the Council to strike out this ruling. I fought the change, and towards the end of my battle received a telegram from the more Scottish Presbyterian Church in Victoria reading, "Fight into the last ditch." I replied, "Have been in it for a fortnight."

The Presbyterian Girls' College is not so fully under the Church as its founders planned but the Council of the College still presents its Annual Report to the Church Assembly.

Before this, I had made another trip overseas, to do another post-graduate course in Britain and to accept a longstanding invitation from Dr Charles Mayo to visit the famous Mayo Clinic in Rochester, Minnesota. I found that Britain in 1927 was a depressing place, with great extremes of wealth and poverty. Wartime profiteers were among the "newly rich," but most people were worse off than before the war. I saw ill-clad, ill-fed paupers on the city streets selling matches and bootlaces — flower girls by their baskets — crippled ex-servicemen squatting by pictures drawn in chalk on the pavements in the hope of attracting alms from passers-by. Middle-class folk were hard hit and living more austerely than before the war, and many of the "old rich" had been obliged to abandon their fine country homes.

But it was good to see my old home again, even though my mother's chair was empty now, and my wife and son enjoyed Scotland and its scenery as much as before. After this my days were full with gaining experience in new surgical advances and techniques. I began at Leeds General Hospital and witnessed a wide range of general surgery performed by men who were leaders in their fields. With Matthew Stewart, the Professor of Pathology and an old friend of mine, I spent a day on duodenal ulcer study.

Next I went to London, and worked with specialists in the surgical fields which were of special interest to me. I saw Sir Berkeley Moynihan perform his radical operations on the stomach at St Bartholomew's, and Sir Thomas Dunhill, at the same hospital, perform general operations and some specially memorable goitre surgery. I studied the upper abdomen with A. J. Walton at the London Hospital, did gynaecology with Victor Bonney at Chelsea Hospital, watched Thomson Walker on prostate work at King's College, and Frank Kidd on kidney operations at his private hospital. Spencer Mort, whom I had succeeded on the surgical staff at Glasgow Hospital, was now administrator of the North Middlesex, and I followed his suggestion to work there with Galloway, a young Edinburgh surgeon.

But not all the time was spent in the operating theatre. I was honoured by an invitation, as a representative of South Australia, to attend a presentation of new standards by King George V to the Household Cavalry regiments. It was a spectacular ceremony, and two of those receiving the standards were Field Marshals Viscount Allenby and Earl Haig— famous men in those days, and part of history now. I saw the Duke and Duchess of York, later King George VI and Queen Elizabeth, return from opening Australia's new Parliament House in Canberra.

My life could have been changed by an invitation to stand as Liberal candidate by Sir Herbert Samuel, but for the second time I could not see myself in politics—and felt even more strongly that my home and future were in Australia.

My wife and son came to London and we saw all the sights together, and after a holiday in Scotland it was time for me to leave for America. My wife decided to return directly to Australia, so I made a lonely, stormy, and seasick crossing aboard the *Berengaria*, then one of the "blue riband" trans-atlantic liners.

New York, even in those days, was noisy, crowded, and dangerous. I was warned not to go down dark streets alone, and during the five days I spent in the city there were four murders. In one of them, the victim's tongue was cut out and nailed to a tree beside his body—apparently a gangland punishment for an informer. Chicago was even noisier than New York, with faster-moving traffic crammed bumper-to-bumper down the streets. I liked it better than New York, especially for its fine sandy beaches along Lake Michigan. When I told friends that I liked their city, but thought the bustle and noise worse than New York, they took it as a compliment. It was the age of "zip, pep, and ginger," as it was expressed to me by a passenger aboard the *Berengaria*, which immediately preceded America's depression years.

It was a relief to get out into the country again and eventually to reach Rochester, Minnesota, only a small town but internationally famous because Doctors Charles and William Mayo had established their Mayo Clinic there. Their development of new medical and surgical techniques and their successful handling of many cases which other doctors had failed to cure, made surgeons and patients beat a path to their door.

I had met Dr Charles Mayo in Macewen's wards in Glasgow, seventeen years before, and was surprised that he remembered me. "What do you want to concentrate on?" he asked me, and I told him, "Abdominal surgery, goitre, and prostate." He put a table in the library at my disposal, introduced me to the experimental institute and invited me to attend, and arranged for me to "sit in" on operations at close range. I was present at the weekly staff discussions, and the combination of expert demonstrations and friendly hospitality made my stay at the Clinic a memorable and rewarding one.

But it was good to be homeward bound again, and I made the long train journey to Vancouver to board the liner for Sydney. At the hotel I met a friend from Adelaide and at breakfast on sailing day he said, "You've been singing like a canary for an hour or more. What's got into you?"

"I'm on the last lap home, and my wife's meeting me in Sydney," I told him.

We sailed at noon, and after lunch I turned into my bunk for a nap. I was wakened at three o'clock and handed a radiogram. My wife was dead.

10

"DAMNED DIRTY NIGGERS"

I WAS HOME, BUT WITH A DIFFERENCE. AT SYDNEY I LEARNT that Rene had died with startling suddenness. She had been speaking to our son Charlie when a vital artery ruptured in her brain, and she died instantaneously.

For fifteen years I hadn't known what housekeeping was, but now I was to find out. The next three years were the most trying of my life—intensely lonely despite the busy days in my consulting rooms and the operating theatre, and full of concern for my son still only thirteen. Soon after I returned home I received a call from Scotland inviting me to return and fight a safe Liberal seat at a bye-election in my home county, and but for Charlie's unwillingness to leave Australia I would have done so. I remembered that Australia was his homeland, after all.

In 1929, as a member of the Council, I was invited to the annual Prefects' Dance of P.G.C., and was introduced to Phyllis Lade. She taught English literature in the Senior School. We stood talking through two dances until Miss Isobel Macdonald, then the Principal, called us to rejoin the official party! We were married just over a year later, to begin a partnership which has lasted for forty-one happy years.

I don't think that either of us realised what battles lay ahead as we became ever more deeply involved with the cause of the Aborigines.

Shortly before our marriage I was consulted by a woman missionary who had been serving on Goulburn Island off the northern coast of Australia. She was suffering from leprosy contracted from the Aborigines whom she had served and it was necessary for me to treat her weekly during the following years. It was natural for me to ask about her life at the Mission and about the Aborigines generally. I was shocked by her grim picture of what was happening to Australia's native people. Among many other things she told me it was common for Aboriginal women to be raped by white intruders who beat up the husbands if they tried to rescue their wives. I found her stories hard to believe and she would urge me to go north and find out the truth for myself. As I shared these things with my wife she too became deeply concerned; it seemed incredible that such things were happening in Australia but in the next few years we heard more and more tales of cruelty and injustice.

Phyllis was to identify herself completely with my cause, "speaking out" to many groups and above all creating in our home a centre of mutual respect between Aborigines and ourselves. The many guests who stayed with us over the years were often shy Pitjantjatjara people who would be put at ease by the efforts of their hostess to learn a few words of their language. Part-aboriginal girls too boarded happily with us for years—three of them being married from our home with Phyllis as "mother of the bride." And myself, whom they called Tjilpi ("old man") giving them away. But all this was far in the future.

In 1933, I heard of the tragedy of Takiar, which made me clench my teeth. It resulted from the Caledon Bay affair, in which troopers of the Northern Territory Police went to investigate a report that Japanese pearl-fishermen had been killed by Aborigines off the coast of Arnhem Land, on the Gulf of Carpentaria. Since the Japanese fishermen were

TOP: The chained and manacled prisoner being examined by the author. BOTTOM: Coober Pedy Post Office in the 1930s

accustomed to raid the villages in search of women, this is not unlikely.

One trooper of the police patrol was killed by Aborigines, and it was proposed to arrest Takiar, as the "chief" of the tribe, and bring him to justice. Instead, two missionaries induced him to leave his wife and family and sail with them on a lugger to Darwin, where he was arrested. Both in Fanny Bay gaol and in Darwin court he was subjected to the callous and inhuman treatment which was customarily meted out to Aborigines in those days. Judge Wells sentenced him to death, but the High Court on appeal strongly criticised the judge, quashed the conviction, and ordered that Takiar should be set free.

According to law, he should have been taken home by the police. Instead, he was left to find his own way home, and was never seen again—or at least not by anyone who was going to talk about it. I have little doubt as to how he met his death.

The woman missionary had stirred my concern for the Aborigines, and the case of Takiar strengthened my conviction that I must "see for myself."

In July 1934, I started on my first trip to the north. There was no regular air service, so the most convenient way to travel to Darwin was by train to Alice Springs and then to board the mail-motor which travelled the 1,000 miles of unsealed road to the coast. The road trip would be a rough experience, but the train journey was a revelation. It went through Quorn in those days, and made frequent half-hour stops to offload provisions for the fettlers' camps along the line; two sheep for killing, vegetables and dry stores, and a supply of water from a tank truck.

Twelve hours after leaving Quorn, we saw our first Aborigines—two full-bloods and several part-Aborigines, some of them very light in colour. This was at Marree, where the flat, sandy desert stretched away for as far as the eye could see. Four hours later a truck loaded high with hay jumped the rails, and the passengers watched as the train crew carefully packed old sleepers under the wheels to lever it back onto the line again. At Curdimurka, the next stop, the guard spent

Top: These charming pictures of tribal mothers and their children demonstrate the family love which is characteristic of Aborigines. Bottom: Children of a nomadic tribe in the desert

two hours telephoning Port Augusta about the faulty truck, which was part of the "mail express" to Alice Springs.

But we were only one and a half hours late in Alice Springs, two days and three nights after setting out. It had been an interesting trip, as the train trundled along through country which for the most part was a desolation of sandy or gibber desert. Obviously it was quite a feat to keep the train running at all through that kind of country, because one of the constant tasks of the fettlers was that of preventing sand from banking over the rails, and the line ran across the dry bed of the Finke River which occasionally would come down in flood and cut communications for days or even weeks. I made one good friend on the trip, the Reverend Percy Smith, one of the Bush Brothers whom I met when the train stopped for breakfast at Ilbunga. I was to meet him often during the next thirty years.

I had let various people know that I was on my way to Darwin, and when I stepped out onto Alice Springs railway station on that Sunday evening one of them came forward to meet me. He was the Commonwealth Medical Officer, Doctor McCann, with another man beside him. "This is Mr Dixon, Doctor Duguid," he said. "Mr Dixon's wife is at the Australian Inland Mission Hostel, and we're hoping that you'll have a look at her in the morning."

Sam Irvine, the mail-motor driver with whom I was booked to travel on to Darwin, was also there to meet me, but I was not to enjoy the drive with him. When I examined Mrs Dixon early next morning I concurred with Doctor McCann's diagnosis that she was suffering from internal haemorrhage which necessitated immediate operation. At nine a.m. I was performing the first major operation that had ever been done in Alice Springs, and Sam was on his way without me. Nevertheless my stay in the Alice Springs area, which was to last for three and a half weeks, was a valuable experience. It confirmed many things that I had been told about the situation of the Australian Aborigines in those days, and opened my eyes to the way in which they were treated.

Mrs Dixon, the wife of a station owner, came through the operation well, and when I called to see her that evening I was introduced to the Padre of the Australian Inland Mission. Almost his first words were, "I believe you are interested in the niggers?"

To hear this from the local leader of the mission maintained by my own church was staggering, but I asked only, "Do you mean the Aborigines?"

"You can call them what you like. They've never been any good and never will be. The best they've any right to expect is a decent funeral."

I was to discover that his attitude was not uncommon. Very few of the white residents of Alice Springs spared the Aborigines as much as a thought, and those who employed them gave them a handful of food and some cast-off clothing by way of wages. I began to see that this attitude had affected that of the local ministers. As soon as people began to know about my interest in the Aborigines, the minister of the Methodist Inland Mission called for a talk with me, and said, "My heart often bleeds for the native people, but if I interfered on their behalf the cattle stations would be closed to me." He felt that he had to choose between ministering to two utterly different flocks—the white and the black.

Percy Smith, the Bush Brother who had Alice Springs as part of his farflung Church of England parish felt a special concern for the half-castes, and E. E. Kramer, a missionary for the Aborigines' Friends Association, cared for full-bloods and part-Aborigines alike. Of the Commonwealth officials, only Doctor McCann and Sister O'Keefe, the matron of the home for part-Aboriginal children, showed real concern for the native people.

I could see that the part-Aboriginal population was increasing at a rapid rate. The white men who despised Aborigines had no compunction in taking their pleasure at the expense of Aboriginal women. Occasionally a white father would maintain his coloured offspring, but most left the responsibility to the government. Percy Smith introduced me to the Bungalow, as the home for such children was called. It was a happy enough place for the babies, toddlers, and older children, but their future held little hope. In their later teens they would be drafted out to work—the girls as servants in township or station homes, the boys to whatever work was available on the cattle-stations or elsewhere. They were not paid in cash, so would have little chance to make their way to better conditions, and the lot of the half-caste girls was tragic. Far too often they became the playthings of white men, including some who were supposed to be their protectors.

On Sunday mornings the children in the Bungalow were divided into three groups, each of which was addressed by a different clergyman — Anglican, Methodist, and Roman Catholic. I attended the Methodist service, and in the afternoon went with Mr Kramer to a service at the gaol. Only two tribal Aborigines were in custody, but as I was leaving the warder told me casually, "One of the troopers is going out on patrol pretty soon. Probably he'll bring in a nigger or two. We need someone to chop some more firewood."

I thought that he was joking at my expense, but found that he had spoken quite seriously. Apparently it was the usual custom.

Mr Kramer also held services at the church he had built for Aborigines in the township and at the Aborigines Reserve. One evening I attended the marriage of two part-Aborigines, and when Mr Kramer asked for their fathers' names the young man gave his but the girl, Clara, answered quietly, "I haven't seen my mother since the last time you asked me, Mr Kramer, so I haven't been able to find out. But I think it was—" and she mentioned the name of a white man known locally.

Apart from the physical deprivations which such youngsters would have suffered from the lack of proper fathers to provide for them, the mental and spiritual deprivations were even more deplorable.

Discrimination against the Aborigines was deeply implanted in every aspect of life. At that time, the only church for white people in Alice Springs was the Methodist. An Aboriginal woman, Nana, who had worked as a housekeeper in Adelaide for many years and was a devout churchgoer, paid a visit to her home town of Alice Springs and went to this church. She was informed that it was not for natives, so rose and walked out. I had known Nana well for many years and knew how greatly she was respected by everyone who had had much to do with her.

The education of children at the Bungalow was negligible, and they were not trained for any occupation. As for full-bloods, they were regarded merely as hewers of wood and drawers of water. "Religion and education spoil niggers," I was told. The full-bloods lived on the Aborigines' Reserve, a mile and a half from town, but only those who were employed were allowed to enter Alice Springs. No shelter or housing of any kind was provided at the Reserve. The Aborigines lived in shacks or humpies thrown together out of any kind of rubbish they could lay their hands on. It must be remembered that, in 1934, the white invaders had been in the Alice Springs area for less than seventy years. The Aborigines and part-Aborigines of the township and the Reserve were the immediate descendants of those from whom the cattlemen, miners, and other exploiters of the Inland had taken the tribal territories on which Aborigines had lived contentedly for centuries. The landtakers had made no attempt to teach the Aborigines how to adapt themselves to this cataclysmic change in their circumstances. They had not been taught to use tools, their hunting grounds had been stolen, their entire way of life destroyed. Yet the white men despised them because they lived in degradation—and because they copied the worst and most commonly-displayed customs of the white man such as drunkenness, often caused by cheap wines and methylated spirits sold to them by whites who were breaking the law.

The whole picture was abysmally depressing, and was made worse by the attitude of some white men of whom one would have expected better things. An Alice Springs solicitor, Mr Webb, told me that he thought "punitive expeditions" should be undertaken against Aboriginal tribes still living further out, in order to "make life possible" for white communities. Yet, on the same day, I spoke to Dow Dow, an old Aranda man who lived at Bond Springs cattle station. He remembered the arrival of the first white men. He and his sister were collecting bush tucker when she drew his attention to a movement in the bush. His father and uncles, hunting nearby, stuck their spears in the ground when they saw the

99

white men. "That meant no fight," said Dow Dow. The Aborigines accepted the white invaders who were to rob them of everything—and then send police patrols against them to keep them in order.

I met Dow Dow again in a later year. It was a drought season, and he was with his grandson and the young man's wife and child. They had to stay with him because, as an old man, he received government rations. As young people, they got nothing. They had to share his food to stay alive—in the country which had once supported their entire tribe.

The comments made by the Padre of the Australian Inland Mission had been a shock, especially since I had thought that the A.I.M. was caring for Aborigines as well as whites. Instead, it was accentuating the division, and when I returned to Adelaide I called on the Director of the A.I.M. to discuss it with him. He was utterly frank. "The A.I.M. is only for white people," he told me. "You are only wasting your time among so many damned dirty niggers."

It is fair to say however that the A.I.M. did a splendid job for the white community, especially for the white women who lived such hard and isolated lives in the outback. Its hostels, always staffed by two fully-trained nursing sisters, have given invaluable medical service where no other existed. They were the wellspring of the Flying Doctor Service, inspired by the Reverend John Flynn of the A.I.M. and made possible by Alf Traeger's invention of the pedal wireless sets which enabled communications between stations and medical centres.

The original "A.I.M." was the Aborigines Inland Mission, founded by Mrs Retta Long. She told me that she called on John Flynn and asked him not to cause confusion by using the same initials when the Australian Inland Mission began work, but he refused to change them. This was unfortunate, because the two organisations operated in very different fields and with completely different methods.

As a doctor, I was appalled by the physical condition of the Aborigines. Its most dastardly aspect was the spread of venereal disease, through pregnancies forced upon Aboriginal women by infected white men. The eyes of all the babies born to these infected women were damaged by gonorrhoea, often with serious impairment of vision. I saw one baby with an eye so damaged that it was likely to be sightless—and it was only one of many born that year similarly affected. When I returned to Adelaide I wrote to the Minister for the Interior, Thomas Patterson, asking for figures on pregnancies and venereal cases among girls in that area. He answered promptly, and his figures tallied with my own.

More insidious, but equally damaging in a different way, was the effect upon Aborigines of the totally unsuitable diet. For thousands of years the native people of Australia had lived on a diet which was largely protein, the raw or partly-cooked flesh of the bush creatures. But this diet was now being replaced largely by carbohydrate, the white man's flour, tea and sugar.

The Aborigines struck a perfect balance with nature. They did not domesticate animals nor cultivate the ground in any way, but roamed throughout their extensive tribal areas and did not settle for very long in any one place. They were in absolute harmony with the land, and many of its natural features were believed to be mythical beings of the Dreamtime, changed into the form of a rock, watercourse, tree, or other landmark. Their complex totemic rituals were religiously observed. Passed on from one generation to another, they taught how the tribe came into being and laid down a complete code of conduct to ensure survival. It was this that enabled them to live off the land, and to find food and water in conditions where a white man would have perished.

The European invasion of the outback destroyed this balance between man and nature for ever. The sheep and cattle of the settlers ate up the ground cover on which the natural food of the Aborigines existed; the kangaroos and other bush creatures were shot for sport or because they ate the feed needed for stock pasture, and the soaks and waterholes were taken over by the intruders. Also, the sacred places of the tribesmen were profaned by the white men.

I saw the result of all this when I visited the cattle stations within a radius of about eighty miles around Alice Springs. The old men and women whom I saw were scraggy specimens existing on government rations: "Not more than 5 lbs. flour, 1 lb. sugar, $\frac{1}{4}$ lb. tea per week." This was a ludicrous diet for people who in tribal days lived largely on raw natural foods. The rations for Aboriginal workers contained insufficient calories for the work they had to do, and their wives and children received even less. With one exception, Undoolya west of Alice Springs, every station had a grossly under-nourished population of Aboriginal women and children.

Government rations were given only to the aged, infirm, and sick. All the Aboriginal women, children, and unemployed men whom I saw in 1934 were undernourished and listless.

I was impressed by Doctor McCann's concern for the Aborigines. He was perturbed by the increasing death toll from tuberculosis at Hermannsburg Mission, eighty miles from Alice Springs, and there was some fear that the disease might spread more widely among the Aborigines. He asked me to investigate, and I paid a two-day visit to the Mission. It was run by the Lutherans, who sent the first mission to the Aborigines in the 1860s, and in 1934 was in charge of Pastor F. W. Albrecht. The mission ministered to the Aranda tribe, once the strongest Aboriginal community of the Centre.

Pastor Albrecht welcomed me and gave me every assistance, because he was equally worried about the prevalence of tuberculosis. I found that the Aborigines were living in thick-walled huts made of mud or clay, with very poor ventilation. They had been built a good many years before, and I felt sure that the infection would continue to flourish under such poor living conditions. I said that the huts should be razed to the ground, and the Aranda elders who listened to my discussions with Pastor Albrecht lost no time in getting to work.

It was the beginning of a new era for the Mission. With his customary vision and enthusiasm, Pastor Albrecht launched an appeal for funds, and when I returned to Adelaide I was privileged to chair a public meeting in the Adelaide Town Hall, which brought a splendid response. The result was the completion of a pipeline to Hermannsburg from Koporilya Springs, four miles away, which among other things enabled the Aborigines to plant a vegetable garden. Improved living conditions and a more varied diet soon resulted in much better health for the Aborigines.

On my first afternoon at Hermannsburg, I had my first experience of seeing the Flying Doctor radio link in action. Pastor Albrecht straddled the pedal-wireless apparatus, pedalled steadily to generate electricity for the transceiver, and called up the headquarters in Cloncurry, Queensland. He was given a telegram from Terowie in South Australia and asked to wait until an urgent call from Innamincka, near the point where the Birdsville Track crossed the Queensland-S.A. border, had been dealt with. I heard the Cloncurry doctor saying, "There's no immediate danger, but I'll fly over if necessary. I'll ring you at seven tonight."

Birdsville was then asked about the weather, there was a long talk with Bedourie in Queensland, and then Cloncurry called Mornington Island in the Gulf of Carpentaria and passed on a telegram from a doctor in Ipswich. It was an object lesson in how the "mantle of safety over the outback," which John Flynn had foreseen as the role of the Flying Doctor service, was beginning to operate.

Next day I was introduced to a handsome, well-built Aboriginal who had just come in from the bush with a thick mulga log nearly as tall as himself. He sawed this into slabs, then used red-hot fencing wire to etch scenes of bush life into their surfaces, which he polished and varnished. Unknown to myself I was watching the first manifestations of the artistic talent of Albert Namatjira, who was soon to act as Rex Battarbee's guide and camel-man on an extended painting tour. For two months he watched Battarbee at work and absorbed all that the artist could teach him, and two years later was on his way to fame as the first Aboriginal artist to paint in the European way. I knew Albert for many years until his death. He stayed with me whenever he visited Adelaide, and some of his paintings are among my proudest possessions.

On the way back to Alice Springs we approached Simpson's Gap at sunset. The cliff glowed red in the setting sun, cattle stood knee deep in the big waterhole, but there was not an Aboriginal in sight. Yet, not so long before, this place had been one of the great centres of tribal ceremonial and family life.

Before I left for Adelaide again Doctor McCann asked me

to have a talk with him. He told me emphatically, "If the black man is to be saved he must be allowed to live in his own hunting and ceremonial grounds. But there's not much chance of that. Cattle and gold interests are believed to be more important. We've knocked down the props on which the blackfellow has leaned for thousands of years and left him completely bewildered. He doesn't know where he is."

Even my brief experience showed me that he was right. I said, "I can't see any future for them until they're treated as human beings like ourselves. So far neither the government nor the churches — except for a few limited missions — have taken a stand on that principle."

McCann was not a man to wait for other people to do things. He was pressing for an Isolation Block to be established for treatment of venereal cases, and soon afterwards in Adelaide I made an urgent appeal for a Public Hospital to be built in Alice Springs, to treat all cases of need regardless of colour or race. At that time, the only place where the sick could be nursed was in the A.I.M. Hostel, but the sisters were not allowed to admit patients with Aboriginal blood.

The Alice Springs Hospital was opened in 1939, but it was not until 1958 that the Executive of the A.I.M. allowed its staff to treat Aborigines.

On the train back to Adelaide, I thought about my final conversation with Pastor Albrecht. He asked, "What do you think about the situation in the Centre now that you've seen it?"

"Ashamed," I told him. "But next year I mean to go further afield, to make contact with Aborigines before station-life overtakes them."

"Then I suggest you go to the Musgrave Ranges, in your own State," he said. "Nobody's quite sure what's happening there."

II

A BEE IN THE BONNET

QUITE SOON AFTER MY RETURN FROM ALICE SPRINGS, I WAS told, "If you don't slow up, you're going to lose friends and patients." Another friend said, "You must be exaggerating. Things can't be as bad as you say."

My trip to the north had stirred me deeply. All that I had been told by the woman missionary with leprosy, all that I had read about the treatment of Aborigines, all that I had seen and learnt in the Alice Springs area, had fired my determination to make the white people of Australia understand the mental and physical sufferings of the Aborigines, and shame them into making radical changes. I spoke frankly, in private and in public, of the facts as I had found them, and gave numerous addresses to church groups and other organisations. One of these had dramatic repercussions.

On 27 December 1934 I gave a midday address to a Presbyterian Fellowship Conference held at Scotch College. In my talk, I said, "The shooting and poisoning of natives that took place in the past are too horrible to recall, and yet occasional happenings of a similar kind still take place in the far outback areas." I mentioned also that I had a photograph of a boy who had been poisoned that year (though he recovered after treatment) by drinking from his own waterhole, and that the wife of a missionary in another State had alleged that if a blackfellow was believed to be a nuisance, he could be disposed of in an out-of-the-way spot. I also pointed out that while various church missions were doing good work along the northern coast in such areas as Arnhem Land, there was unfortunately only one mission in Central Australia (Hermannsburg) which looked after full-blood Aborigines.

Late that afternoon, my wife and I walked out of an Adelaide store to be confronted by a newspaper poster which said in huge type: SWEEPING ALLEGATIONS BY DR DUGUID. When we bought the paper, the Adelaide *News*, we read a gross misrepresentation of my talk. It read as though I had stated that Aborigines were still being killed as in the bad old days without questions being asked, that their waterholes were being poisoned to destroy tribesfolk, and that the churches were apathetic towards the whole problem.

I wrote to the editor of the *News*, asking for an immediate apology, but this request was unheeded. Instead, the paper made a compromise statement, which I refused to accept in spite of my oldest friend in the medical profession asking me, "Have you gone too far, Charles?" Then I received a letter from the Conference, dated 28 December 1934, stating: "We the undersigned members of the Conference who attended the talk given by Dr Charles Duguid on "Our Duty to the Australian Aboriginal" hereby affirm that the report of the speaker's remarks in the *News* of 27 December was not a true or fair record of that talk. No sweeping allegations as stated in the report by the *News* were made by him." This was signed by the chairman, and everyone who heard me speak.

The *News*, at my request, published that letter, but no apology was made until I employed a lawyer. An apology was published on 10 January 1935, in which the *News* stated in part, "Our reporter in this instance put himself and the paper badly in the wrong by paraphrasing Dr Duguid's remarks in such a way as to put words into his mouth which were not actually intended."

A few days later a prominent lawyer, who is now a Q.C., told me, "I thought you were a Scot, but you can't be. You'd have got heavy damages if you'd fought that case!"

"All I wanted was an apology for the misuse of my words—and I was determined to get it," I said.

My whole attitude, which drove me to tell the exact and uncoloured truth about the treatment of Aborigines, earned such comments as, "The man's got a bee in his bonnet. He's an utter fanatic." This remark was made by an Adelaide woman to a visitor from India who later called on us.

Unfortunately the *News* report went further afield than South Australia, and could have done considerable damage both to my reputation and to the cause which I taken up. On 3 January 1935 I had letters from the Secretary of the Department of the Interior, Canberra, and from the Deputy Chief Protector of Aborigines of Western Australia, asking for further information to support what I had said in my talk. Luckily the *Advertiser*, Adelaide's morning newspaper, had published a complete and accurate report of my speech on the day after I made it, so I was able to send newspaper cuttings together with my own explanation.

I had not forgotten Pastor Albrecht's suggestion that I should "see what was happening in the Musgrave Ranges," but I had a lot to do first. 1935 was one of the busiest years of my life. In March, I was called to be Moderator of the Presbyterian Church in South Australia, a position which I accepted after considerable hesitation. I was the first lay moderator in Australia and I made it clear that I would not assume the role of a clergyman but I managed to visit every part of South Australia where there was a Presbyterian cause. In addition I devoted my energies to bringing leaders of the Church of Scotland and the Presbyterian Church in England into contact with the Presbyterians of South Australia. This was done through a series of lunches in which overseas visitors met local ministers, elders and their wives, with my wife acting as hostess.

My main desire was that the Presbyterian Church should take definite action towards helping the Aborigines of South Australia, but I was not able to formulate plans for this any until the end of my year of office. I was also elected President of the Aborigines Protection League, a non-political, non-sectarian league which had been formed years earlier, one heartening proof that not all white Australians were insensible to the plight of the Aborigines. Its main emphasis was on the fact that the sequestration of Aboriginal tribal territories was the crux of all their problems.

My plans to make another trip to the Centre must have become well-known, because on 4 April 1935 I received a letter from Coober Pedy which offered the writer's services as a guide, and asked me to reply to Tarcoola, on the East-West railway. I did not like the tone of the letter and did not answer it, but the same man wrote a month later from Tarcoola and warned me that I should not delay if I meant to go north that year. He claimed to be a missionary to the Aborigines, and said that he would provide stores, camels, and medical supplies for a total of £344. I still did not reply, and his next move was to call at my home, where my wife asked him to dinner so that we could weigh him up. When he had left, our vote was definitely against him being my travelling companion.

As I walked through the city next evening I recognised him again, though he was wearing large dark glasses and was about to pass me. I stopped him, got his address, and called on him next day. His room contained two large home-made calico maps of the north-west corner of the State and an outsize, well-thumbed Bible. His make-believe did not impress me.

A few days later the police rang me. The man had been arrested for false pretences and had given my name. I went to see him in gaol, and he told me in a broken voice that he was a twin. "It is my brother who is guilty, and like Jesus I am suffering for my brother's sins," he told me.

Late that afternoon, H. H. Finlayson, the well-known anthropologist and author of the book *The Red Centre*, called at my consulting rooms. He told me that some years earlier he had travelled in the north-west with the same man and his camels. When they were many miles from civilisation, the man had threatened to desert Finlayson if he was not paid considerably more than had been agreed upon, and Finlayson had no doubt that he would have carried out the threat. So I may have had a lucky escape.

On 8 June 1935 I set out on my first trip to the Musgrave Ranges. It was a carefully planned expedition, to be guided by Reg Williams who was familiar with the back country. We were accompanied by "Robbie" Robinson, a student who was to act as mechanic. You had to be prepared for anything when you took a car into the outback in those days.

It had been a bad season, and we drove in a gale of wind all the way to Wilmington, where my brother George had a farm. His fields were as bare as the road, just spongy dust being whipped away by the wind. Next day was just as bad, and on our way to Marree we found that the road surfaces had been eroded by the wind and we had to travel slowly over the rough metal. In some places the sand had been blown over the road in high sandhills, but we had brought lengths of coconut matting with us and were able to lay our own track for the wheels.

So it went on for the whole 1,000-mile journey to the Musgrave Ranges, a week's travelling over all types of country including rocky creek-beds, sandhills, and the occasional smooth stretch such as the shores of Lake Eyre. The car took a considerable battering, with two tyres blown out by sharp rocks and a cylinder-head gasket blown. The very face of the countryside had been changed by drifting sand since Reg Williams had last been there, and at one time we took a wrong turning which took us to Welbourne Hill homestead—at that time an unhappy place for Aborigines. I knew an Aboriginal man who had been shot on that station in the previous year, and spent sixteen weeks in hospital in Adelaide before his pulped head and shattered thigh healed up. The station owner and his wife kept loaded firearms in the kitchen, and were made very nervous by our arrival. They had expected us to be detectives!

On the way to the Musgraves, it had been easy to see that the white man was still exploiting the Aboriginal woman. When we camped one night we saw two widely separated camp fires in the surrounding bushland, and found next morning that a white man and a native woman were camped in each place. On another morning we saw a white man, his Aboriginal woman, and their three part-Aboriginal children leaving their camp in a dry creekbed not far away.

In the Musgraves we stayed at Ernabella in the most westerly dwelling in South Australia, a partly-built house belonging to Stan Ferguson. It was well-built, looked trim and neat, but had no floor, ceiling, or windows—though a large open fireplace provided welcome warmth when we returned to it in the frosty evenings of the Inland.

Stan Ferguson owned a few sheep, which were looked after by a naked Aboriginal woman, and kept some goats for milk. He had some horses and camels, and used the latter mainly for riding through the back country and collecting dingo scalps from the Aborigines. The house was a focal point for "doggers" who made a living by shooting dingoes for their scalps or trading them from the Aborigines. It was a profitable business for the white man, who received 7/6d from the government for each dingo scalp handed in and often traded them from the Aborigines for a handful of flour apiece.

A rough shelter had been built near the house, and I found that it contained a full-blood woman. "Pica pulka (very sick)," she said, but there was little need for her to tell me that. One side of her nose and part of her cheek were eaten away by yaws— a very contagious tropical skin disease—possibly introduced to the Aborigines by contact with the traders along the northern coasts.

While my two companions got to work on the car to fix it up for the return journey I looked for a guide who would take me further into the Ranges. I made a lucky choice in Gilpin, a fine part-Aboriginal lad of about sixteen with whom I have had frequent contact ever since. He led me into the country of the Pitjantjatjara tribe, which had lived amongst the spectacular scenery of the Musgrave Ranges since time immemorial. They were a fine people with a striking dignity, living naked and with few possessions amid the rocky hills and escarpments of the Ranges, wandering their tribal territory in the constant search for food and water, and yet contented and virile. It was ominously clear that one could not expect them to be left in peace for very much longer. The boundaries of civilisation were

TOP: The cave in which Harold Lasseter died on his search for "Lasseter's Lost Reef." BOTTOM: A wiltja constructed of bush materials

being extended every year, and already white men were in the area to scratch a living from "dogging." I talked to them through Gilpin, and by the time we set off for Adelaide again I was deeply concerned for their future. They were on the edge of a civilisation which had no understanding of them and no feeling of responsibility for them—as our next encounter was to illustrate only too well. We had heard that a white man who had been living with an Aboriginal woman, by whom he had had two children, had recently married a white woman. We wondered what had happened to the children and were trying to find them, and on our way down the track met the white man coming towards us. We stopped, and I asked him where the children were. Quite casually, he said, "Oh, I dumped them and the lubra in the Everard Ranges."

That was all that he knew—or cared. The fact that he had added two more unfortunates to the unhappy community of the part-Aborigines was beyond his caring.

It was a hard trip as far as Oodnadatta. The car was sparking on two cylinders only and we had no spare tyre. We drove across a rocky plateau, then through very rough country, in and out of dry creek beds, through scrub and over rocks and stones. Most of the going was in second gear and my shoulders were aching when I handed over the wheel to Reg Williams, who said, "That track would just about break a snake's back."

We stayed the night at Lambina Station, where Mr and Mrs Charlie Paige made us welcome. We had met them on the way up, and it was the beginning of a long and happy friendship.

Next midday, at Erlyumbina waterhole, we met Victor Dumas, Alan Brumby, and Constable Francis from Oodnadatta. They told us a familiar story. An Aboriginal had been accused of killing a sheep, and the constable was on his way to bring him in to face the white man's justice. There was no question in anyone's mind as to the justice of seizing land which had nurtured the Aboriginal's tribe during ages, so that a station owner could run sheep on it.

Our rough journey ended when we reached Oodnadatta that afternoon, and were forced to stay there a week while we waited for spare gaskets, tubes, and tyres to be sent up the railway line. I filled in the time by helping Sisters McCallum

TOP: Aboriginal children lying behind a windscreen and between the little fires which keep them warm at night. BOTTOM: The occasional result of such sleeping arrangements. When sleeping deeply, a child or adult may roll right into the fire and be badly burnt

and Franks with their patients at the Australian Inland Mission hostel, and learnt at first-hand how much the hostel was appreciated by womenfolk from neighbouring stations.

But the week brought fresh evidence of the white man's attitude towards Aborigines. One instance was of telling significance. The woman owner of a cattle station called at the hostel, accompanied by her daughter-in-law and young granddaughter and a well-dressed part-Aboriginal girl of about seven. The three whites entered the hostel, but the dark child was alone outside for the two hours until they came out again. No person of Aboriginal blood could be admitted to the hostel.

The second instance was far worse. An Aboriginal said to be a "dangerous lunatic" was brought in from a station about 100 miles north, and locked up in the police station. The constable was out on patrol, so his wife asked me to examine the prisoner.

The police blacktracker took me to the tiny dark cell, made of cold stone blocks and slabs, where the "lunatic" sat restricted by a heavy chain padlocked on his neck and handcuffs on his wrists. His sunken face was expressionless.

I asked the blacktracker to take off the handcuffs so that I could examine the prisoner. He was reluctant to do so until I insisted, and then I removed the man's buttonless and beltless shirt, jacket, trousers, and old Army greatcoat. His body felt very cold.

I wrote down my findings as I examined him, and in non-medical terms they could be expressed by saying that he was painfully thin, with depressions above and below the collarbones. His wrists and hands were swollen, with recent chafes on the back of the right hand and lower part of the right forearm—possibly from the handcuffs. His right forearm had had both bones broken at some time, and they had joined in a bent shape because the fracture had not been treated. His shoulder blades, and his back over the left lower ribs, showed recent injury through thrashings. He had fairly recent scars on his chest, and old scars on both forearms and upper arms.

He had been described as "refusing to eat," but was ravenous when food was offered to him. I instructed that he should be fed warm bread and milk, little and often, for the first twenty-four hours, and the policeman's wife looked after him like a nurse. When he was given a full meal, he ate it hungrily.

A month later he was taken to Adelaide to be treated in the Mental Hospital, and was discharged restored to physical and mental health after a stay of two months.

About a year later, I used the man's case as part of a lecture which I gave about my trip to the Musgraves, illustrated by slides taken on the journey. I gave the lecture in a number of places, including a country town where a young man stepped forward at the end of my talk and stretched out his left hand. Holding it up for everyone to see, he said, "That nigger you showed broke a bone in my hand with a hammer when I was breaking him in. What would you have done?"

"I wouldn't have hit you on the hand. You'd have got it on the head!" I told him.

The young man was speechless with rage. Apparently he thought it quite all right to talk about "breaking in" a human being as though he was taming wild animals. It was not hard to imagine the process which had caused the Aboriginal to strike back.

The case reminded me of that of the Aboriginal from Welbourne Hill, with the fractured thigh and pulped scalp. After seeing him I had approached the government and asked for a police patrol to be established for the north of the State, to give some protection to such Aborigines and, if necessary, to station people. An investigation showed that some station owners were in favour of it, but others were not. One man, who dealt in dingo scalps, was quite forthright. "I can deal with the niggers myself," he said. "I once chained a nigger to a post for a fortnight until he told me the truth. I would pull out if a police patrol was started."

Outside Oodnadatta there was a camp for Aborigines; it was alongside the rubbish dump, from which they collected trash to build the hovels in which they lived. Any shelter less worthy of human beings would be hard to imagine.

But there was at least one heartening situation. Two dedicated Londoners, Mr and Mrs Fred Eaton of the United Aborigines Mission, looked after a home for part-Aboriginal children in Oodnadatta. Six children were living with them.

I visited these children every day, and have been able to follow them through their lives with great interest.

The spares arrived, and Robbie soon had the car in good fettle again. We travelled south by the waterless but less sandy back track, and carried a good supply of water with us. 200 miles south, after passing through Wintinna, Mount Willoughby, and Mabel Creek cattle stations—the latter a pioneer venture in those days, but now well-known—we came to Coober Pedy. The famous opal town had not arisen to its present importance, but we were fascinated by the Post Office, general store, and miners' homes; all were excavations in the hillside, protected from the icy winds of winter and the burning heat of summer. The postmaster, then a Mr Moore, handed me a copy of the Adelaide *Advertiser*. "I reckon you can take credit for that," he said, and pointed to a news item describing the Federal Government decision to appoint a doctor to work among Northern Territory Aborigines.

Apparently this arose from a discussion I had had the year before with Mr J. A. Perkins, Minister for the Interior, in Adelaide. I had recommended that a young physician and a bacteriologist should be appointed to investigate the prevalence of leprosy and other diseases among Aborigines of the sub-tropical north. As it transpired, the government decision was fruitless. The salary offered was too small to attract any applicants to a post in a part of Australia which, in those days, was truly back of beyond.

We drove on for another sixty miles until we reached the Dog Fence, which keeps the dingoes away from South Australian sheep and marks the outermost limits of sheep country, and fastened the gate behind us before driving on into the lonely twilight. It was a slow journey along the winding bush track, and there were so many kangaroos about that they jumped across the track in front of us, dazzled by the headlights. One of them jumped clear over the bonnet.

At last we saw the light of a cattle station, and when we drove up to it I was amazed when the door was opened by a woman who had been one of the foundation pupils of Presbyterian Girls' College in Adelaide, Mrs Glen Jacobs, whom I had known as Mary McTaggart. She made us very welcome, and it was good to have a bed again after sleeping on the ground.

The following night was the last to be spent in the open, in the frosty air with the sky above us a glory of stars. By the time we drove into Port Augusta the next morning an important project was taking shape in my mind. I had seen that the Pitjantjatjara people of the Musgrave Ranges were so far uncontaminated by contact with the white man and I was determined that they should be given a chance to survive in their own country. It seemed that the best way to do this would be to establish a Christian mission at the Eastern end of the Ranges, probably close to the spot where we had stayed and that this mission should act as a buffer between the Aborigines and the encroaching white man.

With many ideas about what such a mission should be revolving in my mind we travelled on to Adelaide, calling again at my brother George's farm. The fields that had been dust were now mud, because they had received eighty points of rain while we were in the north.

Back in Adelaide, I made an appointment with Mr (later Sir) Herbert Hudd, the Minister then responsible for Aborigines in South Australia. He gave me a good hearing as I told him about conditions I had found between Oodnadatta and the Musgrave Ranges including the breeding of many children of mixed blood and the inhuman and irresponsible attitude of many men in the area. He asked me to put my report in writing together with more details about the Christian mission I was suggesting.

During the next two months, as I shared with my wife the many disturbing experiences of my trip, we discussed the principles which we felt fundamental to the establishment of the Mission I proposed. The most basic was the conception of freedom. There was to be no compulsion nor imposition of our way of life on the Aborigines, nor deliberate interference with tribal custom. We believed that medical help should be offered at the outset, that only people trained in some particular skill should be on the mission staff, and that they must learn the tribal language. As the economy of the mission developed responsibility should be passed to the Aborigines as soon as possible.

With the setting up of a school the acceptance of the native tongue would be vital and all teaching for the first years should be in Pitjantjatjara tongue. I believe this insistence on learning in the mother tongue was something new in Australian missions of the time. Years later in 1968, when the Government settlement at Amata 100 miles west of Ernabella opened its school, the South Australian Education Department adopted the same principle and was able to borrow Pitjantjatjara primers evolved at Ernabella.

These then were the principles underlying the new mission I was proposing and they were submitted together with my report to Cabinet. The next I heard was when the Chief Secretary, Sir George Ritchie, told me at a Hallowe'en party of the Caledonian Society, "You'll get good news in the morning."

It was good news indeed. The government had accepted my plan in principle, and approved the establishment of a mission of the type which I suggested if I could arrange for it to be run by a responsible church. In addition, the government would subscribe £1,000 if I could collect a similar sum—and it must be remembered that £1,000 was a considerable sum in those days when Australia was only just emerging from the worst of the depression.

This was the seed from which Ernabella Mission has grown—but it still had to be fertilised with a good deal of work. Naturally I hoped that the Presbyterian Church would be the one to administer the mission, and set myself to persuade the church that it was work worthy of her energies. During the following year I spoke at the State Assemblies of the Presbyterian Church in South Australia, Victoria, and New South Wales, and made innumerable contacts of a more informal kind. Some people were enthusiastic, some indifferent, while others could see only the difficulties and problems.

As part of my effort to persuade the government, the Presbyterian Church, and the public in general to concern themselves with the plight of the Aborigines, I persuaded the man who succeeded me as Moderator in South Australia to accompany me on a trip to the outback. He was the Reverend David Munro, and I thought it would be a good idea if he could see for himself that I had not exaggerated my report on the Aborigines, and that it was practicable to institute a mission of the type which I proposed.

Accordingly I had made arrangements to meet Pastor Albrecht of the Hermannsburg Mission and to travel with him into the Haast Bluff area, about 200 miles west of Alice Springs. We set off on 4 June 1936 by train for Alice Springs, and at just about that time the Government Printer must have been printing the Chief Protector of Aborigines report for the year ending 30 June 1936, which read in part: "It appears to be impossible to stop the progress of the white race, even if it does upset the life and habits of the indigenous people. It therefore becomes our duty to buffer the contact in some way so that the clash will not only be gradual, but will in the first instance be with persons who have the welfare and love of the aborigines at heart, and not with those who wish to use him for their own personal gain, discarding him once he has served their purpose. Doctor Charles Duguid has been urging this duty upon the people of South Australia and has been endeavouring to get support for a scheme, which, gaining by the errors of missionary enterprise in the past, will serve to assist the aboriginal to retain his virility and self-respect and save him from the general degradation which usually follows his association with white settlement."

It was an arduous journey by hired car from Alice Springs, travelling through country which had been eaten out by cattle and then eroded by the winds of a prolonged drought. But when we reached the Haast Bluff area we found that the country was in better heart. So far, it had been left to the Aborigines whose methods of food collecting did not destroy the environment in the same way as that of the white man.

About 100 Aborigines were camped at Haast Bluff, of the Pintubi tribe from the Ehrenburg Range and the Gnalias from the Picilli Springs. Both tribes had been forced out of the tribal territories which they had held since time immemorial, but so far seemed to be in good health and spirits. Despite the cold, especially at night time, they were naked, and slept out in the open between little fires sheltered by a brush windscreen. They included a large number of older boys, and one of them, a Pintubi named Tjararu, was one of the brightest lads whom I have ever met, whether black or white. He was eleven then, full of life, and had the Aboriginal gift for mimicry so well developed that he had picked up the Aranda language—and in a very short time was speaking some words of English with the Scottish accent which he picked up from me!

We spent a few days at Haast Bluff with Pastor Albrecht, and saw how the Aborigines looked after themselves by collecting bush tucker. The men went off to hunt wallaby or kangaroos; the women and youngsters gathered seeds, roots, vegetable foods, and the smaller animals.

We travelled on by camelback, skirting the Haast Bluff Range and riding over country carpeted with wild flowers and waving grasses, but then entered a desert of parallel red sandhills. Nothing grew on them but spinifex, and there was not a sign of life in the air or on the ground. On the afternoon of the second day we approached the range which bounded the desert to the west, and the camels padded across grassland once more and between desert oaks which were gay with tasselled yellow flowers. An emu stalked nearby as we headed for a gorge leading into the mountains towards the Wotulpa waterhole, and when we reached it we found that two Aborigines were waiting for us beside a fire. They had followed their custom of avoiding the desert and moving from waterhole to waterhole in the ranges.

We filled our canteens and camped by the waterhole for the night, and I took the opportunity to climb the highest peak and survey the surrounding country. It was easy to see that the best country was out from the ranges.

I could see range after range of mountains, with good country around each range, but between them were great tracts of desert land dotted with saltpans from which fine salt was blowing in the wind. I knew already that tribal Aborigines lived in and around the ranges, where they could find water, game, and vegetable foods except in prolonged drought. But herein lay the root cause of Aboriginal deprivation. When the white man came along, he took this very land in order to fatten his bullocks. The Aborigines at first naturally speared the cattle at the waterholes as they had speared their own game.

The inevitable clash that followed drove them into the wilderness or reduced them to hangers-on at the white man's property, to work for the station-owners for hand-outs of food and old clothes.

The tribal Aborigines had no conception of land ownership. It was impossible for the white man to "buy" land from them, because a tribal territory belonged to the entire tribe and could not be sold by them any more than the people of South Australia could sell their own State. Tribal territory was the means of tribal sustenance—not only physical, but spiritual. They were bound to it by a complex structure of myth and tradition, wherein every physical feature of the land had significance to their spiritual life. When they were driven off their land, they lost their will to live and began the swift degradation which has often been irreversible.

Our party, guided by two Aranda men, made a three-weeks' journey which took us from Haast Bluff to Wotulpa, thence to Mount Liebig, Ayantji waterhole, Warren Creek, Mount Peculiar, Alalbi, Arumbera Creek, over the steep Mareeni Range to Umbartja, and thence to Hermannsberg. It was an exploration of the Australian outback in the days when white men had to travel on foot or on camelback because there were no cars or trucks capable of tackling the many varieties of terrain—sandhills, mulga scrub, rocky gorges and mountain sides, creekbeds and saltpans. Without our two Aranda guides we would have fared poorly indeed. They kept us supplied with game, led us to the waterholes, and showed us where to find water when it seemed non-existent—once by digging three times in a seemingly dry creekbed.

This hazardous travel was a small price to pay for a first-hand experience with Aborigines living in tribal conditions. Apart from those we met at Haast Bluff we lived for two days with a group at Alalbi, and met other groups en route. It seemed to me that these men, women, and children of the Pintubi and Gnalia tribes were very little different from ourselves. The men were as good fathers, the women as fond mothers, and the children as natural as their opposites in the white race. There was, however, one essential difference. They shared everything. If food was available, then no one went hungry. They had no conception of personal ownership, unlike us of European stock who lay claim to everything we can and talk of things being "mine."

All other differences were in non-essentials. They were naked, we wore clothes; we were pale, they were dark; they hunted and gathered their food, we bought ours over a counter; they slept naked between low fires, we slept between blankets.

I found that their health was good. There was one extensive case of yaws for which I gave treatment; there was an old man with a severe burn on his neck, probably caused by rolling into a fire when he slept, a girl with a squint of one eye, and a boy with his heart on the right side of his chest. Otherwise, these naked nomads whom I met on that tour, like those of the Pitjantjatjara met during 1935, were much finer physical specimens than the depressed Aborigines whom we found on cattle stations and in the townships—to say nothing of having the dignity and self-confidence which the other unfortunates had lost.

But, unless some action was taken, these tribespeople would also be driven out of their territory, and know the same kind of misery suffered by those whom white men referred to as "niggers."

It was on such terms that I spoke on my return when I addressed the General Assembly of the Presbyterian Church in Sydney in 1936. Those attending the Assembly had a pretty good idea as to my feelings on the subject. In 1933, when the General Assembly was held in Melbourne, I made a strong appeal for recognition of the worth of the Aborigines and for the church to have a greater concern for their welfare. This had not had any very marked effect. In fact, the Reverend John Flynn told me frankly during 1934 that I was wasting my time, and when I opened my case for the foundation of a mission on new lines I was told by the Secretary of the Board of Missions, the Reverend H. C. Matthews, that John Flynn was doing all he could to prevent it. Yet he was the idealist who had surmounted so many difficulties in order to establish the Flying Doctor service.

I began my appeal by speaking of what I had seen and learnt of the Aborigines during the previous three years, and showed lantern slides of the people and their way of life. On the following day I moved that the Presbyterian Church should accept responsibility for a mission to Aborigines in the Musgrave Ranges, and explained the lines on which it should be run, and the South Australian Government's readiness to help financially. My motion was seconded by the Reverend C. E. Turnbull, and strongly supported, but I could see trouble ahead.

The Reverend W. C. Ratcliffe, of Queensland, moved an amendment which would have postponed the project, and by doing so could have killed it. There was a pause until the Moderator, Dr John Mackenzie, asked, "Is there a seconder?"

"I second it so that it can be discussed," the Reverend Andrew Watson said, and then John Flynn spoke in support of the amendment.

I had no difficulty in countering Ratcliffe's arguments, and the balance was weighted by a senior Presbyterian minister from Queensland. He spoke strongly in favour of my project, said he was puzzled by the amendment and other opposition to the work, and appealed to Ratcliffe to withdraw his amendment. Ratcliffe and Watson withdrew at once, and my motion was carried.

For the time being I felt no triumph in success. I was physically and mentally exhausted by my efforts to swing the feeling of the Assembly onto the side of the Aborigines, not only in my more formal speeches, but in numerous contacts with representatives.

The decision was ratified by the General Assembly authorising its Board of Missions to carry on the work of the new mission through a committee in South Australia, of which I was to be the convener. Late in January 1937 I called a meeting to confer with Mr Matthews, Secretary of the Board, as to the best actual site for the mission. He had supported the project from the moment that I had first suggested it to the Board.

An Alice Springs man wanted it to be established at Opperinna, but I spoke strongly in favour of Ernabella, where I had stayed on my visit to the Musgrave Ranges. I knew that Opperinna, some distance to the west of Ernabella, was not so easy to reach and had poor supplies of water, especially in the frequent drought seasons.

The committee decided on Ernabella, and I was able to tell them that I had already collected £400 towards the £1,000 required to match the government offer. As soon as the decision on Ernabella was announced to the public, and I began to appeal for funds, support came from many sources. However, I did not fail to urge the Presbyterian Church to show continuing generosity to the project—especially from the Smith of Dunesk Bequest to the church, which had been made nearly a century before for the specific purpose of helping the Aborigines.

The bequest has an unusual history. Mrs Henrietta Smith, a member of a well-known Edinburgh family, purchased land in South Australia three years after the colony was first founded. She stated that the proceeds from this land were to be devoted to "The education and evangelisation of the Aborigines of South Australia."

At that time, land in South Australia was still in the process of survey and allocation. A proper Deed of Gift was not drawn up until 1853, but the conveyor, a Mr Barlow of Adelaide, told the Free Church of Scotland that the Aboriginal race was dying out. This belief was widely held at that time.

Mrs Smith was told by the church that the terms of her gift would have to be altered if she wished her money to be used for the cause of Christ. Disappointed though she was, she agreed, but wrote to the Colonial Committee of the Free Church: "I have thought it best that the property may not be lost to the cause of Christ to convey it over to the Free Church of Scotland, trusting and believing that they will not lose sight of the welfare of the Natives for whom it was first intended, along with their other pious objects in South Australia."

By April 1871, Mrs Smith had cause to complain that the money was not being used to help Aborigines, but the secretary of the Colonial Committee replied reassuringly that the fund would be administered according to her wishes. Three months later, she died.

Between 1871 and 1892, the Aborigines' Friends Association received some money from the fund to help the Point McLeay Mission of the Congregational Church. But the South Australian Assembly of the Presbyterian Church then claimed the money, causing the Adelaide *Register* of 3 December 1892 to make the acid comment that, "It seemed natural enough for Shylock to explain ' 'Tis not in the bond,' but for the same plea to be issued by a Christian Church is incongruous to say the least of it."

The Assembly's claim was the first of many happenings which obscured the purpose of the Smith bequest, and so many inaccurate statements have been made about the bequest that John McLellan, Archivist of South Australia, wrote in the *Advertiser* of 12 February 1948 that, "So much misinformation on the subject is now available that it is doubtful whether truth will ever overtake error."

An example of the many inaccurate published statements is one which appeared in a copy of the quarterly *Student World* in 1953. The article stated that Mrs Smith had "lost a son" in the arid regions of South Australia, and that the income from her bequest was to be used for the promotion of the "far away settlers." No trace of Mrs Smith ever having had a son in South Australia, let alone of him dying there, has been turned up despite enquiries within the State and in Edinburgh. The Smiths of Dunesk were a noted Edinburgh family, and the record of such a loss would surely have been kept.

No doubt the well-meaning but misguided Barlow of Adelaide was mainly responsible for the perversion of Mrs Smith's intention, when he reported that the Aborigines were a dying race.

The Presbyterian Church of South Australia gained control of the money in the 1890s. They used it to establish a mission for white settlers, which they called the Smith of Dunesk Mission. In 1933, the money was transferred to the Australian Inland Mission—which as I knew from personal experience would have nothing to do with Aborigines. By that time, the original purpose of the gift had become completely obscured, and at the twenty-fifth anniversary of the founding of the A.I.M., the Moderator-General stated that Mrs Smith founded the Australian Inland Mission. Similar statements have been made on a number of occasions.

When the Ernabella Mission was founded in 1937, it was the first step towards diverting at least some of the Smith of Dunesk

123

Bequest towards the intention of its donor: "the education and evangelisation of the Aborigines of South Australia."

I added £100 to the £400 I had collected, and the balance of the £1,000 was made up by a donation of £500 from Miss McCaul.

Miss Alice M. McCaul, early in the century had a small grocery business on Magill Road, Maylands. I well remember seeing her driving a piebald pony and cart to deliver her goods. Twenty years later an uncle in New Zealand bequeathed her his estate and she was able to retire, moving to North Adelaide. She became a well-loved philanthropist and at her death many years later most of her estate went to the Ernabella Mission and to Scotch College.

We could now claim £1,000 from the government, and press on with the practical details.

In this, I had the assistance of very practical men, not all of them Presbyterians. Mr T. A. Macadam, a leading architect, took charge of the building programme; Mr L. A. Borgelt, a prominent supporter of Hermannsburg and a leading business-man, assumed responsibility for motor vehicles; the Treasurer was Mr H. M. Caire, a city bank manager; the legal member was Mr Howard Zelling, now a Judge of the Supreme Court of South Australia. These men, and many others including Miss McCaul gave generously of their time and energy during the ten years which transformed Ernabella from a rendezvous for Aboriginal-exploiting "doggers" into a thriving Aboriginal community.

But when I was first trying to launch the project, there was a long way to go before the hearts and minds of a great many people could suffer any change in attitude towards the Aborigines. One of my most vivid memories in this respect— probably because it hurt me deeply—is that of the A.I.M. Padre who brought a group of white children down from the Inland to stay by the Adelaide seashore in the summer of 1935-1936.

It so happened that we had a group of part-Aboriginal children staying with us at the same time. I had met them on my first trip north to Ernabella. They were wards of the Colebrook Home at Quorn, and I suggested to Matron Hyde that all thirty-four of them should come down and camp in our Adelaide house and garden during the summer holidays.

It is an index to the feelings of those days that the offer was not taken seriously at first, and that Adelaide acquaintances should have warned me to expect considerable damage to our house and property. They were wrong. The children behaved perfectly, and now, as mature citizens, remember the holiday. Many of them still keep in touch with us and refer affectionately to me as Tjilpi or "old man" just as their elders had.

While they were staying in Adelaide, King George V died in England in January 1936. As Moderator, I called the people of the Presbyterian Church to a Memorial Service, and arranged for the children with the A.I.M. Padre to attend the service together with my group of part-Aboriginals. This annoyed him very much. He rang me, told me that he was making other arrangements for that day, and said, "You've insulted these children—asking them to sit with niggers!"

12

INTO THE PETERMANNS

THE TECHNIQUES OF SURGERY TOOK GREAT FORWARD STRIDES
between the two world wars, and I had planned to make
another trip overseas in order to keep up with the latest developments. My wife and I decided to combine the trip with a
holiday in Scotland which would enable me to introduce her
and our two young children to my eighty-six-year-old father.
I was also to attend an international conference on Church,
Community, and State. The Moderator-General, Dr John
McKenzie, had commissioned me to attend the conference as
representative of the Presbyterian Church of Australia.

So we sailed in February 1937. My son Charlie now in his
twenties took a year off to make the trip with us, planning to
see something of the cattle industry of Scotland and study
wool-classing. After a happy time with the family in Saltcoats
we left him there and I went to London, first taking Phyllis
and the children to stay near her sister in Yorkshire. Later they
came down to Buckinghamshire and I was able to enjoy
beautiful summer weekends with them there.

In London I lodged near the British Post-Graduate Medical

School in Shepherd's Bush. It was a stimulating period for me, spent under Professor Grey Turner, then the Director of the Surgical School. Sir Thomas Dunhill, a graduate of Melbourne University School of Medicine, was responsible for operations on the thyroid and he took me to witness some of the operations which he performed at the London Clinic.

I had a specific interest in cancer of the alimentary canal, and was absorbed by a talk which Grey Turner gave on cancer of the oesophagus. The next morning he spoke to four of us on Gastrostomy as a palliative in cases of blockage of the oesophagus (gullet) and of the methods of feeding required in such cases, when he noticed that I was not paying attention. "You're not with us; your mind is elsewhere," he said, and I said apologetically, "If I didn't know my old chief was dead, I would have said he was speaking to us." I meant Sir William Macewen, and the Professor turned to the others saying, "He's quite right. Macewen's work on the subject has always stimulated me."

Later he was asked to deliver the Macewen Memorial Lecture in Glasgow and wrote to me with a long list of questions on the Macewen outlook on surgery which I was glad to be able to answer.

He introduced me to Gabriel, of St Mark's Hospital, who was then the outstanding surgeon for cancer of the rectum. Gabriel explained his technique to me and invited me to attend several operations. At Grey Turner's request, I also visited the Royal Newcastle Infirmary which had been his training ground.

King George VI and Queen Elizabeth were crowned on 12 May 1937, and the Agent-General of South Australia enabled my wife and me to obtain seats from which we saw the Coronation Procession leaving Buckingham Palace—and the two princesses, still in their nightclothes, peeping from an upstairs window to see what was going on before the procession assembled. Later, dressed for the occasion, they ran across the courtyard in front of the Palace, hopelessly followed by the two ladies in charge of them and then by a gentleman trying in vain with stilted steps and an umbrella to catch up with them!

I finished my studies in London, was rejoined by my family and went to Oxford to attend the Church, Community, and State Conference in July. My quarters were in Worcester College, where I rubbed shoulders with people of many different types from many parts of the world, and I met a number of the leading churchmen, thinkers, and reformers of that time. They included Commissioner Cunningham of the Salvation Army, Reinhold Niebuhr of New York, Dr T. Z. Koo, Professor M. Boegner of Paris, Dr Visser T. Hooft of the Student Christian Federation, Canon Raven of the Peace Movement, Paul Tillich of New York, J. P. R. Maud of University College, Oxford, and the Reverend H. L. Henriod, General Secretary of the Conference. The chairman was John Mott, the "world citizen." The lectures and discussions in which such men participated were stimulating to the highest degree.

Two basic themes of the conference, in that era just before Hitler was to demonstrate the inevitable results of racial and religious discrimination, were peace and racism. Some delegates spoke from personal experience. Dr T. Z. Koo, who was an honours graduate and doctor of philosophy, a dedicated Christian, and a gentleman by any standards, was refused admission to any hotel in Oxford because of his race. There was a flash in his eye when he addressed a vast audience of churchmen from all over the world, and said that he could at least understand the action of a hotelkeeper if the presence of a Chinese on his premises would discourage other business, but he had something very serious to say to the church if it tolerated any kind of discrimination because of race or colour.

Such discrimination was even more common then than now. Later in 1937, a distinguished African gentleman and his daughter could not find accommodation in Edinburgh when they attempted to attend a Christian conference there. They were rescued by Sir John Simon, then Chancellor of the Exchequer, who wired an introduction to a personal friend in the area.

My own contribution to the Oxford conference was mainly on the race question. I emphasised that the church dare not tolerate discrimination in any form, and cited my experiences amongst the Aborigines. The uncompromising statement drawn up by the committee on which I had worked received the unanimous approval of the whole conference.

On 14 October I had the privilege of speaking at a meeting chaired by a very famous Australian, Professor Gilbert Murray, O.M., D.C.L., LL.D., D.Litt. He had left Australia as a young man, and became one of the leading classical scholars of his time.

The meeting, at the Royal Empire Society in London, was under the auspices of the Anti-Slavery and Aborigines Protection Society. I spoke on "The Australian Aborigines and their Future," and illustrated my talk with slides. After this, Professor Murray spoke of his own memories of outback Australia, and shocked the audience by his graphic description of the agonies of Aborigines dying from eating poisoned flour.

For a week after that, the Aborigines were in the news. I was interviewed by the *Manchester Guardian* after the meeting, and the London dailies sent reporters to my hotel. Soon after this, strong criticisms of Australia's attitudes towards the Aborigines were made by two leading Melbourne anthropologists, Wood Jones and Donald Thomson. Their comments, also, were fully reported in London.

My first meeting with Professor Murray developed into a friendship which lasted until his death, and I am proud to have known so great a man. Apart from his academic achievements he was a great administrator and idealist, with an abiding concern for the downtrodden and deprived throughout the world. He was very proud of the work done by his brother, Hubert Murray, for the native peoples of Papua. As Chairman of the League of Nations Union from 1922 to 1938, and President of the United Nations Association until his death, he confronted world problems with his own idealism and hope. My wife still treasures the autographed copy of his translation of *Iphigenia in Tauris* which he sent to her with the inscription "In memory of the evening of 14 October 1937."

We left for home at last, sailing through the Panama Canal and calling at Wellington, New Zealand. Newspaper reporters interviewed me on board and I was asked to give a broadcast on Australia's attitude towards its Aborigines.

Amongst other things I said that, "The government of Australia would be relieved if the Aboriginal race died out, because it would solve the problem." This was repeated in Australian newspapers, and when we docked in Sydney the journalists were waiting for us—with copies of newspapers in which the Prime Minister, Mr Joseph Lyons, denied that his government would be relieved by any such abrupt solution of the Aboriginal question. I believed in my statement, however, and repeated it to the Australian newsmen.

After nearly a year's absence from my practice I had no plans for visiting the outback during 1938, but my wife decided that it was time for her to see the situation for herself. Ernabella Mission, under the Reverend Harry Taylor, was operating by that time, and she was to be its first visitor. She was accompanied by Miss M. E. Eaton, President of the Women's Christian Temperance Union, which was deeply concerned about the status of Aboriginal and part-Aboriginal women.

Phyllis wrote to me from Alice Springs that, "The name of Duguid is met up here with a glassy look or with great warmth!" and she described the experiences of an Alice Springs friend. Phyllis asked this lady why she did not employ an Aboriginal girl in her home, and the friend said that her first objection was to the prevalence of venereal disease and her second to the fact that the Federal government held employers responsible for the good conduct of such girls. This, however, rarely worked out, and our friend would not follow the Alice Springs system of, "Give them an outside room and shut your eyes!"

They visited Hermannsburg, and were amongst the first people to see Albert Namatjira's first collection of paintings— some of which are now valued at several thousand dollars. Albert and Rex Battarbee had just returned from a painting trip to the west, and his paintings were spread out along one of the mission house verandahs. Phyllis was particularly impressed by a painting of Mount Sonder, and when Albert's first exhibition was opened by Lady Huntingfield in Melbourne later that year Rex Battarbee kindly held the painting for our purchase.

In those days, a visit to Ernabella was no simple matter. Phyllis and Miss Eaton had to travel down from Alice Springs to the Finke River, where they were met by Mr Taylor, and then set off on a truck journey from nine-thirty one night until noon next day, with numerous stops including those for petrol blocks and punctures.

They were impressed by the initial work of the Ernabella Mission, and found that Mr Taylor's medical first-aid work was gaining the confidence of the Aborigines. When they returned to Adelaide they helped to form a League for the Protection and Advancement of Aboriginal and Half-Caste Women, and plans were made for a social centre or club at Alice Springs. They had conceived this idea while at Alice Springs and had received a good deal of support, but its implementation was prevented by the outbreak of war. Eventually, the League developed into the Aborigines Advancement League of South Australia, devoted to the welfare of all Aborigines. I was to be President of this enlarged body from 1951 to 1961.

In 1939 I had the privilege of making an outback tour in the company of that remarkable man T. G. H. Strehlow, known to his friends as Ted. Ted Strehlow is the son of a missionary and spent the first fourteen years of his life at Hermannsburg Mission, where he grew up with Aranda children as his principal companions. He learnt their language as though it was his mother tongue, and grew so close to them that he became, in my opinion, closer in thought and feeling to the Aborigines than anyone I know. He is now the Professor of Australian Linguistics at the University of Adelaide, but at that time was Chief Patrol Officer and Deputy Chief Protector of Aborigines in the Northern Territory.

I was in bed with influenza in June 1939 when I received a letter from Pastor Albrecht, asking me to join him and Ted Strehlow on a journey to the Petermann Ranges in the north-west corner of the Northern Territory Aboriginal Reserve. Ted had been commissioned to lead the expedition to find out why so many tribal Aborigines were migrating from the reserve to cattle stations which lay hundreds of miles farther east. He considered the trip to be too risky to undertake with only one truck, and asked for Harry Taylor of the Ernabella Mission to join him with the mission truck.

The thought of an outback journey with such men, and of meeting another tribe, was powerful medicine. As soon as possible, I called at the workshop of Alf Traeger, a patient of mine and the inventor of the pedal wireless which was an essential component of the Flying Doctor service. Apart from calling skilled medical help in emergencies, it had done much to dispel the loneliness of isolated dwellers in the Inland.

With Alf's co-operation, and the assistance of Commonwealth authorities, I was able to take his latest transmitting and receiving set along with us on the trip. It was paid for by citizens of Adelaide, stimulated by an appeal launched by my friend Bob Paton, editor of the now defunct Adelaide weekly newspaper *Radio Call.*

Our rendezvous was at Ernabella on 13 July, and from there we set out through the Musgraves towards the Petermann Ranges. I travelled with Strehlow in the smaller of the two trucks, with the job of taking detailed notes, and Harry Taylor followed with the three-ton Ernabella truck, accompanied by Pastor Albrecht, Ossie Heinrich, who was the motor mechanic in charge of the trucks, and two Aboriginal guides.

It was even heavier going than usual, because rain had been pouring down for several days before we set out and the good soil along the northern face of the Musgraves had turned into mud. The trucks had to grind along in first gear with their wheels sinking or slithering in the mud, and we had to make frequent stops to cool the water boiling in the radiators. Before long we had some qualms about the amount of petrol we were using. We had 160 gallons with us, and decided that we must drive no further than half that amount would take us. We hoped to reach Piltardi, where Ted had arranged for us to be met by camels sent 300 miles from Hermannsburg.

We reached the western end of the Musgraves and turned north towards the Petermanns, and soon drove into a series of individual mountains with great outcrops of rock. It was spectacularly rugged country and made for extremely hard going, so Ted decided to leave the mountains and strike across the desert, in the hope that the rain would have firmed the sand. This worked out very well, and we made a fast run which brought us to Piltardi waterhole at sunset. Here fortune favoured us again, because we saw the flicker of a little fire with a desert Aboriginal and his son sitting by it. He was called Tjuintjara, and Ted realised that he would be just the man to guide us in the Petermanns. Speaking to him in his own language, Strehlow arranged for him to make the trip with us.

Ten camels were waiting for us, but Ted thought that we should make a practice run before tackling the ranges. Camels can be fractious brutes, and it would be better to sort out any problems before going too far. So he asked Tjuintjara to take us on a day's ride to the site of Lasseter's grave, and as we rode along the Aboriginal solved the mystery of the tribal migration to the east. He told us that there had been a prolonged drought in the Petermanns, and that many of the people had died. A number of the survivors had decided that it was better to leave their tribal territory.

However, the recent rains had brought the country to life. The trees and scrub were putting out fresh green tips, and green parrots were fluttering noisily amongst the branches. It was harsh, forbidding territory, and when we reached the site of Lasseter's grave we found that it was an utterly desolate place. His story is well known—that of a man driven on by an obsession for gold, who at last perished alone. Tjuintjara added something to the story by telling us that Lasseter crawled into a cave—which he showed us later—and resisted Aboriginal attempts to help him by firing his rifle whenever they approached. When he lapsed into unconsciousness they carried him out and built a rough shelter round him, and sent a messenger to fetch Bob Buck, a settler whose station was many miles to the east. But when Buck arrived he could do nothing but bury the remains of the man whose name lives on in the Australian legend "Lasseter's Lost Reef." If it had not been for his fear and distrust of the Aborigines who would have looked after him, he would not have died.

Ted was satisfied that the camels would be suitable for the expedition, so we returned to Piltardi and set out again on the following day. He wanted to inspect both sides of the

Petermann Range, and our long camel trip began with a westward ride to the Shaw River. Water was short, so we turned into the range to replenish our supply. We found it at the foot of the mountain, and Ted decided to seek a way through the range at that point. It proved to be a stiff climb, even for camels, and at one point there was only space for one at a time to pad along a ledge.

It was the coldest trip that I have made through the Inland, especially when we were up in the mountains. The wind blew cold, and at night time the tarpaulins under which we slept became covered with frost. Tjuintjara, like all the Aborigines of that area, was stark naked, and carried a firestick to warm himself. He waved it around his body as he walked.

We were the first white men to pass through the Petermanns by that route, and certainly could not have done it but for Tjuintjara's knowledge of the waterholes. Ted Strehlow wanted to find a way to the great range which is aptly called the Ruined Ramparts, but Tjuintjara was now far from his wife and family and was unwilling to proceed until Ted persuaded him to carry on. We climbed down the other side of the range, and passed through row after row of sandhills followed by uninviting country of spinifex, desert oak, and the occasional mallee. Water was hard to find, and in the Hull River we had to dig a deep hole in the creek bed into which the water welled slowly.

At last we rode through a scattered forest of beautiful ghost gums, and came in sight of a striking spur running at an angle from the main range. This was the Ruined Ramparts, and we made camp in the Docker River but were unable to strike water. We knew that, without Tjuintjara's help, we were unlikely to strike it, and Ted assured him that as soon as we found a big water we would all turn for home. Next morning he led us south and then west through the Petermann Range, and at midday brought us to a long deep rock cleft full of water. We were not far from the border of Western Australia.

It was interesting to see how much our ten camels could drink, and we took advantage of the water to wash ourselves and our clothes. We had hardly settled round a camp fire before two naked nomads walked through the bush towards us, and when they were satisfied that we were friendly they brought in another man, three women, one old woman, and three children. They were the first Aborigines we had seen since leaving the Musgraves. We learnt that they had sold dingo-scalps to white "doggers" who had been in the area without permission, so Ted reported the matter by radio to Perth. Later, we heard that two men had been fined, though it was a trifling sum compared with what they would have made from the scalps.

Ted was anxious to make a quick trip back to Piltardi, and for the party of Aborigines to come along with us. They had no food with them, and would have no time to hunt; so we prepared damper for them to carry as rations to supplement the vegetable food they would collect as we travelled.

We met some more naked nomads as we travelled home-wards next day, and they came along with us. One of them was a well-built lad of about sixteen, and we noticed that he was not circumcised—a significant fact, because by that time he should have been initiated. Altogether we met twenty-six people travelling in small parties, and this too was significant. In time of drought, the tribes are forced to split into small family groups which can range widely in search of food and water, and the lad had not been circumcised because the necessary ceremonial corroboree could only be carried out at a place where there was plenty of food and water for the tribal congregation. We learnt that it had been at least three years since any such place could have been found in the Petermanns, and during our journey we saw no kangaroo, euro, wallaby, or emu. We were completely dependent on the stores carried by our camels, and all that the Aborigines could find in the way of "bush tucker" were wild cucumbers and yelka—the roots of grass which grew in the banks of dry creeks. It tastes rather like hazel nuts. The recent rains would make ground feed grow, and wild flowers were beginning to make a fine show, but it would be some time before grass seeds were ripe enough for the women to collect and grind into flour.

It was a cold, rough trip. One afternoon, when we were crossing the Casterton creek bed, we were overtaken by a storm of heavy rain driven by a strong wind. The naked Aboriginal men and women turned their backs to it and sheltered the children by holding them against themselves. At night, everyone received equal shares of the food which Pastor Albrecht prepared for them, and the Aborigines kept warm as they lay between their little fires.

I noticed that the uninitiated lad travelled a little apart from the others, and that every evening a twelve-year-old girl would slip away to take a share of the food to his separate camp. I found that she was his sister, displaying a sense of family love and obligation which was as strong and natural as that between people of any other race. Altogether I found that these nomads of the forbidding ranges and desert country were a delightful folk, and they responded eagerly and happily to my approaches. The children were particularly charming, with the pleasing and remarkable feature of golden hair which greatly enhanced their dark-eyed attractiveness. One of them, Pingeri, was quite blonde. This golden hair gradually darkens as they grow older.

We said farewell to the whole group when we reached Piltardi and loaded the trucks for the return journey to Ernabella, and it was a sad moment for all of us. We could not help wondering what would happen to the little families who were so much at the mercy of their surroundings, but there seemed to be very little we could do for them at that time. The only reward we could give to Tjuintjara, for his faithful service in guiding us through the ranges, was a carefully cleaned oil tin fitted with a handle for carrying. As a nomad, he would have no use for anything which could not be carried in his hands, but even this humble gift was accepted with pleasure. His wife would find it useful for collecting bush tucker and carrying water.

On the way back to Ernabella, we saw that the country was very different from that of the Petermanns. Game of all kinds abounded, and there was plenty of vegetable food. A few miles from the mission we caught up with a group of people whose physical condition confirmed all our findings about the drought and its aftermath. They were so thin that it was easy to distinguish the one Ernabella man, in fine condition, who was leading them to the mission. He told Harry

Taylor that they were Petermann natives, completing a long journey from the drought area.

Arrival at Ernabella marked the close of my third intimate contact with tribal people, under very different conditions from previous associations. In our survey of both sides of the Petermann Ranges we had found only the few survivors who, despite most arduous conditions, remained undaunted.

I stayed on for a few happy days in Ernabella, giving medical treatment to those who needed it and inspecting the sheep camps. I found that on the whole the mission people were in good health, though the bitterly cold weather had caused a number of severe colds and one case of pneumonia.

During that time at Ernabella, I had the privilege of being invited to a corroboree. It was the circumcision ceremony for a youth from the Everard Range, sixty miles to the south, and I must say that the youngster looked thoroughly miserable about the whole affair. We saw his face only once, when he was raised from the prone position in which he was kept for the rest of the time—head covered, on the edge of a circle of men, while one warrior kept a knee on his shoulder and another knelt on his hip. There were two groups of men, about forty altogether, each round a small fire, and they kept up a constant chanting accompanied by a rhythmic thumping on the ground with sticks. The whole ceremony continued throughout the night and well into the following morning.

Back in Adelaide again after an absence of five weeks I recommended that, if another drought should threaten the Aborigines, then food depots should be established in the Petermann Ranges. Thirty years later, special depots were opened and the country was made secure—for tourists.

13

THE CASE OF LALILI

O NE OF THE EFFECTS OF THE OUTBREAK OF WAR, IN WHICH
Australia joined with other democratic nations of the
world in fighting for freedom and justice, was a reduction of
the Federal grant for Aborigines. The money, it was said, was
needed for defence purposes. And, on 20 November 1939, the
Aboriginal Compound at Darwin was taken over for a military
hospital, and its 300 Aboriginal inhabitants rendered homeless. "I am aware of our appalling record in regard to Aborigines, and know of no greater indictment against Australia
than the fate of the original owners of this country," was one
of the remarks made by Sir Henry Gullett, then Minister for
External Affairs, when speaking against the reduction of the
Federal grant.

At about the same time, the South Australian government
passed its new Aborigines Act. This was in some ways an
improvement on the old Act, but had some important draw-
backs. The worst of these was the clause which classified a
person with any native blood in his veins as an Aboriginal.
An Aboriginal could not enjoy full rights as a citizen, so such

a person was placed under the control of a government board. Regardless of his or her education or standing in the community, this part-Aboriginal could not be a full citizen unless granted special exemption from the Act on the basis of "character, standard of intelligence, and development." A limited exemption, which could be revoked at any time during a three year probation period, could also be granted. Complete exemption was subject to the part-Aboriginal proving himself of "such character, standard of intelligence, and development to justify the continuance of the declaration." We would live in a very strange community indeed if the citizenship of every white person depended upon him giving proof of his character, intelligence, and development!

Under the new Act, I was appointed a member of the Aborigines Protection Board on 1 February 1940, and despite the increasing demands of wartime on my private and professional life I decided that I must inspect the reserves, missions, and permanent camps for Aborigines in South Australia. These were widely scattered and, in those days, not very easy to reach. So far as the general public was concerned, it was a matter of "out of sight, out of mind," and despite the devoted work of many people connected with the missions the tone of each establishment was very poor. No attempt was made to fit the Aborigines to stand on their own legs in the general community. They had no regular work or responsibilities and in the main were "hand fed." Young people were not taught any trade or skilled occupation when they left school, and soon degenerated into the idle loafing with which the adults frittered away their time. It is no wonder that they turned to alcohol whenever they could procure it—illegally in those days.

I went first to Point McLeay Mission, on Lake Alexandrina near the Murray Mouth and about fifty miles south-east of Adelaide. Originally it was a Congregational Mission, standing on 4,500 acres of land, and to begin with it had been run on efficient "self-help" lines. There was a smithy, saddlery, carpenter's shop, boot factory, wool-washing plant, orchard, vegetable garden, and fowl run. By 1940, these were all derelict and disused. The Aborigines were provided free of cost with houses, firewood, milk, and medical attention—but what houses! They were all old, and in fact unfit for human habitation. Most of them had cement floors, every one of those I visited had damp showing on the walls, and in several the rain was dripping through the roof onto the beds, which were jammed so closely together that they could not be moved. There were no bathrooms nor water closets, and sewage was carried away in a broken down hand-cart. There was a small church, a well-kept store, and a maternity hospital, but the best building was a modern school with an outstanding head-master, Mr W. T. Laurie.

A total of 450 Aborigines and white people lived there, in what I thought to be very unsatisfactory conditions. I believed that the Aborigines should have been given work, paid for it, and charged for their rent and firewood.

Point Pearce, on the Spencer Gulf and about 120 miles north of Adelaide, was not much better. 350 people had 15,000 acres on the mainland and 7,000 on nearby Wardang Island, but most of this was leased to white farmers. The houses, though stark and unattractive, were better than at Point McLeay, but still needed considerable repair. There was little work for adults, and no attempt to train youngsters leaving school.

My next trip was up the Murray, to visit the mission at Swan Reach eighty miles north of Adelaide. There, I found that two missionaries, a husband and wife, were doing their utmost under very unsatisfactory conditions. The houses were no more than "bag huts," with walls of hessian surrounding floors of earth or cement. About eighty part-Aboriginal adults and children of all ages, together with three full-blood men and one woman, were crowded together in very inadequate space. The well-known blacktracker, Jimmy James, was living there, and I was asked to examine his ten-year-old daughter Eileen. I found her ill in bed with a cough and temperature, and found that the local doctor had made out an order for invalid diet which had been given to a Mrs Schulz, living at Swan Reach on the other side of the river, to send to the Secretary of the Aborigines Protection Board! The government ration of white flour, tea, and sugar, which was useless enough for healthy adults, was lacking in everything required by a sick child.

I was approached by a young part-Aboriginal named Jerry Mason, whom I had observed to conduct the Sunday School in a very capable manner. He was anxious for some kind of training which would enable him to help his people, and I recommended to the government that he should be given his opportunity. He has since become a leader amongst his people at the Gerard Reserve.

On 20 July 1940 we made the long westerly journey to Ooldea, 700 miles along the Transcontinental railway from Adelaide. I had read a police report of 5 July 1939 which stated that there were 300 natives along the line with only sixty blankets between them. Another police report, of 27 July 1939, said that the Mission sent the Aborigines out to hunt the game which was no longer existent in the area, so that they simply drifted to the fettlers' camps along the East-West railway line. The fettlers gave them scraps of meat in return for odd jobs.

When we reached Port Augusta, Inspector Parsonage told me that the Ooldea Reserve community had insufficient food and warmth, and all these grim prophecies prepared us for the worst. Perhaps it was not as bad as we expected, but it was bad enough. Ooldea is a dreary and depressing place, on the edge of the Nullarbor Plain and standing in a desert of sand and stunted scrub. A cutting wind blew for much of the time in winter, and found its way through the doors, floor, and sides of the church building in which the congregation coughed almost continually. 250 full-blood Aborigines lived on the Reserve, and were all clothed. They were supplied with rice, peas, flour, sugar, and tea as a government ration, and so were no doubt glad of whatever scraps of meat they could beg from the fettlers.

The missioner was a young Englishman, Mr Harry Green, who told me that the Aborigines Department had told him to "send the natives out to hunt." He had soon realised that this simply meant sending them to the fettlers' camps, and had ceased to do so.

Only ten out of the whole community had work, with another fifteen being taken on at shearing time. It seemed to me that there was a danger of the whole community, including its fifty children, being turned into paupers wholly dependent upon the government dole.

I returned from this inspection tour to life in Adelaide, with depressing memories of the way in which our Aboriginal community was ekeing out an existence on the furthest fringe of civilisation. Obviously there was a great deal still to be done, and while I was still pondering various courses of action I was horrified by the news of the murder of a man named Lalili.

I had encountered Lalili at Ernabella—especially when I had the task of dressing club wounds which he had inflicted on his wife. He had been reprimanded by the Superintendent for spearing goats belonging to the Mission, and thought that his wife had given him away. He and his family went away from the Mission, as was not uncommon with the still nomadic tribesmen, and in late 1940 his wife and relatives returned to Ernabella in abject grief. They told the Superintendent that Lalili had been murdered by two white men. They said that the men had hit him on the head with the butt of a pistol, tied him to the back of a truck with fencing wire, and driven it to the homestead of the station on which the Aborigines were camped. That was the last they saw of him.

For some reason the Mission did not radio a report to the police, so it was not passed on until the Mission truck visited Finke siding, some weeks later. The police acted at once. Enquiries were made, two men were arrested, and an inquest held at Alice Springs on 29 and 30 January 1941.

Five Aborigines gave evidence, and the exhibits in court consisted of a Luger pistol, a Lee-Enfield rifle, a piece of wire, and a human head. This was said to be that of Lalili, though the government medical officer said it was more like a female's than a male's and that he could not discern signs of injury. Despite this, the coroner found that the two white men had "murdered an Aborigine called Lullilicki or Lollylegs on or about Dec. 14th 1940."

I remembered that Lalili was a powerfully built man with a long dark beard, so it would be impossible to mistake the head of a female for that of such a man. One would have

Top: This historic photograph shows Pastor F. W. Albrecht (right) operating one of the earliest pedal wirelesses which broke the isolation of the Outback. Bottom: Ernabella children playing in the old waterhole

thought that an enquiry would have been made into the death of a female Aboriginal at about the same time, but this did not transpire.

The two men were tried for murder at Alice Springs on 16 and 17 April 1941. Even though it was the invariable custom in the Northern Territory for Aboriginal witnesses to be kept in custody until a trial was over, it was stated in court that three of the five Aboriginal witnesses had "run away." Nor was the arresting constable present to give evidence.

During the trial, the two men admitted that they had gone to the camp of "Lollylegs," searched his ration bags, and decided that they contained food which did not belong to him. After an argument, they covered him with their weapons, tied a doubled length of fencing wire eight feet long around his neck, attached it to the truck, and drove it to the homestead about 600 yards away. The four-speed truck was driven in low gear, so Lalili must have had to run behind presuming that he was able to keep his feet. The two men justified their action with the plea that it was necessary to be "firm with Aborigines."

Their counsel made the obvious point that the head submitted in evidence was not that of Lalili, and the two men were acquitted. However, their permission to employ Aborigines on their property was withdrawn by the Federal government.

As President of the Aborigines Protection League in South Australia, I had been one of those who attempted to find out the truth of the matter before it came to trial. After the inquest, we wrote to the Minister for the Interior, expressing our astonishment that the whole body of the dead man was not taken to the inquest instead of the head only. We pointed out that, although the government medical officer had expressed doubt as to the sex of the head displayed in evidence, it had been exhumed so recently that there should have been no difficulty in telling whether it was male or female. We asked respectfully that the whole body from which the head had been taken should be examined.

Seven days after sending this letter, and nearly two months before the trial, we received a brief letter from the Minister

Top Left: Intjitjinya, an Ernabella girl. Top Right: This blind medicine man of the Pitjantjatjara tribe was photographed at Ernabella. Bottom: Nyinkas: youths who have been initiated and are now about to go "walkabout" and look after themselves in the bush

saying that he was having enquiries made into the matter, and would communicate again immediately he was in a position to do so. Apparently he never found himself in such a position, for we heard no more from him. Nor did anyone see or hear any more of Lalili, Lullilicki, or Lollylegs, as the unfortunate Aboriginal was variously called.

Cases of cruelty to Aborigines were too common to be regarded as the occasional outbursts of ignorant or exasperated men. The Minister for the Interior stated in 1945 that, "In many cases cattle stations are using black labour under almost slave conditions," and this included the actual beating and flogging of Aborigines. In one such case of flogging, reported by a patrol officer of the Native Affairs Department and backed up by a part-Aboriginal stockman who gave evidence that he had helped to tie the victim to a tree, a station owner was found not guilty by a white jury.

When another station owner was found guilty of chaining five men by their necks to fences, trees, and a dray, and assaulting one of them with fists and a revolver, he was fined £135. Several station people said that they thought the verdict to be a "challenge to their control of the Aborigines." They did not state whether anyone was supposed to control the white men.

In September 1941 I made another tour of Aboriginal communities; this time to the camps at Port Augusta, Whyalla, and Iron Knob. Port Augusta, at the head of the Spencer Gulf and 200 miles from Adelaide, was not particularly friendly to Aborigines in those days. When I first went there, in 1935, the Aboriginal camp was a dreadful sight—little better than a rubbish dump in the sandhills and a harbour for derelict human beings. Between 1937 and 1941, the year when the husband enlisted, a missionary couple had worked hard for the local Aborigines. They were Mr and Mrs W. Wyld of the Plymouth Brethren, the Church which maintained a mission at Umeewarra near Port Augusta. Mr Wyld had built a store, a hall, and galvanised iron houses with uneven earth floors— not very attractive homes but at least better than the dirty sand-hill humpies in which the Aborigines lived until he came.

He also worked with Mr L. G. Riches, M.P., the mayor of

Port Augusta, to have the area proclaimed as an Aboriginal Reserve, but another quarter-century had to pass before the government accepted the responsibility for it.

Umeewarra Mission, under Mrs Wyld and her daughter, was in excellent condition and even had a small school. When I returned to Port Augusta I asked why the ten children attending the mission school should not go to the State school in the township, and be taught by trained teachers. But I was told that the Port Augusta folk would not accept the idea, and I thought too that the Brethren did not wish to lose control of their pupils.

Whyalla and Iron Knob, about forty miles from Port Augusta down the Eyre Peninsula, had sizeable native camps. Whyalla was an iron-smelting and shipbuilding city, and Iron Knob, in those days, supplied the iron ore for the smelters and for transhipment. There was plenty of work for the Aborigines, and every coloured man, woman, and child whom I saw was well-dressed and in good physical condition. But they lived in squalor. At Iron Knob, the Aboriginal shelters were only rough huts of galvanised iron, but to the Aborigines' credit the interiors were clean. Empty beer and port wine bottles, many of them broken, were lying everywhere. At that time, it was an offence to provide Aborigines with alcohol, but the police told me that it was impossible to prevent white people procuring liquor for the natives. At Iron Knob one of the police officer's biggest problems was that of keeping some young white men away from the Aborigines' camp.

The Aborigines were almost forgotten in the first World War, but not entirely in the second. On 3 July 1939, the South Australian Council of Churches suggested to the National Missionary Council that a Sunday should be set aside for bringing the claims of the Aborigines before the public. When I was asked what I thought of the idea, I said, "Why only one Sunday? Why not every day of the week?"

Aboriginal Sunday was first observed on 25 January 1940, the nearest Sunday to Australia Day. I spoke at Stow Church in the morning and at St Peter's Cathedral in the evening, and felt that another small step forward had been made.

But the day was to come when I was ashamed of being a

145

Presbyterian. A fine young part-Aboriginal woman who was known to me wrote to the Chief Protector of Aborigines in South Australia to say that she and her husband-to-be, also a part-Aboriginal, wished to be married by a Christian minister. It was known that a padre of the Australian Inland Mission patrolled the area in which the young couple lived; the Protector wrote and asked him to solemnise the marriage. He replied that he had never had anything to do with "niggers," and was not going to start now. When written to a second time, he refused again.

As a last comment on those wartime years, in which our preparations for invasion and air raids by the Japanese were fortunately never to be put to the test, I should mention a telephone call which I received from Canberra. The caller said that the Federal member of Parliament for Adelaide had made a statement in the House which cast doubt on the loyalty of the missionaries at Hermannsburg. They were members of the Lutheran Church and bore German names, though most of them had been born in Australia, but the M.P. suggested that they had secret communication with enemy agents.

My name was suggested as one who had reliable knowledge of Hermannsburg. Hence the 'phone call, to which I answered that the charge was utter rubbish and could soon be dismissed by a proper investigation.

Apparently, some lingering doubts remained. Later, I was told that the Government favoured the appointment of some person of trust to the Hermannsburg Mission until the end of the war, to reassure the authorities. The name of Rex Battarbee, the artist who taught Albert Namatjira to paint in water-colours, was suggested, and though I maintained that the precaution was unnecessary I agreed that he was the ideal man for the task.

Such is wartime, which breeds hate and suspicion like bacteria. But the artist's prolonged stay at Hermannsburg had a fine outcome, in that he was able to guide a number of the Aranda men who wanted, like Albert Namatjira, to try their hand at painting. A number of them have since become well-known for their works.

14

ROCKETS OVER THE DESERT

D URING MOST OF THE WAR YEARS IT WAS DIFFICULT IF NOT
impossible to travel far into the outback, but we were
able to keep in touch with the growth of Ernabella Mission by
letter or by reports which the missionaries made when they
visited the city. So I looked forward to the first chance of
revisiting the mission, and this came in the winter school
holidays in 1946. This time, I set off in company with my wife,
our son Andrew and daughter Rosemary, and one of the first
of our foster children, Sydney James Cook, a homeless full-
blood boy who came to our home when he was six.

Travel from the Finke railway siding to the mission was still
pretty rough, but the children thoroughly enjoyed sleeping in
the open under the splendour of an Inland night sky. When
the truck pulled into Ernabella at last we were greeted with
a great shout of welcome from the Aboriginal community, and
I looked eagerly for one of the girls who had lived with us for
three weeks in the city. I saw her smiling face and called
"Nganyintja!" and she ran forward to greet us. She and my
daughter Rosemary, who had grown very fond of one another

during those three weeks, were soon chatting together as vigorously as any couple of girls who had not seen each other for a while.

At that time, Ernabella was supervised by the Reverend G. Wright, and it was good to see that the mission was developing strongly along the lines which had been laid down in the beginning. The obvious contentment of the men and women who each had a definite place in the community was in striking contrast to the bored idleness of those whom we had seen in other Aboriginal settlements and reserves. Yet there was no compulsion or obligation; whenever a family felt the need to go away and return for a while to their ancient way of life they were free to do so. And it was encouraging to learn that they returned to the mission when their "bush holiday" was over. Sometimes they would be absent for weeks, but the schoolteacher, a member of the South Australian Department of Education, told us that the children could pick up their lessons where they left off and with little need for revision. No doubt the deeply-ingrained Aboriginal instinct for mimicry which is so apparent in their corroboree dances, and their intensely acute powers of observation and memory for minor details which makes them into such expert trackers, are invaluable for children learning more formal lessons.

The lessons were given in their own tongue, Pitjantjatjara, and the children could please themselves as to whether they attended or not. It speaks well for the schooling that there was usually a full turn-up every day. In those years the children still ran about naked, as they would do in tribal life, and when they gathered at the schoolhouse each morning their bodies were dusty with the red sand on which they slept and the ashes of the little fires which kept them warm at night. So their first task every morning was to hose each other down, which they did as gleefully as might be expected with any group of children, and then ran about with their bodies glistening in the sunshine until they were warm and dry. Rosemary enjoyed taking part in this hosing.

While the children were in school their parents and older brothers and sisters did their share of the mission work. Men went off into the bush to stalk kangaroos or bring in firewood;

they chopped wood or worked on the vegetable garden; women milked the goats, and goatherds shepherded them back into the bush to feed; older girls went off to the various staff homes to learn something of the white man's way of life. Shepherds and their families tended sheep at outlying wells.

Naturally I was very interested in the medical services of the mission, and I spent a good deal of time with the patients in the hospital and in assisting Sister Turner in the dispensary. She was one of the busiest people on the staff, and the number of outpatients showed how completely the Aborigines had accepted the white man's medicine. One day I dressed a very severe burn on a baby boy brought in by his mother. He had rolled too close to a camp fire. In my city surgery, I had never seen more loving and skilful handling by a mother of a child who was in great pain.

In the afternoons we enjoyed picnics in the bush or games along the creek, and I was happy to be renewing old friendships. Everyone at the mission looked fit and well; it was a year when there was an abundance of bush-tucker to supplement the government rations and the meat, milk, and vegetables supplied by the mission.

Despite the gradual introduction into the white man's way of life which was being provided by their association with the mission, there was no check upon the Aborigines continuing their traditional activities and rituals. Prominent among these was the training of boys and young men for hunting and fighting. The boys practised throwing light spears at a circle of bark sent spinning along the ground, against the day when they would be aiming at a running goanna, emu, or kangaroo. Many of them were very skilful. As part of a warrior's training, they took turns in spearthrowing at each other. The "target" learnt to be very quick in dodging the weapon by a quick turn of body or leg. One of those who was not quick enough was speared in the knee, and was in my care for several days.

Young men in their late teens, known as Nyinkas, were undergoing initiation into tribal manhood. Part of this process was learning to provide for themselves in the bush, an essential training for a young man who would one day be a husband and father and might have to support his family on whatever he could glean from the harsh outback. So the Nyinkas, including a youngster whom I remembered as being extraordinarily clever with numbers, went far out in the bush and were in fact not allowed to be seen by the rest of the tribe. Like all activities of Aborigines in a tribal condition, the whole ritual of initiation was based on a deep understanding of their ancient environment.

One evening, Aborigines and Duguids sat round a big fire and joined in a song and dance corroboree, and on our last afternoon there was a sports day which included such feats as firemaking, spearthrowing, and running with a billy of water on the head. Nganyintja accompanied us on the truck ride back to the Finke, and she and Rosemary spent two final happy days together. We returned to Adelaide full of pleasant memories, which for me were made even pleasanter by the knowledge that Ernabella Mission was becoming a means of introducing tribal Aborigines into the modern world without the suffering and degradation undergone by native Australians in other parts of the country.

So it was all the more shocking to learn, soon after my return to Adelaide, that the British government wanted to test guided missiles in Australia—and that they wanted to instal a rocket range that would run right through the Central Aborigines Reserve. From the official viewpoint, the situation was ideal. From the rocket base which was to be built at Woomera, the scientists would be able to fire rockets in a straight line for 1,200 miles across "uninhabited" country, all the way to the far north of Western Australia.

But a large part of the area across which the rockets were to pass was the ancient tribal territory of the great Pitjantjatjara tribe—some of whom made use of the Ernabella Mission. When the Commonwealth government agreed to co-operate with the United Kingdom proposals, it was time to protest. Being a member of the Aborigines Protection Board I was a Protector of Aborigines; I could not agree to roads being driven across the Aboriginal Reserve, observation towers erected upon it, and rockets being fired across it.

Many other people were of like mind, and my public protest received wide support. Professor Gilbert Murray, President of the United Nations Association in Britain, gave me his backing. But the governments of the world were once more involved, overtly and covertly, in the struggle for power. Less than two years after the end of the war, the wartime alliances had collapsed and the nations were engaged in a frantic arms race of which the proposed rocket range was only one aspect. Australia, more closely tied to Britain then than now, was co-operating in ventures which must inevitably arouse suspicion and fear in other countries.

The distinguished physicist Mark Oliphant, later Sir Mark Oliphant and now the Governor of South Australia, was emphatic in his warnings that we were on a disaster course. In early 1947 I arranged a public meeting at the Adelaide Town Hall, which was packed with people who heard him make a moving plea that scientists should be freed from the restrictions of secrecy and encouraged to develop the peaceful uses of atomic power. In moving the vote of thanks, I stressed his plea that atomic power should be used to heal, not hurt.

But it was of little avail. Wartime workshops at Salisbury, north of Adelaide, were being converted and expanded to become the Weapons Research Establishment, and it was becoming obvious that our protests against the rocket range were going to be ignored. On 20 January 1947 the Minister for Defence, Mr J. J. Dedman, invited me to attend a meeting of the Australian Guided Missiles Committee at Victoria Barracks, Melbourne, in order to state my views on "measures which might be taken for the safety and welfare of the Aborigines in the Central Reserve." Dr Donald Thomson, the distinguished Melbourne University anthropologist, was invited also.

If the committee members believed that we were going to give virtual acquiescence to the proposal by suggesting ways in which the Aborigines might be protected from it, they were mistaken. Each of us, in turn, spoke in absolute opposition to violation of the Reserve. I said that I was totally opposed to rockets being fired over the Reserve, and would continue to oppose the idea.

The Minister for Defence was not present at the meeting. The committee reported to him, and from what transpired in the Federal Parliament after that I was left in little doubt that I had only been invited to the meeting so that the Minister might tell the House that my objections had been met.

Eventually, the Aborigines Protection Board of South Australia agreed to the proposal for a rocket range through the Reserve. This was too much for me, and I sent my resignation from the Aborigines Protection Board to Sir Malcolm McIntosh, the Minister for Aborigines in the South Australian Government.

However, the sustained opposition which came from many parts of Australia had at least one good result. The Federal Government created a special appointment, an officer who would be responsible for the care and protection of the Aborigines in the Reserve and who would ensure that they had proper explanation and warning when rockets were to be fired. The appointment went to a man who was ideally fitted for the task: Mr Walter McDougall. He was one of the staff of the Ernabella Mission, where he had been supervisor of the sheep flocks, and was already known and trusted by the people of the Pitjantjatjara.

15

EPIDEMIC AT ERNABELLA

T HE FACT THAT THE PITJANTJATJARA TRIBE HAD HAD THEIR
way smoothed into the modern world by the establishment
of Ernabella Mission did not by any means imply that the
whole Aboriginal population of Australia was any better off.
In fact, the greater proportion of white people in outback
Australia continued to regard Aborigines as no better than a
source of cheap labour. Between 1946 and 1951, there was a
repetitive series of accounts of cruel and inhuman treatment of
Aborigines in the Northern Territory. With great courage—
because he had to live in Darwin, capital of the Northern
Territory—the well-known journalist Douglas Lockwood
brought to light some disgraceful instances of "callous, brutal,
and inhuman treatment" of Aborigines in the Wave Hill and
Victoria River Downs areas.

These stories had been told to him by Mr Jack Meaney, a
cattle drover and stockman. They told not only of actual
brutality towards the Aborigines, but of the way in which those
too old or sick to work were being left to slow starvation. The
whole situation was defined as "mass starvation and mass

cruelty," and it was said that "the government is subsidising the pastoral industry with human lives."

Soon after that, a unit went to the Northern Territory to film *The Overlanders*, starring the Australian actor Chips Rafferty. Numerous Aborigines were employed by the unit, which paid them full award rates, fed them properly, and gave them proper beds and bedding whenever possible. For this the film makers were criticised by the local white people for "spoiling the Aborigines." The British director of the film, Harry Watt, told the Adelaide *News* that he was shocked by the way in which Aboriginal workers were "commercially exploited" and "suffering under laws that were distinctly colonial."

It is little wonder that Aboriginal station hands, domestics, and general workers in the Northern Territory went on strike in 1946 and 1947. In May 1946, 800 station hands struck for a minimum wage of thirty shillings a week—and a number of them were arrested.

Two conferences were held, one in Alice Springs and one in Canberra, with the idea of working out better pay and conditions for the Aborigines. But the first was only between officials of the Department of Native Affairs and pastoralists employing Aborigines, and the second was between native welfare officials of the Northern Territory and the States. But no Aborigines were present at the conferences, and trade union officials and journalists were excluded from the first one. When the Minister for the Interior toured the Territory in 1948, he complained that the programmes agreed upon were not being carried out.

The previous allegation that "pastoralists were being subsidised by the government at the cost of human lives" was supported by a report in the Darwin *Standard*. This, in April 1949, wrote about alleged conditions on Wave Hill Station, then owned by the British meat-processing firm, Vesteys. The station employed 250 Aboriginals, the report stated, and alleged that none of them received wages; that rations included tea, sugar, and "a slice of bread and hunk of beef per meal;" and that the seventy Aboriginal children under ten years of age living on the station received no schooling. Few stations provided proper facilities for sleeping, washing, and eating.

The Aborigines did the hard work on food vastly inferior to the white man's, with a consequent lowering of resistance to disease.

"The staple diet for native employees appears to be bread and beef, and not much of that," said an ex-policeman who returned to the Victoria River district after an absence of fifteen years. He said that he noted a marked decrease in the Aboriginal population, which he attributed to lack of nourishing food and lowered resistance to disease. It was a vicious circle. As the Aboriginal population decreased, the station-owners attempted to obtain more work from those who survived —while feeding them so poorly that they were unable to exert the necessary effort. "Niggers, coons, and lazy swine," were the common epithets, and the ex-policeman, G. R. Birt of Adelaide, wrote: "It is ironical that on one cattle station where semi-slavery conditions are particularly noticeable, Sunday school is held regularly for white children only."

But the conscience of the country was slowly being aroused. It was helped to awaken by many prods from such organisations as the Aborigines Advancement League of South Australia, and by the speaking and writing of people who felt as I did. In 1951, the Federal Government created a new portfolio, that of Minister for Territories. Mr Paul Hasluck, now Sir Paul Hasluck, Governor-General of Australia, was the first Minister, and for a number of years he worked steadily at improving the physical condition of the Aborigines. He was equally vigorous in advocating their social acceptance into the Australian community, but that is still a long way from complete realisation.

In the immediate post-war era, the Aborigines of Central Australia were struck a devastating blow by a disease which most white people treat as a run-of-the-mill childhood ailment: measles. It is known nowadays that measles can have lasting side-effects, and when a hitherto untouched community is swept by an epidemic of measles the result can be disastrous.

So it was in 1948. A child returning to his home in Alice Springs from school in Adelaide was the unknowing carrier of the disease, and within weeks it had spread through the Aborigines in the Northern Territory and in northern South Australia.

My first news of it came in April 1948, in a radio telegram from the Reverend A. C. Wright, then Superintendent of Ernabella Mission. He said that the Pitjantjatjara people were suffering badly from measles complicated by broncho-pneumonia. I rang the Aborigines Department, and found that they had been advised of the epidemic but had no doctor who could be sent immediately. I knew that the Commonwealth Medical Officer of Health at Alice Springs, Doctor W. Alderman, had to cover 100,000 square miles in his capacity of Flying Doctor for the area, and offered my services if the Aborigines Department would fly me to the north.

This was arranged immediately. I collected a plentiful supply of penicillin, sulphadiazine, and invalid foods from the Commonwealth Health Department and the Aborigines Protection Board, and took off next morning for Oodnadatta.

There had not been enough time to arrange for transport on from Oodnadatta to Ernabella, but I knew that I could rely upon outback generosity. I was lucky enough to find that Mr Brady, owner of Everard Park cattle station, had come in to Oodnadatta to meet two guests, and he offered me a place in his buckboard.

I did not have to go as far as Ernabella before I encountered the first cases of measles. After spending the night at Everard Park I was driven on to Ernabella, but when we passed through Kenmore Park, a cattle station en route to the mission, I found that the Aboriginal workers were stretched out on the ground, too sick to move. I treated these with the lifesaving drugs which I carried, and was driven on to the mission.

Mr Wright's radiogram had not understated the situation. I found that nearly 300 Aborigines, many of whom had been brought in from outlying stations, were lying in the shelter of hastily constructed windbreaks around the hospital and dispensary, with camp fires helping to keep them warm. Dr Alderman called on the Flying Doctor radio soon after I arrived, and offered to send whatever drugs were needed, but I told him that I had plenty of medical supplies and that the obvious need was for more helpers. The mission staff was exhausted after working eighteen hours a day for nearly three weeks. There was only one trained nurse, and one of the problems which they faced was that of preventing delirious patients from walking away naked into the cold night air. Also, they had to keep fires burning for those who were too sick to do so for themselves.

Miss Clare Harris, a young woman holidaying in Alice Springs, offered to help us, and was flown in to the mission. I sent a radiogram to the Aborigines Department, asking for a nurse and a general helper to be sent, and they arrived soon afterwards.

Measles is an illness in which proper diet and careful nursing are as important as any drugs which can be given. The mission staff had to prepare and distribute special invalid food, coax the worst cases to eat, and at the same time maintain all the regular work of the mission. Not a single Aboriginal was capable of helping out with woodcutting, washing, breadmaking, and so on, and at one time the Superintendent himself was cooking all the food for the patients and taking it to them three times a day.

After a week at Ernabella I had to return to the city, but I could see that the worst of the epidemic was past so far as the mission community was concerned. The same did not apply to other Aboriginal settlements. The disease spread westward and northward, along the railway line and roads, and there were many deaths. Aborigines had no immunity against measles at that time, and when I returned to Adelaide I urged that the Commonwealth Government should maintain stocks of gamma globulin serum so that an immediate vaccination campaign could be carried out at the first sign of another epidemic.

A year later, I made a special visit to Ernabella to estimate the after-effects of the epidemic. I was impressed by the discovery that none of the school children who had been receiving supplementary feeding for several years had died or suffered serious complications. This confirmed what I knew already and what the Aborigines Department should have realised — that meat and milk are essential items of diet for a native people no longer able to forage for themselves in natural surroundings.

16

IN THE NORTHERN TERRITORY

I N A MEDICAL SENSE, THE ABORIGINES OF SOUTH AUSTRALIA AND the Northern Territory have never been so well cared for as they are today. A great deal of devoted work goes on which the public never hears about. In the Northern Territory, Dr W. A. Langsford, Director of Medical Services, has a team at Darwin and another at Alice Springs. They have saved the lives of many young children. In South Australia, the medical care of Aborigines has been supervised for the last six years by Professor G. M. Maxwell, of the Department of Child Health in the University of Adelaide. He has been tackling the serious problems of malnutrition among Aboriginal children, as well as other health problems of which some, in Australia, are almost limited to Aboriginal children.

Typical of these is bronchiectasis. This affliction is commoner in Aboriginal children because they live in wurlies and unhygienic houses, crowded together at night time in a smoky atmosphere from wood-fires, unrelieved by ventilation. Many of these affected children have had some form of more or less unresolved pneumonia preceded by chronic infection of throat

TOP: Tjuintjara, the author's guide through rough outback country, uses the traditional Aboriginal method of straightening a spear shaft. BOTTOM: These nomads of the Petermann area were photographed after it had suffered a three-year drought

and nasal sinuses. The "running noses" and "running ears" so often found when Aborigines are congregated together are evidence of upper respiratory tract infection. The child suffering from bronchiectasis is often listless but this is not due to malnutrition.

Chronic bronchiectasis calls for lobectomy—excision of part of a lung. Sister Anne Hume, a Matron of Warrawee Hostel in Adelaide, told me that in the twelve months ending 31 October 1970 forty-five lobectomy operations had been performed on Aboriginal children ranging in age from six months to eleven years. Most of them were quite well-nourished, and came from missions, government reserves in South Australia, and Aboriginal settlements in the Northern Territory.

Expert treatment of the disease once it has gained a hold is not enough. The only proper cure is by improving the poor social conditions in which many Aborigines still live. The building of hygienic houses should begin at once, and the danger of overcrowding explained to Aboriginal adults and children. It is utterly discouraging to see Aboriginal children, restored to health by skilled medical care and nursing in the ideal conditions of hospitals, returned to the same conditions in which they contracted the disease. They are not even taken back home in the most suitable manner. In this air age, they are still driven many hundreds of miles in well-filled motor-cars.

One can imagine the outcry there would be if forty-five white babies and children had to be brought to Adelaide each year from Central Australia to have portions of their lungs removed as a direct result of living in sub-standard conditions. It is time that a similar outcry was raised on behalf of the Aborigines.

Like most native peoples of the Pacific area, the Aborigines have suffered badly from "imported" diseases brought into their territory by the white invader. Their sufferings have been accentuated by their treatment as sub-humans, with the concomitant low standards of housing and nutrition.

However, it would not be fair to portray the situation without pointing to some of the many attempts which have been made to improve it over the past twenty years. I found some of these

Top: Ernabella Mission in the early days. The central building was the one which the author lived in on his first visit, before the mission was established. Bottom: A schoolroom at Ernabella in 1969

in the far north of the Northern Territory, when I was at last able to make the visit which in 1934 I had had to cut short at Alice Springs.

The Hon. Paul Hasluck, who in 1951 had been appointed the first Minister for Territories, very kindly arranged for me to visit every community of Aborigines in and around Darwin, and I arrived there in July 1951. It was pleasantly warm in the winter sunshine of the airport, where I was met by Mr F. H. Moy, then Director of Native Affairs. I stayed with the Reverend Stewart Lang at the manse of the United Church, and next morning I was called for by Gordon Sweeney of the Department of Native Affairs. I soon perceived that he was putting himself heart and soul into his job and we got on very well together as he helped me to make a thorough investigation of Aboriginal conditions in Australia's tropical north.

Among my first visits was one to Bagot Reserve, on the outskirts of Darwin. It was for full-blood Aboriginals from every part of the "Top End" of the Territory, and we saw people there from every tribe in that area. The Reserve provided free housing, food, clothing, schooling, and hospitalisation, and a good many of the men were taken to work in Darwin every day. They received two pounds a week, but there was no government employment for women.

I was interested in the hospital, where a bright little lass took my hand and walked with me through the wards. Leprosy, which had almost certainly been carried into the Northern Territory by Chinese labourers brought in to build the Darwin to Birdum Railway, was still a problem. I rejoiced, however, to see that children suffering from the early non-infectious stage of the disease like my little guide were being treated in the Bagot Reserve hospital and were no longer being sent to the Leprosarium to mingle with more advanced cases. This was on Channel Island, and when I went there a week later I found that the patients were cared for devotedly by Sisters of Our Lady of the Sacred Heart, assisted by a Brother.

From Bagot Reserve I went to the Aborigines Inland Mission home for part-Aboriginal children, and found that eighty-one children of all ages were being looked after by Miss Shankland in this undenominational mission which does good work in various parts of Australia. A number of them were attending the public school in Darwin.

Next day I called on the Department of Health and talked to Dr Watsford,.who gave me an insight into medical problems of the Territory. Leprosy, hookworm disease, tuberculosis and yaws were endemic, but were being tackled by doctors under Dr Watsford's supervision. They paid regular visits to the missions, government reserves, and outlying camps and stations, in the Commonwealth Aerial Medical Services' planes. The prime lack, however, was that of hospitals, and it was necessary to bring most serious cases to Darwin.

The Aborigines were certainly well-cared for when they were admitted to Darwin Hospital. Guided by Dr Alderman I visited the native wards, and when I entered the men's ward I was greeted by three patients whom I knew. They were from the Roper River Mission, and were friends of our foster-son Sydney Cook who had lived with us in Adelaide for six years. Sydney had developed a great love for horses and skill in handling them, and it was for this reason that we had arranged for him to leave school in Adelaide and go to Roper to help with stock work, while continuing his schooling by correspondence. The three men in Darwin all praised his handling of horses.

The next trip was to Delissaville Reserve, which was reached by a five-mile journey by motor-launch along the channels twisting and turning through the mangrove swamps. The launch was skilfully steered by a full-blood Aboriginal. We carried stores for the Reserve, and were met by Mr Webb, the manager, and a group of Aborigines who unloaded the launch. I found that Mr and Mrs Webb and two Commonwealth Education Department schoolteachers were all keenly interested in the Aborigines in their charge and displayed great faith in them, but it was somewhat depressing to realise that the Reserve was used partly as a disciplinary centre for liquor offences.

In those days, Aborigines were not allowed to drink alcohol or to be on licensed premises, but could be on licensed premises if the hotelkeeper had a licence to employ Aborigines. This in itself created anomalies. Aborigines frequently obtained alcohol, which very often was sold to them by white men in its crudest form such as methylated spirits, and there were numerous cases of Aborigines actually being paid in methylated spirits. Many of them drank simply because they thought that it was a way to make them closer to the white men, who certainly drank full and plenty in the Darwin of those days. But when the white man was hailed into court he was fined five shillings or seven and six, a fraction of a day's wage, whereas an Aboriginal was fined two pounds or so, the equivalent of a week's wages, and was subject to other penalties such as being sent away from the town. This part of the problem has at least been solved by the granting of full citizenship rights to Aborigines, but there is need for the Aborigines to be educated in the dangers of alcohol as a beverage. The same might be said for many white men.

Part-Aborigines, amongst whom there were numerous examples of crosses with Chinese, Filipinos, and Malays, lived on the outskirts of Darwin at Parap and "Police Paddock." White people also lived at Parap, but in both areas the housing was no more than old Army huts, with those on the "Paddock" being in complete disrepair. Sister Shankland conducted a Sunday School there, and Gordon Sweeney told me that she was the greatest influence for good among the part-Aborigines of Darwin. It was miraculous that any message of love and hope could get through to people living under such conditions.

The wages were as bad as the housing. The wage for an Aboriginal stockman was fixed at £1 per week in 1947, but this was not implemented for eighteen months. By that time the pound had dropped in value and a week's wage would go nowhere—and even this meagre basic wage was ignored by many station owners.

Aborigines employed by the government received £2 a week with a few extras, but Darwin prices were so high that it was a struggle to rear a family. Yet many part-Aborigines were making the best of it, and when I called on Mr B. Damasso, Secretary of the Australian Half-Caste Progressive Association, my mouth watered at sight of the tasty meal of fish which he had caught for his family. He and the President of the Association, Mr J. H. McGuinness, called on me the night before I left Darwin. Mr McGuinness was a master carpenter with the

Department of Works and Housing, and was a good advocate for the many needs of his people.

The government in 1951 did not allow an Aboriginal mother to keep her baby if it was of mixed blood unless there was a supporting father, and of these there were few. Such were the children who lived in the Aborigines Inland Mission home in Darwin, while older children were sent from the mainland to live on Melville Island, under the care of the Roman Catholic Church, or to Croker Island under the Methodists.

In those days the missions on the offshore islands were serviced by luggers sailing from Darwin. I had been invited to inspect the mission on Croker Island, so went down to the wharf where the mission luggers were loaded. It was a beautiful sight, with many small craft at anchor on the blue waters and a busy wharfside scene as the little luggers took on passengers and cargo.

I was sailing with the Reverend Ern Clark, who had been a missionary for many years in the Pacific Islands. He led me aboard the Methodist Mission lugger *Arietta*, and introduced me to the young white missionary who was her skipper and her crew of five Aborigines. Two part-Aboriginal children came with us to begin a new life at the mission.

It was a rough passage to Croker, and the children were as seasick as I was when I went down into the cabin to help them. We took some more Aboriginal passengers aboard at Cape Don, and towed their native canoe astern as we plugged on toward the island.

Croker Island, lying two or three miles off the mainland, is about 120 miles in extent. I spent a happy week there as the guest of the Reverend and Mrs F. J. Johncock, who were in charge of the mission, and I thought that it was very efficiently run. The staff and children were keen and lively, and the older Aborigines helped in timber milling, cattle raising, and the making of brooches and other ornaments from seashells. It is a beautiful spot with a true "tropical island" flavour, and I thoroughly enjoyed the magnificent fishing in the blue waters offshore.

The newer houses for the children were good, but the school building was very poor. Despite this, the youngsters obtained some good scholastic results. One could not help wondering what lay ahead of them. As soon as they reached eighteen they were free to return to the mainland, which meant Darwin. Conditions in the town held no great promise for their future happiness.

From Croker Island we flew to Goulburn Island, which was inhabited by members of at least five tribes. This is another beautiful island, with a Methodist mission under the Reverend A. Ellison. He had established a very efficient irrigation system which enabled the mission to grow an abundance of vegetables and tropical fruits, and ample protein was provided by the fish that were easily caught in the sea. The mission had a trained teacher and trained nurse but no hospital nor dispensary — a deficiency which was partly made good by the excellent Commonwealth Aerial Medical Service. It was in constant touch with all the missions along the north coast and gave the same attention to white and dark Australians alike.

The take-off from Goulburn to return to Darwin was rather breathtaking, because the runway was extremely short and we were warned that the aircraft would only just clear the cliff before it became airborne. But we got off safely, and on the day after my return to Darwin I was taken by Brother Lilwall of the Roman Catholic Church on a launch trip to Channel Island. This was the home of the leprosarium, where Aborigines suffering from Hansen's Disease (leprosy) were segregated. Sister Michaelina, the sister-in-charge, kindly allowed me to see patients suffering from all stages of the disease. She had a thorough knowledge of Hansen's Disease and of the methods of treatment which gave some hope to sufferers, and agreed with me that it was a tragedy that early cases should sometimes be housed with the more advanced and infectious cases.

The patients were a little diffident about talking with me at first, but soon realised my concern for their welfare and became most forthcoming. I had a happy talk with a lad of sixteen from Croker Island, who was very like his sister whom I had met at the mission there.

Brother Lilwall was not a medical man but was responsible for the occupation and general welfare of patients. He was doing splendid work, and was encouraged when I told him that satisfying occupation, good food, and proper housing were as important as medicine.

I saw five more cases of leprosy at the Church Missionary Society Mission at Roper River, which I reached next noon after an early flight from Darwin. They were in charge of Sister Erica James, a fully trained nurse who was the only woman on the staff and seemed to be at the beck and call of everyone. She cooked for the staff of seven, and nursed the sick in her lean-to hospital.

Our foster-son Sydney Cook lived at the Aboriginal camp near the mission, so there was a turn-out of the whole community to welcome my arrival by air. He lived with Silas and Rosie Roberts, who were responsible for him, but had meals with the mission staff. When he first arrived there he had difficulty in digesting Aboriginal food, and Silas and Sister Erica arranged for him to have "white man's tucker."

He seemed to be well respected by the Aborigines, especially for his prowess with horses, and was completely accepted by them despite his six years in the city. There were two corroborees while I stayed at Roper River, and he was at both of them. The turn-out of Aborigines was understandably small at the Sunday morning service, since the corroborees had been going on through the two previous nights, but Sydney turned up somewhat late looking sleepy and tousled. He was a good example of assimilation into two worlds, able to dance and sing at the traditional ceremonies of the Aborigines and follow them with worship at a Christian service.

The mission staff were all Bible Institute trainees, though not trained for specific tasks. The Superintendent, Mr Colin Gilchrist, had been a banker, so his administrative background was valuable and he was unfailingly courteous and considerate to the Aborigines in his care. Mr Hart, the stockman, was a vigorous young man who had never even sat on a horse before he joined the mission. He and Sydney hit it off well. "I'm not sure whether I'm in charge of him or he's in charge of me!" he told me as they rode off to a cattle muster.

It was good to see the contentment of everyone at the mission, but my happy stay there ended when I was picked up by the Health Department's aircraft to be taken to see the hospital at Alice Springs, in accordance with arrangements made by Dr Watsford from Darwin.

This trip began with an error which could have ended in tragedy, because the pilot had to refuel the aircraft from drums kept at the mission and was just about to empty the first bucketful into the fuel tank when he discovered that it was water and not petrol! A drum of water had become mixed with those of fuel, and such a dilution in the aircraft's fuel tank could have wrecked her on take-off.

Dr Richard Brock, who was well known to me, was flying as medical officer on that trip, and I was happy to see him again. We flew to Alice Springs by way of Borroloola which, with its three lonesome buildings, was surely the dreariest place I had ever visited, touching down at Tennant Creek for an overnight stay. Here it was bitterly cold and I looked forward to the warm clothes I had left at Alice Springs.

Alice Springs had changed a good deal since my first visit seventeen years before. The war had come and gone, the bitumen road from the Alice to Darwin had been built, air communications were greatly improved, and the masses of men who had passed through the Centre during the war were being followed by the first trickles of what has become an increasing flood of tourists. However, it was good to see and hear that the position of the Aborigines was improving. Mr W. McCoy, then in charge of Native Affairs for the area, told me that the Aborigines of Henbury Station under the management of Mr Pearce were well-housed and receiving five pounds a week—five times what the law at that time demanded. But Henbury Station had always had a good reputation, as is confirmed by T. G. H. Strehlow in his book *Journey to Horseshoe Bend*.

A more significant indication of changing times was the Alice Springs Hospital, for which I had appealed after I first visited the town in 1934.

I met an old friend at the hospital: Sister O'Keefe, who had been in charge of the part-Aboriginal children's hostel called The Bungalow when I first visited the Alice. She knew of my connection with the founding of Ernabella, and when she took me round the Aboriginal section she led me to a bed in the sunshine. "Here is Polly from Ernabella," she said. "And her husband Punch is working in the hospital garden."

Poor Polly had had her right leg amputated because of a fungus affection of the foot—mycetoma or "Madura foot." When Sister led me out into the garden she called "Punch! Punch!" and Punch jumped up from his weeding and hurried across to grasp my hand. He was full of excitement at seeing me again, and told me that he was employed for £2 a week and his keep. It all seemed a far cry from the days when he would have had to live in the "black's camp" on the outskirts of the town.

The hospital contained a good many patients of both sexes and all ages, the majority from Hermannsburg, who were suffering from tuberculosis. That year was about the time when the Commonwealth Government began its national campaign against tuberculosis, and this together with the introduction of the special drugs has considerably cut down the incidence of the disease, but Aborigines seem to be especially susceptible to affections of the lungs.

Tuberculosis, like leprosy, is one of the diseases which flourishes under conditions of poor hygiene, overcrowding, and malnutrition. Such conditions were inflicted upon the Aborigines by the white man. When the first settlers took up land in Australia, the Aboriginal life-style was of a type which did not provide a breeding ground for infectious diseases. They lived in the open air and frequently moved their camp sites, and most of them spent their lives entirely naked. This was in direct contrast to Europeans and Asians of the nineteenth century, who lived in insanitary communities, did not wash very often, and covered their bodies with clothing.

As nomads, the Aborigines had a good sense of personal hygiene. I remember seeing an Aboriginal tribal mother hold out her baby for a bowel motion, and then clean its buttocks by scraping them gently with a flat stone. After that she powdered them with fine sand. By contrast to this, my wife has told me of the expression of disgust on one Aboriginal mother's face when she was staying in our home and was shown how a white mother used nappies for a baby and washed them clean after use.

It is almost certain that the infectious diseases such as yaws, trachoma, leprosy, tuberculosis, upper respiratory tract infections, syphilis and gonorrhoea, were all introduced by white men moving up into Australia from the south or by Asians trading along the northern coasts. I have seen all these diseases among bush Aborigines, to say nothing of the measles epidemics which wrought such havoc at missions, cattle stations, and camps.

This is not to say, of course, that the Aborigines in their natural state did not suffer ill health of one kind or another. In my own experience I have seen congenital faults such as talipes (club foot), hare lip and cleft palate. Aborigines suffer from many burns, often as a result of rolling into a camp fire when asleep, and I have also had to treat spear wounds resulting from quarrels. In winter time painful deep cracks in the soles of the feet, from walking barefoot over rough ground, are not uncommon.

I have also seen cases of mental illness, but it is hard to know whether the Aborigines would suffer in this way when in their natural state or whether such cases are the result of pressures placed upon them by introduction into a new way of life.

After my trip to the north in 1951, I could return to Adelaide with feelings of satisfaction about many of the things which I had seen. Much remained to be done, but a great deal had been achieved, and it was obvious that the attitude of the Australian government towards the Aboriginal people had changed vastly since the days when I accused Joseph Lyons' administration of "hoping that the Aborigines would die out so that the problem would solve itself." The dedicated men and women of the Department of Native Affairs, the Commonwealth Aerial Medical Service, and the various missions of several denominations, were hopeful auguries for the future of the Aborigines.

17

NGANYINTJA AND OTHERS

THE JOURNEYS WHICH MY WIFE AND I MADE AT VARIOUS TIMES over the years to investigate Aboriginal conditions in South Australia and other places have led to our name becoming well known to the Aborigines. So when they come to town, and for one reason or another find themselves in difficulty, they are apt to appeal to us. Hardly a month passes without a call.

One example was that of Sophie Kokum from Penong, on the West Coast. Years after Phyllis and I had visited that area we had a phone call at eleven-thirty one night. It was the driver of a bus from the West Coast, who said, "I've brought in a passenger who can't speak English. Whenever I ask her a question she says 'Doctor Duguid.' Can you help me, Doctor?"

"Put her in a taxi and send her to my home," I told him, and when the passenger arrived we found that she was Sophie. She was suffering from trachoma and had very sore eyes, so we made her comfortable for the night and I drove her to the Royal Adelaide Hospital in the morning.

Quite often we had Aboriginal mothers staying in our home while their children received medical care, and one of these

169

was Gudwin from Ernabella Mission who stayed with us while her son Reggie was an outpatient of the Children's Hospital.

My wife recalls with amusement Gudwin's shocked astonishment one day on North Terrace at the sight of twins in their double pram. The survival of the two babies would never be allowed in the harsh life of the bush.

Many years later her second son, a boy of fourteen, had a charge laid against him by a station owner and was sent to Adelaide for trial in the Children's Court. But the police who sent him south were not happy about the charge, and said as much to the Department of Native Affairs. They asked me to see the boy, who was sullen and unresponsive until he realised that I knew his mother and brother. He gave me the full story then, and the matter was soon resolved. Otherwise he would have been almost certainly convicted.

The Aboriginal tribal tradition of giving "fair shares to all" of whatever provender might be available, thus ensuring that no one should be left out, is so deeply ingrained in them that they virtually take it for granted even in city life, and they will always share whatever they have with those of their own kind. It is a wonderful characteristic, but can sometimes be a trifle disconcerting. One Easter Friday, thirty semi-tribal Aborigines who had a day off from orchard work along the Murray River turned up at our Adelaide home. We were glad to share with them, but it meant a rapid raid around whatever shops were open on that day. On another occasion we met four Ernabella couples after church, and after a chat my wife asked, "What are you going to do now?"

"Coming home with you to dinner," was the immediate reply. We appreciated the implied compliment that we were so much accepted by the Aborigines that it was taken for granted that we would share whatever we had with them — as they would have done with us.

I have often been called to hospitals to see very sick Aborigines sent down from the north, and have twice been able to hasten the release of Aborigines from mental hospitals. It used to be common for Aborigines who could not make themselves understood, or who for one reason or other were considered a nuisance, to be considered insane.

Recently I had an urgent ring from a senior staff sister at the Queen Elizabeth Hospital, who told me, "We have a very sick Aboriginal man who was admitted a week ago. We can't make contact with anyone who knows him, he hasn't had any visitors, and he's turned his face to the wall."

I asked for his name and the district from which he came, and then made contact with the District and Bush Nursing Society—of which I had been President for sixteen years. They gave me all the information I needed, and I went in to see the men. I found that he had been shockingly burned on his face, neck, body, arms, and legs, having rolled into a campfire fully clothed while he was in a drunken stupor. He was too weak to speak, but may have understood my attempts to talk to him, and perhaps this helped towards the recovery which was a tribute to the unflagging care of the doctors and nurses.

A somewhat similar case was that of the Aboriginal boy of sixteen, of subnormal mentality, whom I was asked to see. He came from the Northern Territory and had been in an institution on the outskirts of Adelaide for five and a half years. No one had visited him during that time and the doctor told me that he was deteriorating, so Phyllis and I went to see him at once. After this we arranged for friends to take him for drives and for others to invite him to their homes for a meal. The result was one of many proofs that Aborigines, just like white folk, respond to the feeling that they are of importance to others. The doctor and staff were able to gain a permanent improvement in his condition, and it was soon difficult to believe that he was the same young man as the withdrawn and retarded personality that we met at first.

In my feeling that Aborigines could and should have a place in the whole community of the Australian people, and that they would add a vigorous and useful dimension to our society, I was at variance with a lady whose name was closely associated with Aborigines during the 1920s and 1930s. This was Mrs Daisy Bates, of whom I had known for many years but did not meet until after she had retired to Adelaide. We met at a Government House garden party, and we soon became very friendly. At last she put her hand on my shoulder and said, "I think you are wrong in believing the Aborigines have a future."

"I'm sure they have a bright one when their worth is recognised," I told her.

"No, it's too late," she said. "The Aborigines are dying fast. The only thing we can do now is to try to make their passing easier."

"Mrs Bates, I hope you live long enough to see that you are wrong," I said, and we parted good friends but without changing each other's views. I doubt whether she was able to appreciate the changes which even at that time were coming over the horizon. In her later days she suffered losses of memory and was often found wandering in the street, but my wife and I took it as a great compliment that she always gave our name when she was asked where she lived. Phyllis would arrange for the women police to pick her up and take her home.

Among our Aboriginal friends and foster-children, we cherish special memories of Nganyintja, whom I have mentioned before as an Ernabella friend of ours. Nganyintja is a full-blood Pitjantjatjara, one of the first group of children who formed the Ernabella Mission School. She learnt to write fluently in her own language.

In 1943, when Nganyintja was about eleven, a tribal sister invited her to go on a trip to Coober Pedy, 400 miles from home. Various things went wrong and Nganyintja found herself stranded among strangers who could not speak her language. She could talk little English, but obtained pencil and paper and wrote a letter in Pitjantjatjara to her teacher at Ernabella. The teacher went to find her and then brought her to Adelaide, where for three weeks she stayed with us in our home.

Until her visit to Adelaide she had never seen a train or a tramcar, never seen the sea or a permanent river, had never worn clothes, and had never been inside a city house. But nothing overwhelmed her. She was keenly interested in everything in our home—so much of it opening a new world to her. The almond blossom enchanted her, and she took a great delight in the paintings hanging on our walls. She would not miss her hot bath at night for anything, and the care that she took of her gold-tipped curly hair was an example to most white children.

My wife was determined that she should have clothes as dainty and well-fitting as her own daughter, and it was touching to see the Aboriginal child's pride in nice things and the care that she took of her clothes. Passing on second-hand clothes to Aborigines may be well meaning, but it can be an insult.

The Ernabella teacher was doing a refresher course in Adelaide, and twice took Nganyintja to an Adelaide school. The teachers and pupils were amazed by her speed, confidence, and accuracy in arithmetic. She listened to the school children singing their songs, and when she was asked to sing some of her own she did so readily and without self-consciousness. One afternoon she sang to a full church congregation with natural-ness and feeling.

She spent most days playing happily with my daughter's doll's pram and our beloved little Australian terrier, or lying face down on the lawn and arranging big leaves in circles, playing that they were some of her own Ernabella people. She was never unhappy or tearful, and always willing to help with household tasks or shopping. Every afternoon she waited for my daughter to come home from school, and from then until bedtime the house and garden were full of laughter. Neither knew a word of the other's language to begin with, but the universal language of childhood is one of the most touching proofs that we are indeed "under Heaven one family."

At table, after quietly watching the rest of us, she handled knives and forks for the first time without any awkwardness. No more adaptable, lovable, or co-operative child has ever been in our home, and if she is typical of her race then surely there is no people on earth with a greater genius for co-operation than the Aborigines. It is the tragedy of Australian history that we never recognised this.

While Nganyintja was in Adelaide she was completely unspoilt. She was teacher as well as taught, patiently teaching us some of her language; and learning some of ours. To begin with she was counting the days until her return home, but on the last night she was very quiet as we sat round the fire. She had been happy with us, and in her own way she was telling us so. At the railway station next morning she was as moved as any child is when it comes to saying "Goodbye," and she waved until the train was out of sight, but we were to see each other many times after that. She is now the mother of a large family and has stayed three times in our home. Her eldest daughter, nineteen-year-old Mayana, spent the Easter weekend with us in 1970.

Top: Aboriginal children hose the dust off each other before starting lessons at Ernabella in 1946. Bottom: The first school day at Ernabella, in 1940

18

OVERSEAS AGAIN

FOR TWO OF THE YEARS IN WHICH I HELD THE OFFICE OF President of the Aborigines Advancement League I had consistently encouraged the Aboriginal people to state their own case in public, so that their white fellow-countrymen could hear the facts at first hand. By way of a "training programme" I arranged small meetings at which most of those attending were members of the League, and a number of young Aborigines and part-Aborigines had shown themselves capable of addressing and holding an audience.

Then I took the plunge and booked the Adelaide Town Hall for a public meeting, somewhat to the consternation of my associates. The forthcoming meeting received considerable publicity from press and radio, because so far as anyone knew it was the first time that a Town Hall audience was to be addressed by Aborigines, and even though it was the coldest and wettest night of winter 1953 the hall was packed with people when I declared the meeting open.

We had arranged for Aborigines of different ages to entertain the audience by singing and playing, but the highlight of

TOP: The author's children play with Ernabella children in 1946. BOTTOM: Mrs Duguid with Henry (left) and Charlie, 1964

the meeting came with speeches by five Aborigines:- George Rankine of Adelaide, one of the older leaders of his people, Peter Tilmouth from Alice Springs, Mona Paull, who came from Quorn, Ivy Mitchell and Jeff Barnes of Adelaide.

Each of them spoke quietly without bitterness, and in excellent English, of the disabilities from which they suffered on account of having been born as Aborigines in Australia, and the audience listened intently. One of the young women told the story of two of her friends who had reached the same educational standards as white girls of the same age and then applied for nursing training at the Royal Adelaide Hospital. The Matron would not accept them, and had advised them to return to Alice Springs and begin nursing their own people.

Immediately after the meeting, that matter was taken up officially. It was given wide publicity in the newspapers, and the Royal Adelaide now gives the same training to eligible Aboriginal girls as to any other. Several of them have been appointed ward sisters.

A young part-Aboriginal man told the audience of the way in which he, and those like him, were not allowed first class travel or access to the dining car of the train from Alice Springs to Adelaide when he was on his way down for education and training.

Public reaction to the meeting was most encouraging. For the first time, it had been displayed that part-Aboriginal people needed only the encouragement of those who were interested in them to help them to speak and act for themselves. I have no doubt that the meeting was largely responsible for the rapid correction of some wrongs which were mentioned at that time.

A few months after this, in March 1954, Queen Elizabeth and Prince Philip visited Adelaide for the first time. I had suggested that a party of twenty or so Aborigines from Ernabella should be brought down to see Her Majesty, and the Premier, Thomas Playford, arranged that one of the enclosures on a main street should be allotted to them, an action which gave them great pleasure.

But on their return to Ernabella it seemed that their most lasting memories were not of the crowds and buildings of the city nor even of the royal procession. One of the things which they talked about most was the vastness of the sea, which none of them had seen before. The other was an action of my own.

When the group of Aborigines was ready to leave the city after the procession had passed, we had to attempt a crossing of East Terrace through an apparently endless stream of cars. At last I stepped forward and held up my umbrella, the cars halted, and I led the Aborigines across. I heard later that the incident was re-enacted over and over again at the Ernabella camp site and with unfailing success!

It would be good to think that the Town Hall meeting and the Queen's visit and the fact that Albert Namatjira and another Aboriginal were presented to her by the Federal Government were all tokens of a "new deal" for the Aborigines. Such was not the case. Only four months after the Queen visited Adelaide, Jimmy Gwiethoona died in a prison cell at Nungarin, Western Australia, of injuries which a post-mortem revealed as being a bilateral fracture of the lower jaw and a subperiosteal haemorrhage the size of a two-shilling piece over the right frontal region with some softening of the brain underneath. A police constable was committed for trial on a charge of unlawfully killing the Aboriginal, but on 12 November 1954 the Crown announced that it would not continue with the proceedings because Gwiethoona received his fatal injuries when he "fell over when resisting arrest."

In the Northern Territory during that year, two pastoralists and a drover horsewhipped and assaulted Aboriginal men and women. However, this did not escape notice of the law which should apply equally to all Australians, the pastoralists were fined and imprisoned and the drover fined.

In that same year, my seventieth, I made another trip overseas, with my wife and our children Andrew and Rose-mary. Andrew was on his way to enter Cambridge University to work for his Ph.D. in mathematics, but for the rest of us it was mainly a holiday tour. Phyllis and I attended the Church of Scotland Assembly, at which we had been asked to speak. She spoke on Aboriginal women, I outlined the work of Ernabella Mission and showed that it was the first church venture to put the Smith of Dunesk bequest to its proper use.

We renewed old friendships in London, and in July I attended the Annual Meeting of the British Medical Association held that year in Glasgow, as a delegate from the South Australian Branch. I attended all the surgical sessions, and during the one at which heart surgery was discussed I was sitting near Bill Cleland. I had known Bill when he was a boy in Adelaide, and now he was a leading heart surgeon in London. He told me that within two years it would be possible to operate directly on the heart, with the blood being temporarily bypassed through a heart-lung machine. His forecast was of course quite accurate, and since those days heart surgery has taken the enormous strides which include heart transplants.

We visited our old friends Professor Gilbert Murray and Lady Mary at Boar's Hill, near Oxford, and then travelled across to Denmark. We enjoyed every moment of our visit to that beautiful country, and were especially impressed with the social services and the care of the old age pensioners. In those days, Copenhagen had twelve blocks of flats in different parts of the city, wholly devoted to the accommodation of the aged and with each block under the supervision of a trained nurse. The flats were most comfortable, and the nurse was ready to help the pensioners with their social as well as their medical problems.

Similar homes for the aged were to be found throughout the country, and one of the finest was at Gentofte, near Copenhagen. Here, five blocks of flats had been built so that they all faced the warm southern sun, and the buildings all had the appearance of well-kept private homes surrounded by beautiful gardens. The pensioners were encouraged to bring their own furniture and possessions with them—except for their beds—and their meals were taken to them in electrically-heated containers. "Unfortunately you're not eligible for one of these flats unless you're a pensioner," said the doctor who was showing us round.

I was particularly interested in the care of the aged, especially since I was at that time the President of the District and Bush Nursing Society in South Australia. I had been associated with the D.B.N.S. since my earliest days in Australia, when the nurses made their rounds on bicycles, and knew the value of the work done by the nursing sisters of the Society for old people who needed treatment in their own homes.

In Britain, I was able to see the Geriatric Units which were part of general hospitals. Each had its own outpatients department and short stay and long stay annexes, with a medical staff which included a visiting Consultant Geriatric Specialist. Keen nursing staffs were aided by the vital services of the almoners, who acted as links between hospital and home.

The emphasis in these geriatric hospitals was laid upon helping old people to believe that life is still worth living. As soon as their medical treatment had reached the appropriate stage they were encouraged to get out of bed, to dress and feed themselves, and to move about as freely as possible, with the aid of special equipment if necessary. It was wonderful to see what was possible in rehabilitation, especially for patients who had suffered strokes. Eventually the greater number of the patients would go home; ninety-five per cent of old people in Britain live in their own homes.

I was impressed by the generous time spent by physicians in charge of the geriatric hospitals with the relations of their patients. They welcomed discussion with those who were about to care for aged patients who were ready for home instead of hospital attention, and reassured them that there would be no problems about readmission to hospital if the patient became too difficult to nurse at home.

Also, it was felt that there was need for hostels for the old folk, in order to give helper and patient a complete "holiday" from each other.

The overall organisation of caring for the aged in their own homes was being tackled by the National Old People's Welfare Committee. This committee tried to arrange regular help for routine domestic tasks, to provide a daily hot meal, and to ease loneliness by setting up Old Folks Clubs. In some places, I even found a mobile physiotherapy service. Aberdeen led the way in providing a home chiropody service, and the District Nursing Association in that city had arranged a night as well as a day nursing service. As in the rest of Britain, the District Nurses and the general practitioners of the National

Health Service were responsible for the continuing medical care of the aged in their own homes.

I could see that every effort was being made to allow old people to stay in their own homes instead of shifting them to "old folks homes." In Cambridge, I saw the beginnings of a scheme which provided for five per cent of the houses planned for any new community to be designed specially for the needs of the ageing, with proximity to shops and transport.

The last months of our holiday were spent in Scotland, and Phyllis and I gloried in the beauty of the country of my birth. While we were there I met the family of my old chief, Sir William Macewen, and they urged me to write a memoir of the famous surgeon. They had asked me before, to write his life but it was an impossible task to undertake from Adelaide where I was busily engaged in medical practice. My opportunity to do the memoir came in 1956, after I had been knocked down by a car as I crossed North Terrace in Adelaide. The subsequent period in bed enabled me to get busy, and *Macewen of Glasgow* was published by Oliver and Boyd of Edinburgh in 1957.

The car accident following an operation in 1955, induced me to retire from general surgery. Very soon after that, I was able to make some use of what I had seen of geriatric medicine in Britain and Denmark. The Reverend Samuel Forsythe, founder of the Methodist Old Folks Home at Aldersgate, asked me to act as visiting doctor, and I spent six happy and rewarding years in that position.

Attending the old people had its lighter moments. One tall old man shuffled into the clinic and sat down very slowly, and after I had taken his pulse I asked him to return to his room, get into his pyjamas, and lie on his bed for examination. As soon as I had finished with the other patients I went to examine him, and found that he had a greatly enlarged and very inefficient heart. I used a biro to mark out its width on his chest, and snapped it shut when I had finished. Next day he told the sister, "I've never been examined like that before. The doctor had a wee instrument that went off with a click when he finished using it. It's made me feel better already!"

19

APARTHEID IN AUSTRALIA

I SOON FOUND THAT GERIATRIC WORK DID NOT ABSORB ALL my energies, and after so many years of working with and for the Aborigines my interest in them was as strong as ever. So when my wife and I received an invitation to visit Mrs Neiass of Penong, who was a firm friend of the Aborigines, we accepted with pleasure. We flew over to Ceduna, on the west coast of South Australia, in October 1956, and Mrs Neiass and her son made it possible for us to see a good deal of the Aboriginal situation on the West Coast.

It was not altogether a happy one. The Evangelical Lutheran Mission, at Koonibba, comprised an area of 20,000 acres of arable land, but there was a lack of warmth in the atmosphere of the mission and there seemed little real sympathy between staff and Aborigines. It was saddening to see that a stout railing separated the playing areas of white and Aboriginal children at the main mission homestead, but the schoolteacher and children seemed to have a good relationship.

The Aboriginal homes were very poor, being dark, ill-ventilated, and overcrowded. Many of them had been condemned by the Aborigines Protection Board of that time, but had not been replaced. As we left one of them, a mother hurried after us and begged us to get her child back for her. She poured out her story, and we learnt that her baby had been very ill and had been taken to hospital many months before. Since then the parents had heard nothing and the child had not been returned.

As soon as we returned to Adelaide I made enquiries, and was told that the child had been "placed in a good Christian home in Victoria!" Such a situation was possible under the Aborigines Act of that time. The Aborigines Protection Board was the legal guardian of every Aboriginal child, and could dispose of it as it saw fit and regardless of whether it had parents or not—and without consulting the parents in any way.

Koonibba in 1956 was not a heartwarming place. It was taken over in 1963 by the Department of Aboriginal Affairs— now the Department of Social Welfare and Aboriginal Affairs, which makes no distinction between the social requirements of white and coloured South Australians.

Our impressions of Bookabie, Fowler's Bay, and Coorabie were happier. We called at a number of farms, and met a few full-blood Aborigines and many part-Aborigines. They seemed to be well accepted by their white neighbours and in general showed an attitude of self-respect.

We found a strange situation at Yalata Reserve. The Aborigines had been moved there from the dismal Ooldea Reserve in 1952, and the Government had drawn up an agreement with the Lutheran Church whereby the church was to run Yalata as a sheep farm on mutually agreeable terms, and to provide "education and spiritual guidance." Four years later there was no sign of education having begun. Instead, the Aboriginal men were sitting on the ground, busily at work with new chisels and gouges on the making of "Aboriginal implements." The Superintendent was a young man who had finished his theological training five months before, and I asked him about this activity. He told me that there was a great demand for Aboriginal artefacts among English scientists and technicians from the Maralinga atom bomb testing site. Once a fortnight he "lectured" to the innocent Englishmen, and sold them the artefacts produced by the Yalata souvenir industry.

Yet the only hospital building at Yalata was a large galvanised iron tank cut in half and upturned on the bare earth, with a doorway cut in it. The Sister took us to see it, and showed us where she had confined a mother and delivered her baby on the previous day.

When we returned to Ceduna we visited a small reserve on the outskirts of the town, and found that it was occupied by contented self-respecting people making the best of their conditions without a grumble. The women were thoroughly clean and tidy, and the washing on their lines was white as snow. A husband and wife invited us in for a cup of morning tea, and we enjoyed a chat with them. They were typical of the many fine Aboriginal people whom we met on the West Coast, despite some of its less encouraging aspects.

Not long after that, I was astounded to learn for the first time that the law in South Australia actually forbade association between Aboriginal and non-Aboriginal people—the State's own version of Apartheid. One day a very worried man called at my home in Magill. He was Ephraim Tripp, a respected Aboriginal citizen of Victor Harbor, and he told me that on 15 February 1957 he had a white friend with him in his car. He had known the man since his schooldays, and told me, "His family lives two doors from us and his children play with ours. Well, a policeman stopped us, and told my friend that he was guilty of an offence in associating with an Aboriginal. My wife and I want to get to the bottom of this, but I can't get any satisfaction from the police either in Victor Harbor or Adelaide."

He asked me to look into it for him, and I found indeed that Section 14 of the Police Offences Act of 1953 empowered the police constable to act as he had done. As President of the Aborigines Advancement League of South Australia I laid the matter before the League, and Mrs Iris Schulz, the secretary, prepared a petition and organised a deputation which was supported by various churches and welfare societies. Two members of Parliament, Mr Don Dunstan of the Autralian Labor Party (now Premier of South Australia) and Mr Robin

Millhouse of the Liberal and Country League, introduced the deputation to the Minister for Aborigines, Sir Malcolm McIntosh.

Mrs Schulz presented the petition and spoke on it, and Sir Malcolm then asked me if I would care to speak. I replied that I knew Ephraim Tripp, and that I had known his father and grandmother before him, and then added, "A second case of this kind came to my notice two weeks ago. It happened at Renmark on the Murray. Three young men were stopped by the police when they were going into a dance hall, and one of them, a part-Aboriginal lad, was told that he couldn't go in. His white brothers told the police, 'He's one of us. He's been in our home all his life, and we all went to the same school.' But the dark Australian wasn't allowed to go to the dance."

I felt sure that Sir Malcolm saw the justice of our case. The result came in 1958, when the government repealed the offensive section of the Act.

Soon after this occasion, I was pleased to have another opportunity to visit Ernabella Mission. I arrived on 31 May 1957, and next day motored west with the Reverends V. C. Coombs and J. M. Stuckey under the guidance of Mr John Bennett, the supervisor of sheep. The idea was to find a spot where the soil and water were suitable for an outstation.

Things had changed a good deal since I crossed the Reserve in 1939. In 1946, when the Hon. Mr J. J. Dedman as Minister for Defence was defending the plan for the Rocket Range, he stated that no roads would be built on the Aboriginal Reserve. However, I was not astonished to find that well-graded main roads and many subsidiary graded roads had been run throughout the Reserve. On my 1939 visit the speed of travel through the north-west section of the Central Reserve had been that of camels, doing between twelve and twenty miles a day. Now, it was limited only by the speed of one's car, running over the good roads that were not supposed to exist!

We travelled north of the Musgraves and along the Mann and Tomkinson Ranges to the Blackstone Range in Western Australia, where we found the operations of the West Mining Co., a Canadian firm which was searching for nickel and copper. Assays of ores brought up by drilling were carried out in a modern laboratory.

Mr H. Lane, the supervisor, gave us shelter from a rainy night on his verandah, and on our homeward journey next day we saw clouds of screeching galahs wheeling around the waterhole at Mount Davies, in the eastern Tomkinsons, on which his company depended. I thought that the Tomkinson country was the most suitable land for the proposed out-station, but it was somewhat remote from the mission.

When we returned to Ernabella and I had a proper chance to look around, I realised that the Aboriginal children were thinner than I had ever seen them. The mission medical officer, Doctor Jean Davies, was deeply distressed by the number of babies who were dangerously ill with pneumonia and diarrhoea, and they too were very thin. The Ernabella community had just passed through another measles epidemic in April and May, and it had hit hard. Most of the patients had been children, both dark and white, who had not been at the mission during the 1948 epidemic. The white children recovered, but twenty-four Aboriginal children and two adults died of complications with underlying sub-nutrition.

Such a record, in an Aboriginal community which all concerned with it had hoped would set an example to the rest, was most perturbing. The present state of child-health on the mission left very much to be desired, and I was determined to find out why.

I found a variety of reasons. It transpired that, for some years past, cattle stations had been encroaching upon large tracts of country over which the Pitjatjantjara people roamed in search of food. In 1956, the year before my visit, a plague of grasshoppers had ravaged thousands of square miles of country, causing a shortage of game and vegetable food. For the first half of 1957 there had been a drought which further checked the natural food supply. And, for the past twenty years, constant hunting for game and foraging for bush tucker by the mission Aborigines had thinned out supplies within accessible distance of the mission.

All these factors gave a reasonable explanation for poor nutrition in a community which depended upon hunting and

185

foraging for its food. But Ernabella Mission had always supplemented the Aborigines' natural diet, though in the beginning it was expected that bush tucker would be the main diet and mission supplies would make up any deficiencies. Now, it seemed that the position was reversed. Fewer and fewer people were going out hunting and gathering and so the mission food would have to be the sustaining diet and bush tucker the supplement.

So it was necessary to find what was lacking in the mission diet, and for six days I attended the preparation of every meal, tasted every item of food and drink, and noted the ingredients of every meal.

The deficiencies soon became apparent. At that time, a full-blood Aboriginal named Kitty was in charge of the ration store, with several Aboriginal helpers. They served a total of 350 Aborigines living at the mission, and I found that out of all these people it was only the working men who received enough meat in their stew—though it was hard to tell whether this was by accident or design. The amount of meat received by women and children was negligible. Infants were suffering from lack of supplementary feeding and vitamin concentrates, largely because of the fact that tribal and semi-tribal mothers kept babies on the breast until they were two or three years old. Since those days, Professor G. M. Maxwell and Dr. R. B. Elliott have stated that supplementary feeding should begin at six months.

This problem was compounded by the fact that the goats were being milked by untutored semi-tribal women. Goat's milk was in short supply, and what was available was freely mixed with water. The tea, coffee, and cocoa served to the Aborigines were all unpalatable, especially the latter two. They were merely luke-warm water with a slight coloration. The centre of all the bread and damper that I sampled was soggy, no jam was served with it during my six days' inspection, and syrup only once. I did not see any cheese, and no dessert was served at midday meals.

Meat of various kinds, even that of birds and reptiles, has always been the main article of diet in tribal life, and if this could not be provided at Ernabella then I felt that a protein substitute must be found. Pregnant and nursing mothers must have extra food, and proper baby scales were needed for weekly weighing of the babies whose weights should be recorded regularly.

All the problems were inter-related. Poor nutrition meant poor health; poor health meant lowered resistance to disease; lowered resistance meant fatalities from such epidemics as measles; the new roads across the Reserve, and the increased numbers of motor vehicles, meant that the mission community was in frequent contact with Alice Springs and Finke, with almost certain danger of recurrent epidemics. So the answer was to build up the health of the people, especially the children, with proper nutrition.

When I returned to Adelaide and had had time to think it over, I felt that something had to be done at once to supply ample protein to the Ernabella Aborigines. With the concurrence of the Reverend Ian Silke, then Moderator of the Presbyterian Church in South Australia, I appealed to the Church for funds to send full protein dried skim milk to Ernabella. The response of church members was so hearty that it enabled us to send up the dried milk in hundredweights at regular intervals, together with baby scales, hospital scales, a vitamiser, and general foodstuffs and supplies.

The Commonwealth Department of Health sent me their improved Ration Scale for Feeding Aborigines, which would eliminate sub-nutrition at all ages. I recommended that it should be adopted at Ernabella.

To tackle any recurrence of measles, I recommended that the General Secretary of the Board of Missions should be notified immediately a case was diagnosed. As a medical member of the Board resident in Adelaide, I too should be notified, and would take the responsibility of negotiating with the Aborigines Department and the Department of Health for a supply of gamma globulin to be flown at once to the mission, to inoculate those who had not yet contracted the disease.

There was one more Ernabella problem to be solved — employment. Most Aboriginal women at the mission were employed in craft work, teaching, hospital work, housework, and cooking. But the men did not have enough to keep them busy. Before Ernabella Mission was founded the people of the Musgraves still retained their ancient and well-balanced social, cultural, religious, and economic life. The very idea of the mission was to help them to retain this balance even though it was threatened by the incursion of the white man, but it had now become obvious that for a variety of reasons the Musgrave people had become largely dependent upon the mission. Therefore it was the duty of the Presbyterian Church to introduce some form of economic development which would support the Pitjantjatjaras in their own country.

Such jobs as sheep shearing, well sinking, and fencing were all necessary, but were spasmodic or seasonal. The sheep had to be looked after all year round, but did not employ all the men. So I felt it was time for cattle-raising to be established as another means of employment, and recommended it during two successive years to the Board of Missions. My persistence was rewarded and the idea accepted.

But all the problems of Ernabella were not yet solved. In 1958, I was happy to find a vastly improved appearance in the people of the mission, and the quantity and quality of food served to the natives in the dining hall was incomparably better than in the year before. However, it was still obvious that leaving the preparation and distribution of food to semi-tribal natives was not yet a good idea. I saw that they still could not cook a European-type diet properly nor share it out fairly. A mass of glutinous porridge was left in the bottom of saucepans for want of stirring, the children spilt too much of their meals when carrying them from counter to table, and the lion's share of the meat in the stew still went to the menfolk.

It was equally clear that proper supervision of the kitchen and dining hall could not be expected from a small and over-worked staff. The Aboriginal population had increased considerably, while the staff remained the same. Sister Ramm, the nursing sister, now had to supervise the dietary scale of mothers, babies, toddlers, school children, and adults. This meant almost constant work for her and extra duties for other members of the staff. The Minister Superintendent, the Reverend J. B. Edenborough, was so heavily involved in checking and ordering stores, handling accounts, and attending to clerical details that he carried a heavy load on top of his ministerial duties. The Industrial School had been closed for lack of a teacher, thus depriving young Aboriginal men of training in carpentry and other skills.

On the credit side was the fact that, in July of that year, the Aboriginal toddlers were able to combat an outbreak of gastroenteritis. Only three out of thirty-four toddlers were badly affected, and they recovered quickly from an attack of what was identified in Adelaide as *Shigella ambigua* from stools sent down to the Institute for Veterinary and Medical Research. The reaction of the Pitjantjatjara people was to burn down their greatly improved wiltjas, on which I had complimented them when I arrived, and build new ones elsewhere. That was the tribal way to fight infection. When I returned to Adelaide I sent up apparatus for saline infusion in case of further outbreaks, so that there would not be any deaths from dehydration.

The mission staff were unanimous in praising the beneficial results of the skim milk protein, but the problem of food wastage and unequal distribution remained. It was solved very sensibly when a new superintendent, the Reverend W. H. Edwards, was appointed to Ernabella. He worked out a system which enabled the Aborigines to buy their food at the store and cook the meat ration themselves, so that each member of the family received a fair share from the mother.

I made another visit to Ernabella in the following year, this time in company with my friend Newton Brooks. We planned to go as far as Ayers Rock, and drop in at Ernabella both going and returning. Newton's rate of travel was rarely under ninety miles an hour when he was on anything like a good road, and it took only two days to drive to Ernabella via Port Augusta, Kingoonya, Coober Pedy, and various cattle stations. I was glad of a day's rest at Ernabella before we drove on to Mulga Park Station, where I examined several sick people including a dangerously ill Aboriginal baby. I advised the station owner to ring the Flying Doctor, but found afterwards that he did not do so.

At last, after a final sixty miles of struggling through soft sand with our tyres let down for traction, we reached Ayers Rock. This massive monolith, which to the Aborigines had been a centre of religious and ceremonial life, had by that time already become a rackety tourist centre. A brand new house of compressed straw, built for the Ranger in charge of the area, stood a short distance from the rock. "Well, I'm blowed," he exclaimed when he saw us, and pushed his hands down the sides of his waistband—the characteristic posture of my old friend Bill Harney who has become known to so many Australians by his books about the Aborigines.

"My mate Tom who cooks for the tourists at the camp is an old patient of yours," he told me. "He's a new man since you fixed him up, but he doesn't hit it off too well with some of the Yanks. There are mobs of them, and they must have plenty of dough. Some of them have been all over Australia in taxis, and Tom says that they know more about Aborigines than we do."

We drove over to see Tom, and Bill told me to lie low so that we could surprise him. Tom was stoking a big fire when Bill called to him, and when he came over to the car and saw me he was so excited that he practically pulled me out of it.

We had dinner in the big dining hall built for the tourists, followed by an avalanche of questions from North American tourists. Bill took me back to his new cottage, in which he had not even slept so far, and said, "You sleep in that bed and don't get up in the morning until I bring your breakfast. What about bacon and eggs?"

"That will do me fine," I said, but I was wakened at eight-thirty a.m. by a constant rattling of the stove. I walked into the kitchen in my pyjamas, and found Bill wrestling with a stove jammed with blackened wood. "I don't understand these new-fangled things," he said. "I could have had your breakfast ready an hour ago out in the bush."

"Bill, you haven't pulled the choke out," I said. "Give me a match."

The excitement was too much for the bushman; he walked outside. "Come here," I said as he returned. "Didn't you know you have a flush toilet?"

"No, I don't. What is it, anyhow?"

Top: Children at Goulburn Island. Bottom: Northern Territory children suffering from Hansen's Disease (leprosy). Photographed at Channel Island, Darwin

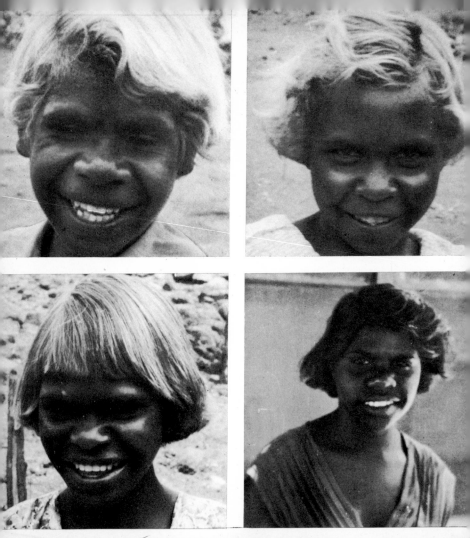

No one knew bush Aborigines better than Bill Harney, but he was less at home with modern amenities.

On the way back to Adelaide we picked up Lucy Turner, our foster daughter who had been holidaying with her friends at Ernabella. We drove the 300 miles to Oodnadatta, where we were invited to lay out our swags on the verandah of the United Aborigines Mission hostel. The part-Aboriginal children living there were of many shades, some of them being almost white.

Constable Francis, the local policeman, showed me three new houses provided by the Aborigines Department. "I wouldn't mind having one of them to stack my wood in, but that's all," he said. He was right, because the "houses" were simply open galvanised iron sheds; freezing in winter and roasting in summer. I have never met another policeman who had more sympathy for the Aborigines' problems than Constable Francis.

It was a rough trip south to Marree, through sand in which a number of vehicles had sunk to the axles. We had similar problems, and I had the task of opening and closing all the gates. I was glad of the welcoming meal provided by the Matron of the District and Bush Nursing Society at Marree, and to drop into bed. I was State President of the D.B.N.S. at that time, and spent next day in admiring recent developments at the hospital. It was a very far cry from the D.B.N.S. facilities which I had known when I first arrived in Australia, when the nurses had to ride along the bush tracks on bicycles in order to reach their patients.

After that it was a fast trip home through Leigh Creek, Copley, Hawker, Quorn and Port Augusta, passing down the western side of the Flinders Ranges and into the southern spurs. It is one of the most spectacular areas of the State, and we saw many emus near the road or on the skyline. The only blot on the landscape was the settlement at Copley, where the part-Aboriginal community had made themselves shelters out of flattened kerosene tins. I took some photographs, with a sense of shame that our wealthy and beautiful country could do no better for this portion of its people.

TOP: Some Aboriginal girls from Ernabella. Tinpulya and Tjunkaya are at top: Nyukana and Tjikalya beneath them. BOTTOM: The author prepares to give the bride away on a foster-daughter's wedding day

20

MOVING FORWARD ?

T HE DECADE FROM 1960 TO 1970 WITNESSED A GREAT increase in public concern for the Aborigines, together with big steps forward by the Commonwealth Government. The first of these came in 1962. On 18 April 1961 the Minister for the Interior, Mr Freeth, moved in the House of Representatives that a Select Committee on the Voting Rights of Aborigines should be appointed. On 12 May the Sergeant-at-Arms and Clerk of Committee, Mr A. R. Browning wrote to me. He said in part that, "the Select Committee would welcome evidence from you on the subject in the form of a detailed written statement." Naturally I was in favour, and sent off my statement. On 12 October the Committee met in Adelaide, and I was given a lengthy interview. The following year the Commonwealth. Government granted voting rights to Aborigines.

The next great forward move was the referendum of 1967, in which for the first time the entire voting community of Australia was given the opportunity to indicate its feelings about the Aborigines. The result of the referendum allowed amendments to be made to the Constitution, so that the Commonwealth government could legislate for the Aborigines, in the States as well as the Northern Territory.

But some consciences were being disturbed long before that. By the time the second World War broke out, Australians with any sense of justice could see that it was time for Aboriginal conditions to be improved. The war itself proved that Aborigines could serve the country with skill and courage, but in its immediate aftermath the progress of Aborigines towards acceptance and equality was too slow for many of their white fellow-Australians. The 1967 referendum clearly demonstrated the concern which most Australians felt for the future of the Aborigines. And this concern, though not always well-informed or well directed, steadily grows. It is imperative, however, that we all move forward together. The Aboriginal race has increased considerably since 1939, but the increasing numbers, greater mobility, and better education of the Aborigines have brought their own problems. In the past, the white newcomers refused to co-operate with the Aborigines; today, a clamant minority of part-Aborigines refuses to co-operate with the white people or with the rest of their own race. There is increasing talk of "Black Power," and propaganda couched in the language used by some Negroes of the United States. Such isolationism will benefit neither the Aborigines as a race nor Australia as a nation.

The essence of true co-operation was put finely in an editorial "Who is My Neighbour?" in the 19 December 1959 issue of the *Medical Journal of Australia*. The writer said: "Jesus of Nazareth gave the world a new concept of neighbourliness. He made it clear that to Him a true neighbour was one who, moved with compassion at finding a fellow-man in distress, leapt over barriers that would stop a lesser man whether they involved national hostility, practical difficulties or what you will, and gave what help He could."

For nearly two centuries, the Aborigines have been the equivalent of the robbed and beaten man on the road to Jericho, and it has needed countless Good Samaritans to put them on their feet again. It is difficult to know whether that need is really past.

After the 1967 referendum, the first move for the advancement of Aborigines was the formation in 1968 of a Council for Aboriginal Affairs in the Prime Minister's Department. Doctor H. C. Coombs, one of Australia's most brilliant minds, was appointed Chairman, and in the Federal Parliament the double portfolio of Social Welfare and Aboriginal Affairs was given to Mr W. C. Wentworth.

These two men, who enjoy a fine reputation for their concern with social problems, personally investigated the situation of Aborigines in many parts of the Commonwealth. Positive action was soon forthcoming in a variety of ways. Among these is the Capital Fund for Aboriginal Enterprises, which is intended to help Aborigines who wish to launch out on their own account. It does not simply lend money to an Aboriginal who, for example, wishes to start a business, but ensures that the applicant is properly trained and involved in all aspects of the undertaking before the loan is granted. Such money is lent only for income-producing enterprises, with the aim of helping Aborigines to stand on their own feet.

The number of houses available for Aborigines, whether in the cities, towns, or in the country, is still far short of requirements, and too many Aborigines are still at the mercy of grasping landlords. But the Commonwealth and State Governments are co-operating in making provision for the basic needs of Aborigines, one of these being housing.

The education of Aborigines—and it should be remembered, of course, that this word includes all people of part-Aboriginal descent—has received special attention. The responsibility for educating them at primary and secondary levels is the responsibility of the State governments, just as it is for white children, but a special Commonwealth grant is available to help in this. For youngsters who wish to stay at school beyond the age of compulsory education, the Commonwealth provides Aboriginal Secondary Grants awards. The parents are paid $200 per annum for school, clothing, books, and similar essentials, and $240 to $300 per annum as a living allowance if the child is living at home. If he has to attend a school away from home, then the full boarding costs are paid, the school receives payment for special compulsory fees, and each child receives weekly pocket money. This is a far cry indeed from the schooling which I saw given to Aboriginal children at "The Bungalow" in Alice Springs in 1934.

Should the Aboriginal student wish to proceed to tertiary education, including technological training, and should he qualify to do so, then the Commonwealth pays a living allowance of $1,100 per annum, pays all compulsory fees, gives a textbook and equipment allowance of up to $100 per annum, provides an allowance for a wife and children, and covers the travel cost of students who must live away from home to complete a course.

Nor have Aborigines who missed out on education been forgotten. Those who wish to acquire work experience and training which would equip them for continuous regular employment may take advantage of the Employment Training Scheme. This provides a living away from home allowance, pays for necessary travel, and subsidises the employers of Aborigines who have had no previous regular employment.

The toughest knot for the government to untangle is that of land rights. In the Australian legal sense, the Aborigines do not own a square yard of the continent over which their fore-fathers roamed. With the exception of the Aboriginal reserves and unalienated Crown land, the whole of Australia's grazing land is in the possession of people of European race, whether companies or individuals.

The story of this seizure is an indictment of the whole white race. When the British first took possession of Australia the Aborigines were treated like vermin, to be shot or poisoned or driven from their tribal land. Such incidents were particularly bad in the Centre, in Queensland, and in the Northern Territory, where gigantic areas were taken by force. Some-times, such areas did not even come into the possession of white Australians. For a long time, the two largest cattle stations in Australia were owned by British interests. These were Wave Hill and Victoria River Downs, of 6,000 square miles and 5,000 square miles respectively plus a number of large outstations. On these great tracts of land cattle were raised for export and for making into Bovril extract of meat. I well remember as a youth in Scotland an advertisement showing a bullock in an outsize teacup, with the caption, "The strength of an ox in a teacup!" The millions who enjoyed their cups of hot Bovril had no idea that it had been produced for them with the aid of Aborigines living in conditions so degraded that they were only a step from slavery.

Such conditions have been improved by the present owners of the properties, but it is still a staggering thought that the contracts under which they are leased by the Commonwealth government cannot be changed until 2004. Yet Aboriginal tribesmen will be capable of managing their own cattle stations long before that, and the enormous lift in Aboriginal status over the past forty years gives some indication of what may be expected of them. In 1930 it was believed that the Aborigines were dying out, and some Australians hoped that they would. To claim at that time that they were people of worth and ability was to be branded a fanatic — as indeed I was.

For those Aborigines who wish to repossess the "land of their fathers" in order to embark on such enterprises as farming and stock-raising, the Council for Aboriginal Affairs provided the scheme under which they may obtain long-term government loans. I am confident that the Council will not allow land to be bought by Aborigines at such exorbitant prices that they would prevent these ventures from being an economic success.

But, not unnaturally, a certain proportion of Aborigines claim that land should be returned to them without cost. Some groups have even taken it over. They state, with justice, that the land was seized from their forefathers without payment, without legal contract, and often at the barrel of a gun. The whole problem of land rights is likely to cause considerable trouble in the near future.

After the first seizure of lands, the governments of those days attempted to regularise matters by creating the reserves on which tribal Aborigines could continue in their age-old ways of life. Unfortunately, such reserves have never been sacrosanct. To my own knowledge, excisions of land from reserves have taken place on eight occasions over the past fifty years. The worst example was the addition to a cattle station of a huge area of rich pastoral country in Arnhem Land. The pastoral map of the Northern Territory shows clearly where it has been taken over.

Such interference with reserves continues. Under the present law, the Aboriginal reserves in the Northern Territory belong to the Commonwealth, and not to the tribesmen. They can be altered by proclamation, and until the law is changed the Aborigines cannot legally own the land or look forward to any security of tenure.

As recently as May 1971 I met James Galurrwuy, a tribal Aboriginal from the eastern end of Arnhem Land. Mr Galurrwuy, who is tall, good-looking, well-dressed, and the owner of a pleasing and persuasive voice, was educated at a mission in the Arnhem Land Reserve. This is land which sustained his forebears since the Dreamtime, yet at the age of twenty-two he was obliged to tour the country in support of his people's claim to ownership. They had never doubted that the land was theirs—until an international mining company, with Commonwealth government permission, moved in and wrecked the countryside.

Mr Galurrwuy is definite in his demands, but like most full-blood Aborigines he is not tainted with bitterness. "The land is ours," he said. "We don't want the government to boss us. The law will have to be changed. If profit-making companies want to use our land, it will have to be on our terms—and the companies must have our permission before they start operations."

In this regard, it is interesting to recall the assurance given by the Hon. Paul Hasluck, as Minister for Territories, when he addressed the House of Representatives in 1963. He said: "Country with economic potential in reserves is to be held untouched until such time as the Aboriginal wards can themselves share in the benefits which arise from its development." This assurance is still, technically at least, government policy.

But how many Members of Parliament know what the land means to tribal Aborigines? Are they aware that the land on which Aborigines live is part of their very being, that their entire social, cultural, and spiritual lives are so integrated with the land that when they are separated from it they become dejected, lose interest in life, and pine away? As James Galurrwuy put it—"An Aboriginal deprived of his tribal land is like a leaf torn from its tree."

As citizens of Australia, Aborigines must be given a stake in their own country. Young full-blood Aborigines on the reserves wish to develop them in the interests of their own people, and it is our sacred duty to help and not hinder them in this development.

Too many examples show that we hinder as much as we help. When the first township was built by the white intruders on Yirkalla Reserve, the Aborigines appealed against the granting of a liquor licence. They knew all too well what damage is caused to families and individuals by free access to alcohol. The Licensing Court upheld the appeal, but the decision was reversed when a further appeal was made by liquor trade interests.

A month after I met James Galurrwuy a highly intelligent Aboriginal woman in her forties, a Mrs L., called at our home to discuss the work she was doing in Aboriginal family education under the direction of the Van Leer Foundation. This project is a far cry from the denial of family human rights which she and her brother suffered at the ages of seven and nine. As naked bush children, they lived with parents on a cattle station near to Leonora, in the east of Western Australia. The Chief Protector of Aborigines at that time, acting within the law, had the children removed from their parents and placed in an institution.

After some time, the Protector visited them in the institution, told them that their parents had died, and advised them to forget about the old life they had lived. Not until long after they had left the institution did they discover that their parents had lived for twenty years after their alleged "death." The girl, as she grew up, took every opportunity to study, qualified at the Singleton Bible College, and is now an outstanding leader.

But such incidents cause one to remember the speech of Alexander Hamilton, the American statesman, in which he said: "Indeed I tremble for the future of my country when I reflect that God is just."

21

MALEVOLENCE AND BENEVOLENCE

THE DEVELOPMENTS OUTLINED IN THE PRECEDING CHAPTER, together with the increasing involvement of State and Commonwealth governments in Aboriginal affairs, may cause some of those concerned with the status of Aborigines to feel that the biggest battles have been won. Yet the hardest battle of all, that of securing complete acceptance of Aborigines in the hearts and minds of their fellow-Australians, may still lie ahead.

During the decade 1960-1970, in which such great forward steps were being made, I was still actively interested in Aboriginal welfare and in wide contact with those of similar interests. In 1965, I received a letter from a man who had driven up to Darwin, who wrote: "the drive up from Alice Springs was most unpleasant, what with continuing heat, very strong hot wind and sand first night out camping, and the following unhappy circumstances. We stopped to help a stranded Aboriginal family with a broken down car, and found they had been standing beside the Stuart Highway for some twenty hours—a family of six including three children, without food or water. After supplying them with a drum of water and a heap of food we went on and reported the matter at Wauchope, the next town. Reply: 'Let them walk in (twenty miles) they've been walking all their lives!' However, the police at Tennant Creek said they would send some sort of help." The stranded family was ninety miles from Tennant.

This was an attitude of downright malevolence. But there is an attitude of unimaginative benevolence (damaging in its own way), which is sometimes present even in those who are in fact working for the Aborigines. In 1960 I visited Papunya settlement on the Pintubi Reserve, and asked the Superintendent if I could see two men known to me, Tjararu and Warangula. "They're not here," he said.

"I think they must be," I told him. "This is their country."

I spoke to some of the Aborigines, and they told me that Tjararu was building a stock yard five miles away. We drove down, and saw four Aborigines lifting massive timbers with backs to us. Even so, I recognised Tjararu at once. In the evening he took me to see Warangula. Later, I described the two men to the Superintendent, and he said, "Oh, those are Johnny D and C-two!"

Next morning, I noted that the schoolchildren were being taught in English, a completely foreign tongue with no relevance to their old way of life. I did not meet any staff member, on any settlement visited that year, who had any knowledge of the native tongues.

In the Papunya dining hall, I saw the Aborigines file in three times a day, and sit on chairs at tables with knives, forks, and spoons in front of them. The Commonwealth government was certainly feeding those who might otherwise go hungry, but it seemed hardly right to hustle them at such a speed into the western way of life. Such things as the above are illustrations of the "unimaginative benevolence" which is concerned with filling the bodily needs of the Aborigines, while overriding basic human dignity.

The visit was part of a trip which I made in 1960, just before the immense job of packing up and moving out of the property at Magill which had been the family home for forty years. With the goodwill of Mr Paul Hasluck, (now Sir Paul Hasluck,

Governor-General of Australia), I stayed at the government settlements in the southern half of the Northern Territory: Warrabri, Yuendumu, Papunya, Areyonga, and Amoonguna. They were all part of Mr Hasluck's plan to revolutionise conditions for tribal and semi-tribal natives.

I set out to see them in the pleasant company of Patrol Officer Tony Giddings, who undertook the task of driving me around. Our first visit was to Warrabri, the oldest, smallest, and most highly developed of the settlements, covering seventy square miles and set like an oasis in the scrub 100 miles south of Tennant Creek. To emphasise that we were leaving the bush, a water tower and the greenery of a park attracted the eye. There was an ablution block, kitchen, dining room, school, hospital, and training centres. The Aborigines had two types of houses, either aluminium or cement block, and the staff lived in good homes raised on piles.

Yuendumu, our next stop, is only 200 miles to the south-west of Warrabri as the crow flies, but very much further by road. Tony decided to try a short cut which proved to be "the longest way round," because the car was soon thoroughly bogged in sand and had to be dug out!

Yuendumu covers 850 square miles, with conditions very similar to those at Warrabri, but I found the semi-tribal folk there to be much more enterprising. Two men ran a very productive vegetable garden, and sold the produce; others were turning out a steady supply of mud bricks. But the most interesting feature was the quarry. Some of the Aborigines had noticed an outcrop of good rock, and had already sunk a good-sized hole and quarried a quantity of stone. A good example of Aboriginal "free enterprise" taking the white man's example as a lead, because the Aborigines in their tribal state never used stone as a building material.

Papunya, the next settlement, was linked with a cattle-raising project at Haast Bluff, from which all its meat was obtained. Papunya was in its infancy in those days, with many buildings recently constructed or in course of erection, and most of the Aborigines still lived in the same type of wurlies to which they had been accustomed in their semi-nomadic life. Kitchen, dining hall, dormitories, school, hospital, church, manual training centre, garage and workshop, power house, staff houses, stockyard, and cement brick houses were all rising out of the desert and showed that it was to be a thriving centre. It was here that I met "Johnny D and C-two," as the superintendent called them, and when Tony Giddings reported back to Bill McCoy, then Superintendent of Native Affairs at Alice Springs he told him of his astonishment that Tjararu had recognised me after a gap of twenty-four years. "I'm not so surprised," Bill told him. "It would have been something new for Tjararu to see a white man at Haast Bluff in 1936, and there could only have been one who talked like the Doctor!"

From Papunya we drove to Haast Bluff to see the beginnings of the cattle-raising project, and saw yard-building and fencing while other men searched for water. Like Areyonga, our next stop, Haast Bluff had originally been a food depot started by Pastor Albrecht and supervised by Aranda tribesmen from Hermannsburg. In 1954 they were taken over by the Commonwealth and run as Aboriginal settlements by the Northern Territory administration.

I had a happy stay at Areyonga, because I knew several of the staff and a number of the Aborigines. There has always been much coming and going of the Aborigines between Areyonga and Ernabella, especially when corroborees were on. However, I was not so happy with conditions there, because most of the buildings were old and inadequate.

The final visits were to Amoonguna Settlement, seven miles from Alice Springs, where building had only just been completed and there was nothing else to see, and to Jay Creek, thirty miles south of the township. Then home again, to join my wife in the immense task of sorting out the accumulations of forty years before we left the old home.

Phyllis and I returned to Alice Springs in 1964, and found that the first and most obvious change had occurred through the legalisation of drinking by the Aborigines. In 1934 I used to see drunken white men lying in the gutters; now it was the Aborigines. The white man's privilege had become the black man's curse. Women as well as men were drinking in the hotels, and a chance remark which we overheard revealed a new attitude to Aborigines. Outside the Riverside Hotel some white children were annoying their mother, and she snapped, "If you don't stop that nonsense I'll put you in the black bar!" We found that there were two bars: one for whites, the other for blacks. Shades of apartheid!

Many other things had changed—including the fact that we were flown to Ernabella aboard a small aircraft of Connellan Airways, instead of making the long and weary trip of days gone by. It was good to see the old place and old friends again, especially Tjuintjara, the man who had guided us through the Petermann Ranges in 1936. We met him when John Bennett, in charge of the sheep, took us on his ration tour to the sheep camps and parties cutting timber and erecting fences on the limits of the property. The fences were as straight as a die. Tjuintjara lived in a well-made wiltja alongside the fencing camp, and was so excited when he saw us that he begged Phyllis to let me stay!

In 1964 and subsequent years, Phyllis and I continued our work with the Aborigines Advancement League of South Australia. We visited many of the Aboriginal settlements, and found many signs of the all too slow but steady progress being made.

In November 1964 we stayed at the Gerard Aboriginal Reserve, on the River Murray eleven miles from Berri. It was at that time a model settlement presided over by Mr Jack Foot, a man of vision and practical experience. This property of 5,000 acres was taken over by the Government of South Australia in July 1961 from the United Aborigines Mission. At the time of our visit there was a population of 150, equally divided between full bloods and part-Aborigines, and all of them seemed to be proud of the place and their part in it.

Mr Foot was supported by a keen staff of six—two women and four men—and training was given in mechanics, carpentry, building, agriculture and sheep work. Housing varied, and was being improved; employment was no problem as there was more work than workers. Education was compulsory. Nearby Winkie school, to which most of the Gerard children went had 170 pupils—Greeks, Italians, Aborigines, and white Australians in nearly equal numbers. Opportunity classes at the Berri school had proved a great stimulus to some of the Aboriginal children, who had missed schooling in their earlier years but responded rapidly to extra individual attention.

The Settlement had a well-defined lay-out, of staff housing area, administrative block, Aboriginal housing area, community block, church, tennis courts, co-operative store, gymnasium, pre-school centre, hall and oval.

I was most impressed by the fruit production in that year. There were 600 peach trees of seven varieties; 2,000 citrus trees—oranges, lemons, grapefruit, and mandarins; 2,000 grapevines, and one and a half acres of tomato plants. These were only the beginning of a well thought out plan. It was estimated that by 1970 Gerard would be supplying fruit to all Aboriginal settlements in South Australia and the Northern Territory. The Department of Agriculture supervised all plantings; soil tests were made by them and all trees and vines planted had the Department's certificate.

Mr Foot told me that when full production of the area was under way, work for about forty Aborigines would be available for the whole year and up to twenty more during harvest period. This ambitious practical concept received a severe set-back when Jack Foot was sent elsewhere by the Department of Aboriginal Affairs.

Gerard had the great advantage of beautiful river scenery and fertile irrigated land. Davenport Reserve, on the outskirts of Port Augusta had neither. The sandhills on which Davenport was eventually built were those which I visited in 1935 and 1941, to find derelict humpies occupied by ill-clad and impoverished Aborigines.

As already mentioned the missionaries of the Plymouth Brethren came to the rescue with the founding of Umeewarra Mission, and the provision of religious instruction, a school and a hall.

Late in 1964 the Government Department of Aboriginal Affairs decided to take responsibility for the area and it was created a Reserve. In February 1965 a resident superintendent was appointed and a considerable building programme was begun. By the end of May, when my wife and I visited the

Reserve, there was already a modern, well-equipped cash-store which had been built by Aboriginal labour under the supervision of a building expert.

Housing varied greatly. Ten two-roomed galvanised iron shelters with cement floors had been especially built as being the most suitable for near-primitive semi-nomadic Aborigines, who preferred to build fires on the floor. This need was strongly stressed to us by the woman Aboriginal welfare officer, Mrs Rachel Brady, who was showing us the homes. But even the three bed-roomed homes with wood stove, electric lighting and power and water laid on could not all have been regarded as finished housing. That this was the opinion of the Aboriginal Affairs Board can be judged by its annual report four years later, which stated in part: "With Commonwealth housing becoming available more families will be able to leave the Reserve during the coming year. This will allow less sophisticated Aborigines to settle at Davenport and progress through the stages of housing to outside employ-ment and housing off the Reserve."

At this time there was still an Education Department school on Davenport although many of the Aboriginal parents sent their children in to Port Augusta to school. But the Reserve school was closed when Mr R. R. Loveday was Minister of Education, and the policy of integrating Aboriginal children in the Port Augusta schools has been adhered to except for the pre-school centre at Umeewarra on the edge of the Reserve.

One of the first things done by the Government in 1965 was the planning of an Old Folks Amenities block. By May 1965 a fine beginning had been made, with the erection of Matron's Office, a dining room, kitchen, and bathroom for the pensioners. The first twelve two-roomed pensioner's cottages were being started nearby. Roads had been put down, and a fine tree planting scheme for the whole Reserve had commenced.

On subsequent visits in the years following we found steady progress, not only in roads and buildings but in employment of Aborigines as assistant carpenters, plumbers, gardeners, and bus drivers. Mrs Rachel Brady, already referred to, continued to give outstanding service, and some Aboriginal people were employed in clerical duties. The people at Davenport had elected their own Aboriginal Council which handled applications for houses on the Reserve and permits for all visitors. This was no light responsibility, as Davenport not only supported permanent residents but had to cater for transient Aborigines from the north and west. Numbers came to Port Augusta for medical treatment, including maternity cases. Not only did the mothers stay at the Reserve in the rooms provided but fathers and children often came too, waiting till mother and baby were ready to go home. At any one time there would be about 300 Aborigines, most of them part-Aboriginal with some full-bloods from outlying districts, on the 200-acre Reserve.

The aim of the Superintendent was to make Davenport Reserve an acceptable suburb of Port Augusta. He has had many problems to face but five years of energetic and enthusiastic work have seen him well on the way to realisation of his goal.

In October 1965, Phyllis and I made another visit to Point McLeay Reserve which in addition to the 3,000 acres on Lake Alexandrina had 3,000 acres of scrub land eight miles inland. This was known as Block K. The population of Point McLeay had dropped to 140 including 35 school children. Housing varied greatly. By far the best were the fibro-plastic houses with three bedrooms, sitting room and kitchen, at a rental of $2.50 a week. Some houses cost $1.50 a week, and I was informed that twenty of these old houses were to be demolished. All inhabited houses now had bathroom, toilet and laundry, the toilet connected to a septic tank.

In recent years many young Aborigines had moved in to the outside community. That was to be expected, but not the steady decline of the Reserve. If water was pumped from the Lake, as it is pumped from the River Murray at Gerard, a flourishing settlement of great potential could soon be created. However, that would need a more powerful pump, and new pipes to get rid of the gross leakage from the old ones which we noticed.

Employment was almost at a standstill. Only fourteen men,

including three semi-invalids, had regular work. Three boys were employed, but there was no outlook for girls.

The adult wage was $28 a week. Milk cost five cents a pint, mutton ten to fifteen cents a pound, and firewood thirty cents a bag. The store, run by an outside store-keeper, opened thrice weekly. Maternity cases and emergencies went to Tailem Bend hospital, thirty-two miles away. At the Reserve, a clinic was held once a month by the Tailem Bend doctor. On Tuesdays and Thursdays a bus ran from the settlement to the Surgery at Tailem Bend, the fare being paid by the passengers. There was no trained nurse at Point McLeay and no woman welfare officer.

The Reserve had a dairy herd with modern milking machine. Many cattle had been sent away and the flock of sheep greatly reduced because of lack of feed.

Block K had been only partly cleared and was in a sorry state. Neglect of the land had spread to the buildings at Block K — the windows of an unoccupied modern house, and of an up-to-date shearing shed, had been smashed by week-end rifle shooters. Back at the village I found that the old people did not wish to leave the spot, some of them being of the opinion that development at Point McLeay was being slowed down purposely. In the two days we stayed at the Reserve I was happy to meet many of the old brigade. David Unaipon aged 94, once a guest at our home, was still mentally and physically alert. He asked about our children, Andrew and Rosemary, whom he remembered well, and he proudly showed us his latest invention. Annie Rankin who made beautiful flowers from pelican feathers, and her husband Kendall, were there; Frank Lovegrove was still in charge of the electric plant, and his wife welcomed us to their home. Sumners, Rigneys, Wilsons, Karpanys, Karpinyaris and Gollans were still to the fore. It was my sixth visit to Point McLeay during thirty-seven years, and I left it somewhat depressed and puzzled as to its future. Mr Watson, the able and conscientious superintendent, and his wife, were doing what they could to brighten the people who did not seem to know what was coming next.

In that same year, my wife and I made a two-day visit to

Point Pearce Reserve. The village housed 330 Aborigines of the third and fourth generation from the full-bloods; the farm land covered 13,000 acres. There was no woman welfare officer and the trained nurse was soon to be only part-time. The school, under the Education Department, had a head-master and two woman assistants. Fifty per cent of the children, whose parents happened to be interested in education, attended regularly, but every morning the headmaster had to round up the other fifty per cent. Children from Grade IV upwards went to an outside State school by bus. The Kinder-garten Union of South Australia had opened a well-equipped pre-school centre with a fully trained kindergarten teacher in charge of thirty tiny tots.

Most of the houses for Aborigines were old, although water and electricity were now connected. Five three-bedroomed houses were expected to be finished soon. Deep-drainage was then only under construction. Several large buildings were new to me—a mechanical work-shop, a carpentry store, and an implement shed in process of building. There was need for a modern craft-room to create interest and give employ-ment. Too many young people, male and female, were just hanging around. "Two-up" was played every day by children and teenagers and alcohol was still a problem. Point Pearce showed improvement on past visits but the old feeling of depression was still in the air. But there were such bright spots as the schools and the playgrounds; the children were better dressed, and less shrinking than before. Also a better policy was being evolved, for soon after our visit residents were paid more realistic wages. They were then expected to pay some rent for their houses and to buy their own milk, meat and medicines which had previously been free. In other words the days of the "hand-out" were coming to an end.

Among all the social and legislative progress made for Aborigines in Australia, no measure has been more spectacular in its implications than the Aboriginal Lands Trust Act (1966) of South Australia, sponsored by Mr Don Dunstan who was then the Attorney-General and is now Premier of the State. Under its provisions, a Board consisting of three people of Aboriginal descent was set up. All unoccupied reserve lands in South Australia were to be placed immediately under control of this Board; later, all occupied reserves under government or church control would be transferred to the Board if the residents agreed. Such a decision would be made by the self-governing Aboriginal Councils on the reserves.

While the Act was still being debated, considerable effort was made to grant to the Aborigines the full mineral rights of their reserves, as part compensation for the deprivations which the race has suffered. But the measure was defeated. When the Act was passed, it included provision for mineral rights to remain vested in the Crown, and for the Treasury to make grants to the Aboriginal Lands Trust from any royalties received from such rights.

The Lands Trust Board has met with frustrations and difficulties, but the Act which brought it into being is surely the greatest single event in the struggle for recognition of Aboriginal rights. Is it too much to hope that the Federal government may yet cede its reserve lands to their Aboriginal inhabitants by a similar Act?

In June 1969 we travelled by the modern train to Finke, a township in the Northern Territory, 880 miles from Adelaide and 150 miles from Alice Springs. We were met by Margaret Bain, an Ernabella staff member who some years earlier had shown deep concern for the Aborigines at Finke railway siding. She was living in a caravan at the camp, and as a dedicated Christian was making the needs of the dark people her responsibility. The Aborigines were living in make-shift humpies among sandhills to which not infrequently young station workers went in search of women. Too many of the Aborigines had become heavy drinkers, but some of the people were responding to Margaret's intelligent handling of difficulties and her unfailing love. They wanted housing-blocks of land in the township, blocks which they had already selected. They asked in their own words, that a fence be erected round each block "to keep out dogs and drunks," and specified that water be laid on to each house "for drinking, washing and toilets." At the time, no water was available except what they could collect at a distance from a leaking tap. The people we met knew that if they were allowed to live in the township they would receive the same police protection as white folk and could expect to have water laid on. In the sand hills they were on common ground with no protection.

Finke had changed since I knew it first in 1934—when it was an expanse of sand with a single railway track running across it. The change had not been entirely good. The hotel was a wayside inn, which must supply alcohol or food on demand at any hour of the day or night. We stayed there on the Friday we arrived, to find that the rooms and amenities were not very good but that the food was excellent. On our return we stayed at the hotel on a Saturday. Drinking, singing and shouting in the bar began at nine p.m. and continued unabated till midnight, when the crowd moved out as the doors were closed. A minute or so later there was a knock on the door, it opened, and drinking and noise continued till one a.m., when the door closed again. But the noise went on outside; I got to sleep at four-thirty a.m. All the drinkers I saw that night were white people, and one of them consulted me in the morning because he was vomiting blood.

After Sunday breakfast, Margaret took us to the simple service with the Aborigines. When it ended I was paid a moving compliment in a short speech by Ginger, the second son of my friend Tjuintjara. John and Jan Langbridge, the Ernabella teacher and his wife, who had invited us to be their guests, drove us there in their Landrover. We travelled most of the 200 miles on a new very wide well-graded tourist road that runs 300 miles from Finke to Ayers Rock. Soon after leaving the main road we came on a group of Ernabella people collecting rabbits for a mobile refrigerator. They were all old friends, and we had a happy talk with Peter and Tjalara and their four children, Alec and Mayawara and their four children, and Nyinguda with her two children and brother. Nyinguda's late husband, Eric, was a genius at mental arithmetic. I wasn't in the hunt with him.

On Sunday at Ernabella there was a service in the Church at 10.30 and one in the camp at 6.30 p.m. I missed several faces I used to see at Ernabella; some of the people were at a corroboree at Everard Park, and many who used to live at the Mission were now permanent residents at the Government reserve at Amata, 100 miles further west. As soon as the morning service finished I was surrounded by mothers all of whom I had seen grow up from early childhood. Yukari came forward first, then Nura, Ankuna, Purki, Imbidi, Tjuwilya. Nearly all these mothers had four or more children. I was sorry to miss Tjikali and her husband Colin; they were at the corroboree. Later I met Nukana, and with her the girl I used to call "little Gudwin" and her three children, Numalka and her three and Yipiti who was Kuyata before her name was changed. Next day we visited the upper and lower schools supervised by John Langbridge and Rhoda Jenkin, and paid several visits to the craft room. John Bennett took us to the sheep camp at Duguid Bore, and pointed out Mount Duguid, the highest peak in a range some miles off. At Womakata camp we met Sandy, his wife and children, his sister Patjiparan and her children. Sandy was the eldest of a family of five all of whom I had known since children, the others were Henry, Patjiparan, Tjikali, Yipiti. I spent most of the morning at the hospital, greatly improved with its bath, four showers and four flush toilets. It had grown like Topsy from a poor start. We spent a day at the Fregon outstation stopping on the way at Shirley Well. Paddy and his wife, parents of Tjalara, were in charge of sheep kept there as killers for Fregon. At a camp nearby we met Iwana and her baby, Angela looking very happy at seeing us again, also a sister of Tjalara, as distinguished looking as Tjalara herself, and several others.

The air strip at Fregon, the work of Aborigines under the Superintendent's direction, was the finest I had ever seen in the back country. Grant McTavish was a key man on cattle. I was happy I had persisted on the Board that we should run cattle. Bob Capp, the teacher, had mastered the Pitjantjatjara language.

At the cattle camp on the way back to Ernabella we met Albert, a powerful six-footer, in charge of the men. He gave me a very warm handshake as we left. I remember his grandfather well and once took his photograph. Next day I had a happy time with the younger children at Ernabella. This year they called me Tjamu (grandfather). Ken Macdonald, the industrial manager, showed me the garage, his office unit, the huge shed that housed his larger vehicles, and the fine new engine house with the 240 volt generator to supply lighting and power. That afternoon I took photos of school children playing games conducted by the teachers.

Nganyantja, then expecting her eighth child, was very disappointed that my wife and I were unable to get over to see her at Amata, the Government settlement where she now lives, but Charlie her husband drove the hundred miles to see us. Brenton and Douglas came with him. Douglas went south every year for fruit picking and has picked up white workers' attitudes on wages and conditions.

The camp site of the Aborigines, about a mile from the mission buildings, was a disappointment. There was litter everywhere, too many dogs, and something new—many second-hand motor cars, a few of them broken-down hulks. It is understandable that Aboriginal people should like means of transport rather than houses in fixed spots; they have always been accustomed to move from place to place. Families are now much larger and they can all travel in comfort in a motor car. Perhaps the car is becoming a status symbol in the Musgrave Ranges, as it is in the cities of the south. It was a shock to see another breakdown in tradition at Ernabella—the revolt of the nyinkas. In the past, fathers and uncles trained the boys in their teens before sending them out to fend for themselves. They were trained in the use of spear and woomera for killing of game, shown where water could be found in the country over which they would roam, and instructed in the life history of plants. When the period of instruction was over the nyinkas went bush for several years, out of contact with the tribe until they had attained manhood. It was taboo for them to come in contact with the opposite sex. In 1969 the nyinkas had not "gone bush;" they were living in a camp half-a-mile from the main camp, and I saw a lad ride to the edge of the main camp and speak at length to a girl of his own age. That was a serious breach of nyinka discipline.

Change of life at the Mission was inevitable, and various factors have been at work. It may be that the fathers and uncles are now more interested in mastering the motor car than in training their sons and nephews for the future. It could be that the lads are no longer interested in the traditions of the tribe. It is certain that the gradual change envisaged by the Mission has been accentuated by many things. In recent years an increasing number of people from the south, with many different interests, have worked around the Mission and the nearby Government reserve at Amata, thus making contact with the Aborigines. Apart from this, more Aborigines have come south, some to do seasonal work, others to enter hospital.

In 1969 the most important feature of the Mission had not altered—the understanding of the Pitjantjatjaras and the happy relation between them and the staff. I have never been so warmly welcomed by my dark friends since I first met them as tribal nomads in 1935. I think they realised 1969 was likely to be my final visit to the Mission but they did not forget me. In 1970 and 1971 an increasing number of Pitjantjatjara folk came south to learn new skills and some came to be instructors at Pitjantjatjara language courses. All got in touch with me and called again before they left for home. Yet forty years ago it was commonly said that Aborigines never show appreciation for anything done for them—one of the many lies of the past.

22

A SUMMING UP

MY LIFE HAS SPANNED AN ERA OF ASTOUNDING CHANGE in human life, literally from the stage coach to the Sputnik—to say nothing of such things as the moon landing, which in my youth were only the dreams of writers like Jules Verne and H. G. Wells. I can remember seeing what must have been one of the last stage coaches in Britain. It ran between towns in Derbyshire, and I can recall my excitement at the sight of the four horses, the driver, and the man beside him with a long horn which he blew as the coach approached Chapel-en-le-Frith, the town where I was staying. "Penny-farthing" bicycles could be seen occasionally, though they were being superseded by the "safety" bicycle. When I arrived in Australia in 1912, Cobb & Co's coaches were still running to some outback towns.

As I look back over the years, change has been so dominant that I seem to be living in a different world from the one I was born into. In the latter part of my life changes have come rapidly, but significant changes were occurring even when I was a boy.

When my family went for summer holidays to the isle of Arran, in the late nineteenth century, it was a place of peace and quiet where motor cars were unknown. I well remember the first car to arrive in my home town, Saltcoats. It belonged to my uncle, a shipbuilder on the Clyde, and he sent my aunt and cousins in it to pay us a surprise visit. It was driven by a chauffeur, whom I accompanied on an errand to the town to buy some extra provisions. Sitting beside him, I made a secret resolve that one day I would own a motor car like my uncle. No one in those days ever dreamed of the time when the majority of families would run cars, and of all the problems which they would bring into our lives.

It was in my uncle's house that I first spoke on a telephone. I had to "ring up" by turning a handle which rang a bell, and then give the number I wanted to an operator in the exchange. In those days, a telegram was regarded with suspense; one always feared that it might contain bad news. Most business transactions were by cash; I had never handled a cheque until I settled in Australia.

I can remember the first train to run through Saltcoats on a Sunday and the consternation it caused among the Sabbath-observing folk of the town. Flight, the greatest development in transport, still lay ahead. I was nineteen when the Wright brothers made the first successful powered flight—over a distance shorter than the length of a modern jumbo jet.

Entertainment has changed, too. From the joy of "magic lantern" shows I have lived through the days of "movies" to "talkies" and then to radio and finally television in the home. Radio and television have been great discoveries, but for effective presentation of personalities they are far behind the stage. A supreme artist on stage becomes one with his audience. I shall never forget the first time I heard Harry Lauder, in 1914, when the packed audience in a Melbourne theatre seemed to become one family through the magic of his personality. I was to meet the great Scots entertainer in later years, and on the last occasion, in 1936, he was so upset by the news of the abdication of King Edward VIII that he would not leave the railway station when he came off the East-West express in Adelaide en route for Melbourne. He refused the offer of Sir George Ritchie, then Chief of the Caledonian Society of Adelaide, to give him a sightseeing drive around the city, and told me, "What I want is a cup of tea." So we had one together in the station buffet before he went on to Melbourne.

Medical development was slow in the early years of this century. The great discoveries of anaesthesia, antisepsis, and X-rays had been made, but when I graduated in 1909 we still had to prescribe such crude drugs as opium and digitalis. The active principles were not discovered until later. Insulin, discovered in 1922, for the control of diabetes, was the first of the specific drugs; the "wonder drugs," such as penicillin and the sulfa derivatives, did not come into general use until the early 1940's. By the middle of the century many powerful drugs of a specific nature were on the market, and have been of immense benefit to mankind. They have been of great assistance in limiting the spread of tuberculosis, and psychiatrists have used them to enable sufferers from mental disorders to return to normal life. Among all the advances in twentieth century medicine, few things are more striking than the completely changed approach to mental illness. At one time little could be done for people suffering from mental disturbance, many of whom were likely to end their lives in an "asylum."

For people in many parts of the world, modern medicine has brought a freedom from suffering which once was undreamed of. Such diseases as scarlet fever, diphtheria, typhus, typhoid, cholera, tuberculosis, smallpox, and pneumonia, which less than a century ago were all too frequently fatal, are now rare and comparatively easy to cure. Also, doctors have taught the public how to take an intelligent attitude towards health and hygiene. This together with the vastly improved living conditions for many people of the western world has given a much longer expectation of life to the average person. And so we face new problems in care of the aged and control of population!

Surgery has taken gigantic forward steps, though even in my student days such men as William Macewen were laying the groundwork of many modern techniques. One of the

A SUMMING UP

most publicised procedures, because it is the most dramatic, is open heart surgery and the transplant of hearts, but countless operations are performed every day which at the beginning of the century were unimagined. The last few decades have seen the emergence of specialist surgeons, who give their attention in depth to limited fields of surgery. All surgeons — and their patients — have benefited by the development of modern anaesthesia. Early in the century, chloroform on an open mask was the usual anaesthetic in Scotland; in England it was ether on a closed circuit. They were unpleasant methods by comparison with the modern one of induction, which has proved most acceptable to the patient.

Allied to the scientific and technical advances in medicine have been the great administrative advances. I was closely associated with one of these, the District and Bush Nursing Service, from my very early years in Australia. When I first arrived, the nurses went their rounds in small buggies or jinkers, later superseded by bicycles. It was a common sight to see the District Nurse in her navy and red uniform cycling for many miles in the country or suburbs, with her medical basket firmly strapped to the handlebars. On the River Murray, they used rowing boats. Originally, the nurses were expected to serve chiefly the poor of the community, but in later years the Society has undertaken general home nursing wherever it may be required. Excellent co-operation between District Nurse and local doctor has always been an outstanding feature, and there is no doubt that the D.B.N.S. is one on which the community will make increasing calls. After being President for sixteen years, I was honoured to be made a Life Member.

The Royal Flying Doctor Service, the Commonwealth Medical Benefits scheme, and other administrative advances have done much to ease the burden of sickness upon the average Australian, just as other social services have helped in other ways.

By contrast, change and development in another sphere have immensely increased human misery. Scientific and technical progress have made modern war into a process which involves the entire populations of combatant countries,

217

and its side effects are incalculable. The crime and violence which plague so many communities today are the direct result of the way in which two world wars and numerous smaller conflicts have eroded those moral standards which, once destroyed, are so hard to rebuild. It is heartening to hear modern youth proclaiming loudly that any war is too much, but world stability will never be achieved until each nation is prepared to forego a measure of its national sovereignty and co-operate in a properly supported United Nations with power to keep the peace.

Of all the changes which I have seen since I arrived in Australia sixty years ago, none has been so great as the altered attitude towards the Aboriginal peoples. As a youth in Scotland, I heard about the cannibals of the South Sea Islands and about missions to such places as Africa, India, and China, but the Australian Aborigines were never mentioned. To most of the world, they were unknown. Many Australians were almost as ignorant; as late as 1930 it was believed that the race would die out. A number of Australians hoped that they would. But, since 1939, the Aborigines have been increasing steadily, which is a joy to those of us who stood by them before they achieved recognition. In my book *No Dying Race*, and in this one, I have written about the ways in which Aborigines were treated before the average white person's attitude towards them began to change. This change of heart is not yet complete, and is not helped by the "Black Power" tactics of a clamant minority of part-Aborigines, but at least it has begun. I have been privileged to play some part in this.

Religious belief and observance have not escaped the sweep of change. The church has lost much of the influence it had when I was a boy, partly because science has probed the secrets of nature so deeply that it has tended to undermine a simple faith. The vast upheavals of the two World Wars also helped to weaken the faith of many practising Christians, so that their children were not brought up with a deeply-founded belief.

Yet, even amid the rapid change and increasing materialism of today, there are many signs that people seek faith in a

Power greater than themselves. The "Jesus movement" among young people, informal though it may be, is a sign of this. And to me there is one thing which remains unchanged in a ceaselessly changing world—the astonishing power of selfless love. I have seen its manifestation in many places and in many ways throughout my long life. It remains for me the ultimate solution to the world's problems.